GUARDS WITHOUT FRONTIERS
Israel's War Against Terrorism

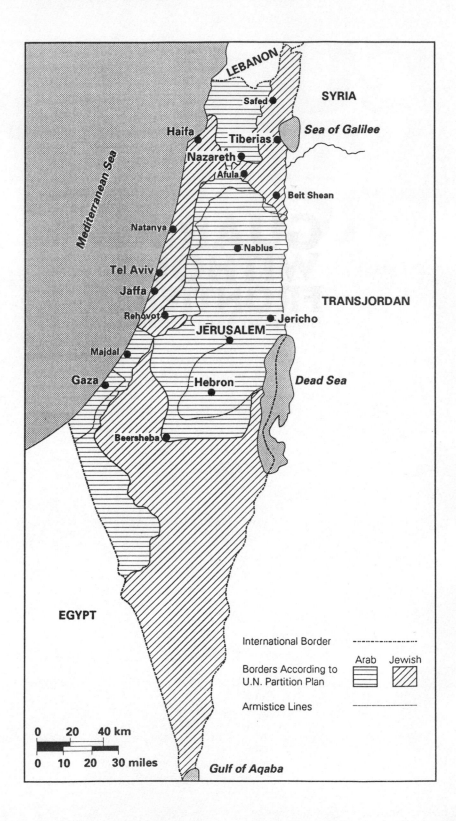

LEBANON

SYRIA

Safed

Haifa

Sea of Galilee

Tiberias

Nazareth

Afula

Beit Shean

Mediterranean Sea

Natanya

Nablus

Tel Aviv

TRANSJORDAN

Jaffa

Rehovot

Jericho

JERUSALEM

Majdal

Hebron

Dead Sea

Gaza

Beersheba

EGYPT

International Border

Arab   Jewish

Borders According to
U.N. Partition Plan

Armistice Lines

0   20   40 km

0   10   20   30 miles

Gulf of Aqaba

GUARDS WITHOUT FRONTIERS

Israel's War Against Terrorism

SAMUEL M. KATZ

ARMS AND
ARMOUR

First published in Great Britain in 1990 by Arms and
Armour Press, Villiers House, 41–47 Strand, London
WC2N 5JE.

Distributed in Australia by Capricorn Link (Australia) Pty.
Ltd, P.O. Box 665, Lane Cove, New South Wales 2066.

British Library Cataloguing in Publication Data
Katz, Samuel
Guards Without Frontiers: Israel's War Against Terrorism.
1. Israel. Counterterrorism
ᶜ I. Title
327.12095694
ISBN 0-85368-930-X

Cartography and charts by Sampleskill Ltd., London

Designed and edited by DAG Publications Ltd. Designed
by David Gibbons; edited by Michael Boxall; layout by
Anthony A. Evans; typeset by Nene Typesetting Ltd.,
Northampton; camerawork by M&E Reproductions,
North Fambridge, Essex; printed and bound in Great
Britain by Mackays of Chatham, Kent.

Contents

Principal Palestinian Terrorist Organizations

El-Fatah: Palestine National Liberation Movement. Currently based in Tunis, with bases in Lebanon and Jordan and access through Egypt. Commanded by Yasir Arafat (Abu Amar). Includes *Force 17*, Arafat's élite personal bodyguard force and commando strike unit, and *Force 14*, the nucleus of a Palestinian Air Force.

PFLP: Popular Front for the Liberation of Palestine. Syrian- and Libyan-sponsored, and commanded by Doctor George Habash.

DFLP: Democratic Front for the Liberation of Palestine. Based in Syria, and commanded by Nayif Hawatmeh.

PFLP-GC: Popular Front for the Liberation of Palestine General Command. Backed by Syria and Libya and long believed to be an arm of Syrian intelligence. Commanded by Ahmed Jibril.

As-Saiqa: Vanguard of the Liberation War. Originally a Syrian-sponsored force, although believed to be controlled now by Libyan elements. Commanded by Issam el-Qadi.

Abu Nidal Faction: Black June Revolutionary Council. At times financed, controlled, and used by Iraqi, Syrian, and Libyan intelligence, this notorious group is commanded by Sabri al-Banna alias Abu Nidal.

PCP: Palestinian Communist Party. Based in Syria, and commanded by Suleiman Nejab.

PLA: Palestine Liberation Army. Consists of Palestinian soldiers serving in the Jordanian and Syrian armed forces.

ALF: Arab Liberation Front. Currently commanded through Iraq, and commanded by 'Abd el-Rahim Ahmad. According to recent intelligence reports, the ALF has consolidated its forces and capabilities with Abu Nidal's Black June.

15th of May: 'Abu Ibrahim Faction'. Intelligence reports list 15th of May as an integral element of Iraqi Military Intelligence. Based in Iraq, and commanded by the elusive Muhammad 'Amri (Abu Ibrahim).

el-Fatah (renegades): Palestine National Liberation Movement. Separated from Arafat's *el-Fatah* in 1983. Supported by Syria, and commanded by Sa'id Mussa Ma'arara (Abu Mussa).

PARC: The Palestine Arab Revolutionary Committees of the Arab Liberation Movement. Libyan-controlled, and commanded by Ziad el-Khumsi.

PLF(1): Abdul 'Abbas Faction of the Palestine Liberation Front. Tied to Jordan, and commanded by Muhammad Zain 'Abbas (Abul Abbas).

PLF(2): Talat Ya'aqub Faction of the Palestine Liberation Front. Controlled by Libya, and commanded by Talat Ya'aqub.

PLF(3): 'Abd el-Ghanem Faction of the Palestine Liberation Front. Libyan- and Syrian-backed, commanded by Abd el - fatah el-Ghanem.

PPSF: Palestine Popular Struggle Front. Libyan-financed and controlled, commanded by Doctor Samir Ghusa.

MPLA: Popular Arab Liberation Front. A small, Libyan-supported group commanded by Naji Alush.

PFLP-SC: Popular Front for the Liberation of Palestine Special Command. Obscure organization commanded by Salim Abu Salem (Abu Muhammad) with leanings toward the People's Democratic Republic of Yemen.

Border Guard—IDF Rank Comparisons

Border Guard / Police Ranks

Shoter – Policeman
Rav-Shoter – Master Policeman
Samal Sheni – Second Sergeant
Samal Rishon – First Sergeant
Rav Samal – Senior Sergeant
Ra'sa'r – Senior Master Sergeant

Mefakeach Mishne – Deputy Inspector
Mefakeach – Inspector
Pakad – Senior Inspector
Rav Pakad – Chief Inspector
Sgan Nitzav – Second Superintendent
Nitzav Mishne – Deputy Superintendent
Tat Nitzav – Superintendent
Nitzav – Chief Superintendent
Rav Nitzav – Chief of Police

IDF Equivalent

Turai – Private
Tar'ash – Lance-Corporal
Rab'at – Corporal
Samal – Sergeant
Samal Rishon – First Sergeant
Rav Samal – Senior Sergeant
Ra'sa'r – Senior Master Sergeant

Sag'am – Second Lieutenant
Segen – First Lieutenant
Seren – Captain
Rav Seren – Major
Sgan Aluf – Lieutenant-Colonel
Aluf Mishne – Colonel
Tat Aluf – Brigadier-General
Aluf – Major-General
Rav Aluf – Lieutenant-General

Preface

Originally, this book was conceived as a testament to the unheralded courage of the Israeli National Police Border Guards in their battle against Palestinian terrorism and, more specifically, for the brilliant counter-terrorist/guerrilla campaign their outnumbered and overwhelmed forces performed in Lebanon in the wake of the 1982 Israeli invasion. I was fortunate enough to have spent a great deal of time with many Border Guard officers and policemen; from the jovial commander of one of the Northern Brigade companies whose rapport with his men was awe-inspiring, to the career sergeant who spent many a sleepless night inside the Lebanon waiting in ambush for senior terrorist leaders. They fought with the skill and courage of the very best IDF units, and displayed the cunning intuition of the world's finest detectives in their search for the perpetrators of terror past and present. The war also introduced their élite anti-terrorist rescue unit known as the *Ya'ma'm*, a product of the 1974 Ma'alot massacre. During this campaign, the Border Guards suffered heavy casualties in fire-fights with well-armed terrorists, and two particular incidents entered the Border Guard vocabulary as the 'Two Tyre Disasters': a mysterious 1982 gas burner explosion in their first HQ in the Lebanese port city of Tyre, and the 1983 Shi'ite suicide truck bombing of their second Tyre compound cost them dearly. In all, Operation 'Peace for Galilee' cost the Border Guards more than 50 dead and scores of wounded. It was a phenomenal price to pay. Their total force constituted less than one per cent of the total Israeli forces in action yet they incurred well over ten per cent of the casualties. Theirs was a story which needed to be told.

As I began to research this project, however, certain developments regarding terrorism began to unfold in Israel which eventually determined the format of my book. There was the hijacking of the No. 300 bus travelling from Tel Aviv to Ashqelon in April 1984, which ended when an IDF 'élite' unit stormed the bus, killing two terrorists and capturing two others. The prisoners were killed hours later by agents of Shin Bet, Israel's General Security Services, during 'routine questioning'. That incident unravelled the once top secret activities of Shin Bet in public and revealing fashion. Then there was the IDF/Navy's destruction of a merchant ship off the coast of Israel in April 1985, which was carrying more than 20 highly trained and heavily armed

Palestinian terrorists. Their mission was to land in Israel, storm the Ministry of Defence complex in Tel Aviv, and kill the Defence Minister, Yitzhak Rabin. The serious consequences for the State of Israel had the attack succeeded shed a well-deserved light on the vigilance of Israeli naval terrorist interdiction operations in the country's stormy coastal waters. And in October 1985, Israel's never-ending campaign against terrorism took on a new turn when the Israel Air Force journeyed 1,500 miles, the farthest Israeli forces had travelled since the Entebbe rescue, to bomb the Tunis headquarters of *Force 17*, Yasir Arafat's élite praetorian guard. The raid was in retaliation for the murder, days earlier, of three Israelis on a yacht in Larnaca harbour, Cyprus, by three *Force 17* members. It demonstrated to the world that Israel's resolve in fighting terrorism knows no frontiers or boundaries.

Finally, there was what became known as the 'Bus of Mothers'. As my wife and I prepared to board a flight to Israel on 7 March 1988, we heard news reports that a three-man PLO (*el-Fatah*) team had infiltrated into southern Israel from Egypt, and hijacked a bus carrying female workers from Beersheba to their jobs at the nuclear facility at Dimona. When the terrorists began massacring the hostages, the *Ya'ma'm* burst into action and killed the three Palestinian gunmen. The attack was an attempt by the PLO to assume leadership of the then four-month-old Palestinian *Intifadah* (literally shaking off or uprising) which had engulfed the Israeli-occupied West Bank and Gaza Strip. The terror raid near Beersheba, like the foiled April 1985 raid on the Ministry of Defence and countless others before that, was masterminded by PLO deputy chief, Khalil al-Wazir, better known by his *nom de guerre* Abu-Jihad (or 'Father Holy War'). Few could have predicted the subsequent Israeli reaction; but the April 1988 assassination of Abu-Jihad in his Tunis villa brought back memories of the efforts of the Mossad hit teams to strike back against the leaders of the Black September Organization during the 1970s.

I decided to examine Israel's all-out war against terrorism in an inclusive fashion, discussing all her 'guards without frontiers'; from intelligence agents in the capitals of Europe, to policemen in the ancient alleyways of Jerusalem. It must be understood that such a topic deals with information that is mostly of a highly sensitive nature – even if dating back a decade or more. The Israeli defence and intelligence community is extremely tight-lipped and *fanatical* when it comes to security considerations. Although this book, in its manuscript form, has undergone the scrutiny of the Israeli Military Censor's Office, it is hoped that through a compilation of the most accurate foreign and Israeli sources new light can be shed upon past and present Israeli intelligence, military and police counter-terrorist operations, both in the Middle East and points beyond. In addition, and through the assistance of the Israeli National Police, who were justifiably interested in having their unheralded participation in this all-out war told, new and quite fascinating information regarding the efforts of the Border Guards, their anti-terrorist commando unit, and the National Police Bomb-Disposal Squad can be disclosed.

This book could not have been possible without the assistance and friendship of a good many people. I offer my special thanks to the Border Guard Chief Superintendent, Gabi Last, whose impatience for a written testament of his men's epic campaign in Lebanon will now, it is to be hoped, be satisfied. I offer my sincere gratitude to the Border Guard Chief Inspector, Nachum Mordechai, whose tenacious approach to his work and love of his men will leave a lasting impression with me; and special thanks to Master Sergeant Yoel Baranas for his photographs, and to the rest of the professionals of the Border Guard Northern Brigade stationed in Safed, Zichron Ya'akov and points beyond. I should also like to thank the Police Minister, Lieutenant-General (Res.) Haim Bar Lev; the National Police Bomb Disposal Unit Commander, Shlomoh Aharonishky, for giving so unselfishly of himself; the Police Operations Commander, Meshulam Amit, for giving me a few gracious moments from his hectic schedule; and most especially Superintendent Ruth Schlesinger, whose assistance made a great deal of this book a reality. I would also like to thank the very friendly and extremely courageous men of the Police Bomb Disposal Squad stationed in Holon, who, due to security considerations, must remain anonymous, but whose openness allowed me to witness their gallant efforts at first hand, and share in their experiences.

I wish to thank also Andreas Constantinou for his, as always, superb technical assistance, and Joseph S. Bermudez Jr., whose help regarding Syria clarified many mysteries. I wish to thank Chris Westhorp of Arms & Armour Press, whose help and editing skills were of great assistance. Last, though certainly not least, I wish to offer very special words of thanks to three members of the Elyakim family: two present, and one former. In many ways, this book, like others before it, would not have been written had it not been for the incessant efforts of my father-in-law, Nissim Elyakim, who tirelessly acted as a messenger, transferring the manuscript to and from the Censor's Office. His kind actions, and uncanny ability to produce miracles amid a labyrinth of bureaucratic indifference, were of monumental importance to me, and I shall forever feel indebted to him. I should also like to thank my sister-in-law, Sharon Elyakim, for her never-ending consideration, and for the very important articles, periodicals, and photographs she faithfully sent me. Finally, and with great affection, to my wife Sigalit, who was always by my side helping me with interviews, the logistics of writing such a book and most importantly, giving me her love, patience, sweet smile, and support.

This book is dedicated to the men of the Border Guards Northern Brigade, and to their families, and to the memory of their fallen.

Samuel M. Katz
New York, September 1989

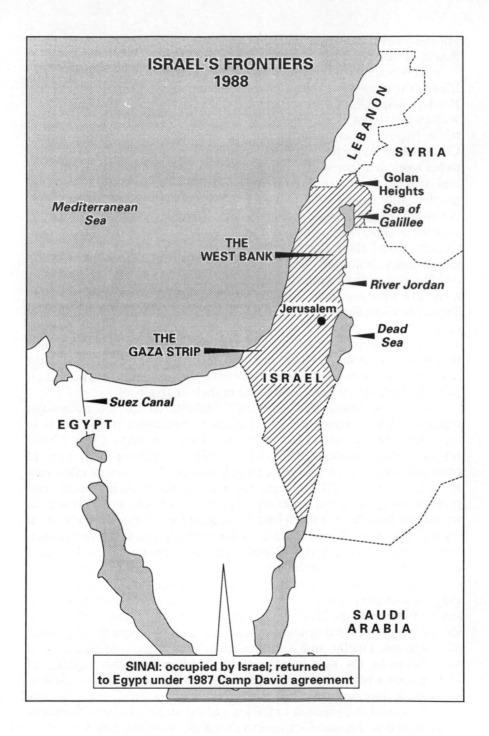

ISRAEL'S FRONTIERS
1988

LEBANON

SYRIA

Golan
Heights

Sea of
Galilee

Mediterranean
Sea

THE
WEST BANK

River Jordan

Jerusalem

Dead
Sea

THE
GAZA STRIP

ISRAEL

Suez Canal

EGYPT

SAUDI
ARABIA

SINAI: occupied by Israel; returned
to Egypt under 1987 Camp David agreement

Introduction

'Armed struggle is the only way to liberate Palestine. Thus it is the overall strategy, not merely a tactical phase. The Palestinian Arab people assert their absolute determination and firm resolution to continue their armed struggle and to work for an armed popular revolution for the liberation of their country and their return to it. They also assert their right to normal life in Palestine and to exercise their right to self-determination and sovereignty over it.'

(Article 9: the Palestinian National Covenant)

This is the story of one nation's war against organized terrorism. It is a tale of revenge, untold brutality, vigilance, all-out warfare, covert assassinations, national conspiracies, private suffering and, of course, courage. The opening chapter was written in the summer of 1956, but to this date still knows no ending.

13 July 1956. In a small, unobtrusive article in the prominent Cairo newspaper *El-Ahram*, the death of one Colonel Mustafa Hafaz was announced: the cause of death was attributed to his Russian-made jeep detonating a 'Zionist' land-mine near his home and office in the Gaza Strip. The article emphasized the fact that the late Colonel Hafaz was, 'One of the heroes of the Palestine War, and fought hard to liberate her from Zionist occupation.' The Israeli Press, however, had a different opinion. The respected daily *Davar* stated that Colonel Hafaz was the head of Egyptian-sponsored Palestinian terror attacks and had been murdered by Palestinian refugees seeking revenge for the hundreds of refugees he had sent to their deaths in 'pointless' guerrilla raids against Israel.[1] What both these obituaries failed to mention, as a result of strict orders issued by the Israelis and Egyptians, was that Colonel Hafaz had been assassinated in an Israeli military intelligence operation. It was Israel's first true statement of her will to combat terrorism, a legacy which remains the cornerstone of Israeli policy today.

Colonel Hafaz was assigned the Palestinian Desk in 1949 and authorized to set up large-scale espionage rings for operations against Israel's southern frontier. He had one of the most brilliant minds in Egyptian Military Intelligence, and was a rarity in as much as he had achieved his high rank through ability rather than through political allegiances and affiliations. Unlike the majority of Egyptian officers he

15

cared little for the class system brought on by rank and showed great affection for his men and their problems. He also understood a major Israeli weakness: her porous frontiers. In 1952, there were 3,742 illegal crossings into Israel from Arab territory. The young Mustafa Hafaz realized only too well that such poorly fortified frontiers provided an invaluable opportunity for him to attain his objectives against the Jewish State. He soon began organizing armed forays into Israel by displaced Palestinians from bases inside the Gaza Strip. Egyptian military control of refugee life in the squalid, miserable Gaza camps was all-pervasive. Those with money, ability and foreign connections quickly fled, leaving only the poor, illiterate and bitter; men who, once properly cajoled, were only too willing to sacrifice themselves and cross into Israel to commit acts of terror.

These infiltrators became known as the *Fedayeen* or 'Men of Sacrifice', and they targeted civilians living on remote agricultural settlements in southern Israel in an attempt to instil fear into the hearts of all Israelis. Mustafa Hafaz's Fedayeen were so successful that in the spring of 1955 an Egyptian Army Fedayeen Battalion was formed with the specific military objective of sowing murder and terror inside Israel. Colonel Hafaz now became known as the Commander of Palestinian Intelligence.[2]

The Israelis had long been aware of Colonel Hafaz's career and they tried in vain to terminate it. On 30 August 1956, a three-man sapper squad from Unit 101, Major Ariel 'Arik' Sharon's famous though short-lived counter-guerrilla force, destroyed Hafaz's home during a larger raid against Palestinian Fedayeen targets in Gaza, but, luckily for the colonel, he was out that evening. This failure alerted Hafaz to the fact that the Israelis were on to him and he was thus able to use his vast network of spies inside Israel to escape further harm. As a statement of his disregard for such Israeli attempts on his life, Colonel Hafaz then increased the Fedayeen operations. Although bold retaliatory operations by IDF paratroops were ordered following each major Fedayeen outrage, rarely a day went by without an incident; such was the atmosphere that an innocent drive in the Negev Desert was turning into a military operation. As the Fedayeen attacks slowly moved to within 18 kilometres of Tel Aviv it was finally decided that bold, and urgent action was needed.

Israel's patriarch and Prime Minister, David Ben-Gurion, was vehemently against assassinations as an instrument of national policy. He believed that Israel had to perform at a moral level above that known to the Arabs, and that the very survival of the State depended on the morality of its policies. Others, who had survived Hitler's Europe and fought the Arabs on equal terms, however, argued that survival meant the ends justifying the means, especially in a Middle East where such Talmudic reasoning would not prevent murder and destruction. Colonel Hafaz's counterparts in the shadowy war of the minds, officers working for *A'man* (literally the Hebrew acronym for 'Intelligence

Section', or 'IDF Military Intelligence'), therefore laboured feverishly to fabricate an ideal plot.

The man in charge of the silencing operation was Colonel 'R', a highly experienced Military Intelligence officer whose identity remains a state secret to this day. He had begun his intelligence career in the Haganah's élite Pal'mach (Strike Companies) where he served as an intelligence scout for the legendary 3rd Company. He was subsequently promoted to Haganah's intelligence service known as *Sha'i* (Information-tion Service), and then to the IDF Intelligence Corps. Working with Colonel 'R' was Major 'S', a graduate of the Scottish University in Jerusalem, and control officer of the failed network of Egyptian Jewish spies who were eventually captured during Operation 'Suzannah'* in 1954. The unit assigned to 'R' and 'S' was in Southern Command, and consisted of twenty officers, all known to one another by code-names beginning with the Arabic *Abu* (Father of ...). Considering the importance of their work, the intelligence unit was poorly supplied, as were most IDF units in the 1950s. Even though telephone lines and vehicles were considered a luxury, they were under intense pressure from the Chief of Staff, Lieutenant-General Moshe Dayan, and Military Intelligence boss Major-General Yehoshofat Harkabi, to emulate the innovative ragtag commandos of Unit 101 and take the war into the enemy's territory.[3]

After mounting an intensive intelligence-gathering effort against the Fedayeen in Gaza, using Arab agents to operate communications and photographic equipment, Colonel 'R' came to the conclusion that killing Colonel Hafaz could not be delegated to a commando-type operation such as the Unit 101 attempt three years earlier, for the simple reason that he was heavily guarded, and very cautious. The officers considered mailing him a booby-trapped package from a post office in Gaza, or delivering a gift of poisoned fruit, but both were rejected because they were impracticable and they contradicted the IDF's strict policy of *Tohar Haneshek* (Purity of Arms) which forbade the killing of innocents. Colonel 'R' knew that they needed a special package: it had to be very important, very tempting, something Colonel Hafaz would be sure to handle personally and which could easily get through his tight ring of bodyguards. When news of a double agent inside Military Intelligence's Southern Command network reached Colonel 'R', all the loose ends came together.

His name was Suleiman Et-Tlalka, and he was a volunteer servant to the Israeli cause. He was a 25-year-old Bedouin from Rafah, known for his cunning personality. He was also a ruthless spy, who had been recruited and controlled by none other than Colonel Hafaz. The Israelis

---

* An ineptly conceived and amateurishly executed rogue operation of IDF Military Intelligence's mysterious special operations force, known as Unit 131, to turn Western sentiment against Nasser's Egypt by initiating a campaign of terrorist bombings of Western installations and to blame the acts on the 'Muslim Brotherhood'. Following several failed attacks, the perpetrating group of sleeper agents – in fact, a firmly entrenched fifth column should war erupt – made up entirely of Egyptian Jewish Zionists were captured and imprisoned after public, and politically damaging, trials.

had suspected that Et-Tlalka was both 'batting and bowling', but his true identity was not confirmed until his controllers asked him to provide them with information regarding a certain Egyptian base in the Gaza Strip which they were interested in attacking. Intelligence reports the following day from a reliable source revealed that the base's garrison had been tripled. Colonel 'R' knew that the manipulation of a double-agent was tricky, but in this case, in order to assassinate Colonel Hafaz, it was a necessary task. He summoned Et-Tlalka and ordered him to deliver a package of 'new codebooks' to Israel's master agent in Gaza, Lutfi El-Achawi, who just happened to be Gaza's Police Chief, and a loyal Egyptian who had actually never worked for the Israelis. Colonel 'R' knew that Et-Tlalka would take the package straight to his controller.

The biggest problem for Colonel 'R' was authorization. His unit had been careful not to embark on any 'independent' operations, especially after the disastrous Operation 'Suzannah', when official denials had placed the lives and careers of professional intelligence agents in severe jeopardy. Initially Major-General Harkabi was sceptic-al about the assassination plot, but, with his trusted Colonel 'R' providing him with the target, the method and the means, he was sold on it. After obtaining the booby-trapped package from the Intelligence Corps Research and Development Department, Colonel 'R' raced the goodies from HQ in Tel Aviv to the Egyptian border in such haste that he even ordered his commandeered driver and jeep to run over the motorbike of a Military Policeman who had foolishly tried to issue the intelligence team with a speeding ticket![4]

At their base in southern Israel, Colonel 'R' and his staff of officers explained the delicate assignment to their excited agent. To make sure that Et-Tlalka's curious nature wouldn't lead to the detonation of the carefully constructed bomb, they showed him a notebook with codes in English and then told him they were wrapping it in an adjacent room. As the sun set over the Mediterranean on 11 July 1956, Colonel 'R' and two officers escorted Et-Tlalka to the border where, after a handshake and an *Insh Allah* (God Willing), the double agent headed off on his mission. When Colonel 'R' looked through his high-powered field glasses and noticed Et-Tlalka heading in the direction of central Gaza rather than towards the home of the Police Chief, El-Achawi, he knew the bait had been taken. It would now be but a matter of time.

Suleiman Et-Tlalka reached Colonel Hafaz's headquarters just before midnight, where he found the Egyptian intelligence master in conversation with fellow officers. It was six years since he had been assigned to the 'Palestinian Desk' of Egyptian Military Intelligence and he had just returned two days earlier from a back-slapping visit to his bosses in Cairo. Initially, the heavily armed sentries outside Hafaz's HQ refused to allow the Bedouin to see the Colonel, but after hearing that his best agent had invaluable material, Hafaz ordered Et-Tlalka in at once!

At first, Colonel Hafaz refused to believe that Chief Inspector El-Achawi was an Israeli agent. He had worked side by side with the Fedayeen and Egyptian Intelligence, and was considered above suspicion, although there was some speculation that he was dealing with the Israelis in order to protect his hashish smuggling enterprise. As he opened the package, a small piece of paper with Arabic script on it glided out, followed by a thunderous blast which killed the 34-year-old Colonel instantly. He was buried with full military honours in his native Alexandria. Fedayeen raids stopped for ten years.

The assassination of Colonel Hafaz sent a message to the Arab world louder than even that fatal blast in Gaza: Israel would utilize all the resources available to her to combat the dire threat which organized terrorism posed to her existence, and she would eliminate every would-be terrorist leader she could locate. In the thirty years since the appearance of the Fedayeen and the death of Colonel Hafaz, Palestinian terrorism and Israel's efforts to thwart it have taken on an entirely new appearance. The Palestinians surrendered their attempts to wage war inside Israel in exchange for performing on a much larger stage, one served by the international media and intended to convey their desperation to world opinion. Although terrorist attacks against Israeli border settlements have continued to this day, turning towns like Ma'alot and Nahariya into international definitions of horror, Israeli and Jewish installations abroad have also been targeted for destruction, including Israeli diplomats in Washington, DC, Jewish worshippers in Istanbul and Olympic athletes in Munich. The poorly equipped Fedayeen warrior of ages past was replaced by the suitcase bomb, by the masked gunmen holding hostages aboard a bus and by such men as Sabri Al-Banna, better known to the world as Abu-Nidal, considered by most intelligence officers to be the world's most dangerous terrorist.

Few countries can boast Israel's intransigent stance against terrorism, but then few countries have such capable forces at their disposal. The Mossad, Israel's foreign intelligence service, has long been considered one of the world's most professional of its kind and has devoted much of its efforts to infiltrating and destroying the various Palestinian terrorist groups. The Shin Bet (Hebrew acronym for General Security Services), Israel's combined secret service and counter-intelligence force, has long been regarded as a crack organization not to be crossed, and it too has dedicated much of its manpower and resources to protecting Israel from terrorist attack.

Yet beyond the cloak-and-dagger world of the intelligence agent, Israel has had to rely on other forces for its survival. These include the highly professional men of the *Mishmar Hagvul* or Border Guards, a para-military police force whose efforts in protecting Israel's borders and points of entry have become legend, including one of the world's most successful counter-insurgency campaigns performed in the maelstrom of Lebanon. Assisting the Border Guards in interdicting terrorist infiltration has been the ultimate barrier Israel can deploy: her battle-tested army, the Israel Defence Forces. Its ground forces along the frontiers and its small though potent navy have done their best hermetically to seal the frontiers; in doing so they have often defeated grandiose attempts by the Palestinians to disrupt the very fabric of Israeli society. When attacks have succeeded, the might of the Israel Air Force has retaliated in kind, often in spectacular fashion. Lastly, there is the Israeli National Police and, more specifically, its élite Bomb Demolition Squad, or sappers. Made up of volunteers who deal with explosives with skill and courage, they are on call throughout the nation and respond every day to calls of suspicious objects which need to be identified, isolated, and neutralized!

The struggle against terrorism has been, at different times, both one of Israel's most secretive campaigns and one of its most overt. Israel has never admitted dispatching Mossad hit teams throughout Europe and the Middle East in order to kill the perpetrators of the Munich Olympics massacre. Although the motive and method of attack were undoubtedly Israeli, Jerusalem would never acknowledge its direct participation. Even after the foiled Mossad attempt to kill the Black September operations chief, Ali Hassan Salameh (the infamous 'Red Prince'), in Lillenhammer, Norway in 1973, there was silence. The shroud of secrecy has lasted to this day, when Jerusalem denied any involvement in the April 1988 assassination of the PLO deputy commander, Abu Jihad, in Tunis. The Shin Bet's role in this war had also remained a highly guarded secret until a public incident (the killing of two captured bus hijackers in 1984) brought their activities to light. Other facets in the war, however, are highly overt. A visitor to Israel is reminded of the nation's vigilance the moment he arrives at Ben-Gurion International Airport and notices heavily armed policemen wearing the Border Guard's trademark – the green beret. If that thought-provoking reality evades you, the constant howl of sirens from the Police Bomb Disposal Squad jeeps is a powerful reminder of exactly what kind of threat Israel faces 24 hours a day, and what it is prepared to do to defeat it. For more than twenty years, Israel has waged this incessant counter-terrorism campaign, understanding only too well that defeat results in the deaths of men, women, and children whose only crime is that of being an Israeli or a Jew. The men and women of Israel's intelligence and military community realize that it is their efforts that provide their citizens with a shield, ensuring that holiday travellers aboard an El Al flight will never again be hijacked and that housewives in Nahariya will never again be forced to witness the savage murders of their husbands and children by revolutionaries seeking publicity in the name of Palestine. It is a war in which the world is their battlefield and no act or risk is too great. From the tarmac at Lod to the streets of London, from the back alleys of Tel Aviv to the exclusive beachfront of Tunis, Israel's guards are without frontiers, having crossed the boundaries of nations, and of the imagination, to ensure that no harm comes to the nation, the people, and the beliefs they have sworn to protect.

1. Mossad

Background to Terror
The Years of No Return, 1967–72

If the countless hours of propaganda beaming from Egyptian radio were accurate, 1967 should have been *the* year of glory for the millions of Palestinians who were living as refugees in camps in Lebanon, Syria, Jordan, and Egypt. President Nasser's promise to push the 'infidel' Jewish State into the Mediterranean was crushed one very sunny June morning, when the might of the Israeli Air Force destroyed Arab air power in one brilliant gambit and, in the process, secured the outcome of the third Arab-Israeli War. It was a conflict which lasted only six days, but which changed forever the face of the Middle East. Not only did the State of Israel emerge from the June 1967 War as the dominant military power in the region, but Palestinian hopes of regaining their homes through a victorious *jihad* were once again shattered. The most ironic tragedy was the fate of a million Palestinian refugees living on the West Bank of the River Jordan and in the Gaza Strip. They had escaped from an infant Israel in 1948 and had nurtured hopes of one day returning to their homes in the vanguard of a victorious Arab army of liberation. They now found themselves under the control of a much more powerful Israel and the hope of liberation became a distant fantasy. A time of desperation was at hand.

Egypt, Jordan, and Syria had denied the Palestinians the legitimate opportunity to face Israel at the conference table and negotiate a just peace to the Arab-Israeli conflict. They had instead manipulated the various Palestinian liberation movements, such as the Egyptian-sponsored Fedayeen of the 1950s, to commit acts of terror and sabotage against Israel in order to satisfy their own specific political agendas. In a January 1964 meeting of the Arab League in Cairo, President Gamal Abdel Nasser bullied the other heads of state into creating an organization to represent the Palestinians' efforts to liberate their homeland from Israeli clutches; the Palestine Liberation Organization (PLO) commanded by Ahmad Shuqairy was born.

The PLO created a governing body known as the Palestine National Council (PNC) whose covenant decreed that 'Palestine is an

Arab homeland' (although they denied claim to the now contested West Bank, controlled by Jordan's King Hussein, and the Gaza Strip, controlled by Nasser's Egypt), and that 'Zionism was imperialist, racist and fascist'. To turn the dream into reality, the PLO created an indigenous army of liberation, the PLA (Palestine Liberation Army), which had units conveniently stationed in Syria, Jordan, and Egypt for quick cross-border operations against Israel. The PLO also called for Arab unity as an integral fact of Palestinian liberation, but Nasser soon took control of the 'Palestinian Cause', much to the alarm of the Jordanians and to the anger of the Syrians. The Syrian Army's Intelligence Commander, Colonel Ahmad Sweidani, reacted by actively recruiting Palestinians throughout the Middle Eastern diaspora whom he intended to train as a convenient pro-Syrian Fedayeen force. In Beirut, his agents found eight politically aware Palestinians, led by a Cairo-born engineer named Yasir Arafat, who had founded an organization of their own called 'The Movement for the Liberation of Palestine'. They received political help from the Ba'ath Party in Damascus and were given Syrian funding and military training. Shortly afterwards the Palestinians renamed themselves *el-Fatah*, the reversed initials of their name in Arabic: *Tahir al-Hatani al-Falastini*.[1]

On 1 January 1965, on a murky winter's morning, a guerrilla from *el-Fatah* crossed the Jordanian border near the Sea of Galilee, and planted a small explosive device alongside the National Water Carrier. Although it was a minor incident causing little damage, it was the genesis of today's Palestinian terrorist movements.

Three years later, the Palestinian revolution and the Middle East were turned upside down. Israel's pre-emptive strike of 6 June 1967 secured her a military victory of unimagined proportions. In just 144 hours, land, air, and sea units of the Israel Defence Forces (IDF) had captured the Sinai Desert and its Palestinian ghetto of Gaza from Egypt; the West Bank of the River Jordan with its 800,000 Palestinians, from Jordan; and the ultra-strategic Golan Heights from Syria. The Palestinian dreams of recovering Haifa, Ramla, Jaffa, and Jerusalem were now apparently lost forever. Spurred into an immediate guerrilla war against Israel, the Palestinian liberation groups, led by Yasir Arafat's poorly supplied *el-Fatah* 'commandos', tried in vain to initiate an effective guerrilla movement from within the Israeli heartland. Infiltrators were quickly hunted down in a counter-insurgency campaign conducted with brutal efficiency by IDF élite forces in the desert wasteland of the Jordan Valley and the fertile splendour of the Beit Shean Valley. Yasir Arafat's *el-Fatah* had long opposed direct acts of terror against civilian targets in Israel and abroad, hoping instead to emulate the 'popular struggle strategy' of guerrilla warfare which had proved so successful for the Viet Cong and the Chinese Communists. It never materialized; as will be examined later in this book, the Shin Bet confiscated the Jordanian police files on known PLO commanders and operatives, and were able to neutralize resistance in the newly occupied territories.

With the inhospitable terrain of much of the West Bank and Gaza Strip working against Palestinian plans for a traditional guerrilla struggle, a new theatre of operation and an innovative approach was urgently required. With the 'Flower Children' in the United States influencing the 1968 leftist Students' Rebellion in France, the time appeared ripe to open up the Palestinians' European front.

Doctor George Habash's Popular Front for the Liberation of Palestine (PFLP) had for years been a pariah among even the more eccentric armed groups which made up the PLO. Habash and his deputy commander, Wadi Haddad, both West Bank Christians, were unique in that their motives were not based purely on the yearning for a Palestinian homeland, but instead centred around a Marxist-Socialist idea of a Pan-Arab revolution. Naturally his extreme politics made many leaders in the Arab world very wary of him, but Habash had the gift of insight and knew exactly how to thrust the plight of the Palestinians on to the world stage. On 23 July 1968, a three-man PFLP team hijacked an El Al (Israel's national airline) flight from Rome to Tel Aviv and sought sanctuary in Algeria.* It was the first act of Palestinian terror to strike outside the confined battleground of the Middle East and would forever change international air travel for hundreds of millions of passengers.

Habash and Haddad justified their act of air piracy by claiming that since El Al had been used to transport arms, and was piloted by a reserve IAF (Israel Air Force) officer, it was a purely military target. The PFLP, however, were not content with hijacking attempts; when the Shin Bet responded with stringent security arrangements for El Al, the PFLP mounted machine-gun and rocket attacks against taxiing El Al aircraft in Athens and Zurich in 1968 and 1969. European governments were outraged by this war, which they cared little about, being waged on their territory, and were forced to escort El Al take-offs and landings with armoured cars and heavily armed troops. This act outraged Habash who called it 'obscene' and he responded in kind with an obvious strategy: strike at any airline servicing Israel. On 29 August 1969, an American TWA jet *en route* from Rome to Tel Aviv was hijacked by PFLP gunmen and taken to Damascus. The PFLP's un-molested attacks against commercial air travel continued, culminating in spectacular fashion on 6 September 1970 when, in a bold and all-inclusive terror offensive, the PFLP hijacked four airliners and attempted to bring Israel and much of the world to its knees. A TWA flight *en route* from Frankfurt to New York and a Swissair aircraft *en route* from Zurich to New York were successfully seized and flown to Dawson's Airfield in the middle of the Jordanian desert near Zarga,

* The commander of that El Al hijacking team, known by his *nom de guerre* of Captain Rifa'at, would continue his terrorist career with spectacular success. His luck ran out on 9 May 1972, however, when he was killed by IDF *Sayeret Mat'kal* commandos who, dressed as mechanics, stormed a hijacked Sabena airliner at Lod Airport. This act was the first 'Special Forces' rescue of hostages.

while a Pan Am flight from Amsterdam to New York was taken to Cairo.

The fourth aircraft to be hijacked was an El Al flight from Israel to New York via Amsterdam. Both Habash and Haddad, in planning 'Skyjack Sunday', hoped to seize as many Israeli hostages as possible and ordered three of the PFLP's best, including Leihla Khalid† (*femme fatale* of the revolution, and successful hijacker of the TWA flight to Damascus) and Patrick Arguello, to seize the Israeli aircraft. Fifteen minutes after the take-off from Amsterdam, Khalid and Arguello (a third terrorist failed to reach the airport in time to board the flight) announced to the passengers that the aircraft had been seized. An armed Shin Bet agent reacted immediately, shooting and wounding Arguello with a .22 calibre Beretta automatic, and Khalid was wrestled to the ground and subdued by an angry passenger. After landing in London, a tug-of-war ensued between armed El Al security officers and British Police. The El Al crew was urged on by Major-General Aharon Yariv, head of Israeli Military Intelligence and future architect of the Israeli intelligence war against Black September, who had been travelling incognito aboard the aircraft *en route* to an intelligence conference in London.[2] The British eventually won their battle for Leihla Khalid and whisked her off to Ealing Police Station. It would, however, be a victory they would soon regret. On 9 September, the PFLP hijacked a BOAC aircraft *en route* from Bombay to London and flew it to Dawson Airfield in Zarqa. Their obvious demand to British authorities: free Miss Khalid at once!

The series of events was climaxed by the dramatic filmed destruction of the three airliners in the Jordanian desert and it appeared, at first, to be a Palestinian victory, but it was in fact a prelude to disaster. For Jordan, Skyjack Sunday meant an end to their much-tested restraint. For years, the Palestinians had been transforming parts of Jordan into a heavily armed, uncontrollable mini-Palestinian state, and the tempers and frustrations of both King Hussein and the Palestinian leadership had been simmering for some time. Furthermore, Israeli retaliatory raids for acts of Palestinian terror had forced a large section of the Jordanian population in the Jordan Valley to flee in haste, which served to exacerbate King Hussein's dilemma. The Dawson Field escapade was the proverbial straw which broke the camel's back, an ominous threat to the King's power following closely on two unsuccessful assassination attempts by Palestinian elements some weeks earlier. On 16 September, King Hussein unleashed his vengeful Bedouin brigades into the refugee camps near Amman. In brutal and tenaciously contested close-quarter fighting, the Jordanians were merciless and inflicted a decisive defeat on the Fedayeen. The results of the 'Civil War' were immediate and

---

† While it is common for women to take up arms in the Palestinian cause their employment as equals to men runs counter to Islamic tradition. The apparent contradiction has not proved susceptible to Israeli attempts to manipulate it for intelligence ends, according to Uri Dan, author of *The Finger of God: Secrets in the War Against Terror*.

far-reaching. The PLO was flung into disarray and sought a new refuge in Lebanon, while Arab unity on the Palestinian question was destroyed. For the Palestinians, it became known as 'Black September' – a disaster on a par with the creation of the Jewish State, and one which they swore to avenge.

Out of this anger was born the Black September Organization, one of the most feared terror groups modern history has known. Their desperate acts were initially directed against the Hashemite Kingdom of Jordan and included the cold-blooded assassination of Jordanian Prime Minister Wasfi a-Tal in a Cairo Hotel on 28 November 1971 – followed by the subsequent drinking of his blood by the perpetrators of the ghastly crime. Other attacks soon followed, including the 15 December 1971 shooting of Jordan's Ambassador to the Court of Saint James's in London, the bombing of the Jordanian Embassy in Geneva and the execution of five Jordanians, suspected of being Israeli agents, in Cologne on 6 February 1972. The Arab world stood ambivalently silent while Black September engaged in 'justified vengeance' for alleged Jordanian crimes against the Palestinian people, then they vociferously and joyfully embraced the organization when its attacks against Israel began. All along, the PLO's top leadership claimed it exercised no control over the activities of the secretive Black September Organization. In fact, it had been covertly created by Yasir Arafat himself, and commanded by his deputy and intelligence chief, Abu Iyad, as a secretive action group which would terrorize the enemies of Palestine without incurring negative publicity for the politically moderate PLO. 'The suffering of the Palestinians', they argued, 'would become the suffering of the entire world.'

The first Black September attack against an Israeli or 'pro-Israeli' target was the sabotage of oil tanks at Ravenstein in The Netherlands. Other similar incidents soon followed, but they resulted in minimal loss of life and property, having 'more bark than bite'. That soon changed on 8 May 1972, when a two-man, two-woman Black September team hijacked a Belgian Sabena Airlines jet on its way to Israel. The audacious move was a clear and resounding signal that Black September meant business. Even though the hijacked airliner was subsequently stormed and the hostages freed by a unit from *Sayeret Mat'kal* (the IDF's élite and highly secretive General Staff Reconnaissance Unit), Black September was on the map; the war had only just begun.

The year 1972 continued to be a banner year for terrorist operations against Israel when three members of the Japanese Red Army, working on behalf of George Habash and the PFLP, committed one of the worst massacres yet. Arriving at Lod International Airport on a routine flight from Rome on 30 May 1972, the three Japanese gunmen entered the customs hall just like any other incoming travellers entering the Holy Land. Once their luggage was recovered they opened their bags and each removed Czech VZ-58 7.62mm assault rifles with 30-round magazines, and several Russian F-1 anti-personnel grenades from false bottoms in their cases. During the next seventeen seconds they fired more than three hundred rounds and threw two grenades, which carnage resulted in 27 dead and more than 70 seriously wounded; mainly Puerto Ricans on a religious pilgrimage. The only terrorist taken alive, Kozo Okamoto, was given an 'intensive' interrogation which provided an invaluable insight into the vast international network of alliances the Palestinian terrorists had established world-wide.‡

This same 'international network' working on behalf of the Palestinian revolution (although for the PFLP-GC this time) was in action once again on 16 August in Italy, when an explosive device hidden in a booby-trapped turntable detonated on board an El Al flight from Rome to Tel Aviv. The Captain's tenacious flying skill and an increased fortification of El Al fuselages to cope with such explosions combined to prevent a mid-air massacre. Nevertheless, the explosive device, brought on board by the innocent Dutch girlfriend of a 'handsome' Palestinian,§ punched a 40-centimetre wide hole through the aircraft body. Preventive security measures had for once succeeded in thwarting a Palestinian terrorist attack, but there would be no such luck during Black September's next, and most audacious, European operation.

The 1972 Olympics in Munich was a milestone for the West German people. Hosting the international games of peace was a rite of passage for that nation from its Nazi past into a much prayed for, peaceful German future. Munich, it was hoped, would soon be remembered as the site of Olympics sport competition, and not the site of Chamberlain's bamboozlement by Hitler. Yasir Arafat, Abu Iyad and Black September's infamous 'Red Prince', Ali Hassan Salameh, had somewhat different plans.

According to Willie Voss, a neo-Nazi German criminal who had served as liaison for the Palestinians inside Germany, the thought process behind the Black September operation in Munich began in Libya during the spring months of 1972. A high-level Black September operation and intelligence team met in the Libyan capital, Tripoli, to co-ordinate their efforts with their sleeper agents in Europe, their commanders in Lebanon, Libya and Syria, as well as the top PLO leadership in Beirut who enthusiastically approved of Black September's master stroke.[3] On 5 September 1972, as the world marvelled at the exploits of Soviet gymnast Olga Korbut, and American swimmer Mark Spitz, the 6,000 journalists and TV crews covering the athletics were to switch their attention to something of a totally different nature, a life and death drama where the Olympics message of international

‡ Okamoto was released from an Israeli prison in 1985, together with 1,150 convicted Palestinian terrorists, in a highly controversial exchange with Ahmed Jibril's PFLP-GC for three IDF soldiers kidnapped in Lebanon.
§ Despite their equal, though sometimes sexually abusive treatment of female Palestinian guerrillas, the 'Palestinian Movement' made it a feature of their work to exploit 'foreign' women in this fashion; this was only one of a number of other similar incidents which have continued until today.

co-operation and brotherhood would soon be forgotten in a hail of murderous gunfire.

Just before dawn on 5 September, eight Black September terrorists, clad in track suits and carrying travel bags, climbed over the fence surrounding the Olympics village and sprinted towards 31 Connolly Strasse, home to the small Israeli Olympics team. The Black September force had been carefully screened and selected for their murderous task. The leader, Mohammed Masalhad, was an architect who spoke fluent German and English and had even been on hand during the construction of the Olympics Village. The others included a terrorist known only as Toni, a guest worker in the Olympics Village kitchen, who spoke fluent Hebrew. They soon located the rooms of the Israeli team and began their attack with military precision. The combative though fatal efforts of the wrestler, Joseph Romano, and his coach, Moshe Weinberg, to deny the terrorists entrance to their quarters provided enough warning for a good many of the athletes in a nearby room to escape. Armed with AK-47s and grenades, however, the Black September squad succeeded in seizing nine hostages with relative ease. The Munich operation had been given the code-name Operation 'Berim and Ikrit', the name of two Christian Arab villages which had surrendered to the Israelis without resistance in 1948. The name was chosen by Fakhi al-Umari, a member of Black September's internal security department, also known as the 'Killer Section'.[4]

Masalhad's demands, issued to the West German officials and soon after to much of the world's media, were impressive: he ordered the release of 200 Palestinians and Lod Airport murderer, Kozo Okamoto, held by the Israelis, plus the release of Red Army Faction leaders, Andreas Baader and Ulrike Meinhof, in custody with the Germans, all in exchange for the 'living' Israeli hostages who would be released in an unspecified Arab capital. If their demands were not met within the designated deadline, they would kill one hostage an hour. Through her Defence Minister, Moshe Dayan, the Israeli premier, Golda Meir, strongly reiterated Israel's traditional public stance of 'never negotiating with terrorists'. With little room for manoeuvre, the Germans were forced to wait and see in a situation which called for a decisive response. As Masalhad's deadlines were pushed back and back, the Germans began to grow ever more desperate, even offering the terrorists money and women. The offers were foolish and disrespectful to the fanatic dedication of a terrorist; they underscored the lack of understanding the world had for the Black September Organization. Such men and women were not common criminals, nor profit hungry; as Masalhad would reply to his German negotiators, 'Money is not important and neither are our lives.'

The West German Federal State of Bavaria was not equipped to cope with such a débâcle during its well-publicized Games of 'peace and joy'. West German police, sporting track suits and submachine-guns, had staked out the Israeli quarters and had taken up firing positions in the hope that they would find a terrorist in their gun sights, but in reality there was little they could do. Hoping as a last resort to ambush the terrorists on open ground at Fürstenfeldbruk NATO Airfield and free the hostages unscathed, the Germans agreed to the terrorists' demands for safe passage to the Arab capital of their choice. They agreed to take the terrorists and their hostages in two West German military Bell-205 helicopters to a prepared Lufthansa jet for Tunis. German officials never intended to allow the incident to be exported and urging the Germans on in their hard-line stance was General Tzvi Zamir, the unobtrusive Mossad chief, who had flown to Munich together with an Arabic-speaking Shin Bet agent to supervise the unfolding events.[5]

The events of the next few hours were utterly terrifying and confusing. West German police snipers had insufficiently prepared their operation, expecting far fewer than eight gunmen. Armed only with bolt-action snipers' rifles, and with no firm military or police back-up, they were heavily outgunned for a potentially desperate fire-fight. Major-General Tzvi Zamir had urged a more forceful military effort, but Bavarian police officials did not take kindly to suggestions made by Zamir and the very experienced and outspoken Shin Bet officer.

Under the gloomy darkness of an autumn sky, the beating noise of three helicopter's rotor blades (two carrying the terrorists and hostages, and the other carrying a team of German negotiators and the concerned Israeli contingent) signalled the commencement of the showdown. As Masalhad and a comrade walked confidently back to the helicopters after inspecting the prepared Lufthansa Boeing 727 airliner and declaring it to their satisfaction, a police sniper in position on the control tower roof opened fire. His lone shot was followed by a sputtering barrage from the four other police snipers whose crackling rifle shots engulfed the silent tarmac. The terrorist walking with Masalhad was killed instantly, but Mohammed dived into the shadows of the dimly lit airfield and fired a deadly burst at the control tower from his AK-47 assault rifle which killed the poorly concealed police sniper. After a six-minute fire fight, in which an additional two terrorists were killed, a stray bullet struck a master electric cable and the dim lights illuminating the airfield were doused.

For the next ninety minutes, a tense stand-off ensued between the five surviving terrorists, the German police officials, and the Shin Bet agent. At a few moments after midnight, the remaining terrorists decided to act. They leapt into the firing position and deliberately raked the two helicopters holding the hostages with automatic fire as well as tossing in an anti-personnel grenade for good measure. The nine Israeli athletes had no chance of escape. In the subsequent orange glow of an explosion the helicopters and their condemned hostage cargo detonated into a fireball. Major-General Tzvi Zamir observed the eerie scene in horror and disgust while the Shin Bet officer exploded in rage. The thought of 'what might have been' had Israel been allowed to assume command of the situation would forever haunt the Mossad chief.[6]

During the fire-fight between the terrorists and the German police, who by now were reinforced with armoured cars, Masalhad was killed and the remaining three captured. Initially, the media had learned of the rescue attempt and had prematurely reported the rescue of the Israeli athletes. At 0300 on 6 September, however, a press conference disclosed the tragic results of the mêlée. The following day, 80,000 people attended a memorial service at the main Olympics stadium. This solemn event was followed by the return of the eleven murdered Israelis to Israel, where a period of national grief and outrage engulfed the nation.

For the perpetrators of the crime and their supporters, Black September's moment of glory at Munich was a national victory. In an interview given to the Arabic journal *As-Sayyad* on 13 September 1972, Doctor George Habash's ecstatic reflections on the Black September operation were shockingly expressed:

'A bomb in the White House, a mine in the Vatican, the death of Mao Tse-tung, an earthquake in Paris could not have echoed through the consciousness of every man in the world like the operation at Munich … The choice of the Olympics, from a purely propagandist viewpoint, was 100 per cent successful. It was like painting the name of Palestine on a mountain that can be seen from the four corners of the earth.'[7]

Although most of the civilized world was horrified by the murders at Munich – hundreds of letters in the international press labelled the terrorists as 'scum of the earth' and 'degenerate heroes of the sewers' – nowhere was the shock more heartfelt than in Israel. Its response was a series of massive air strikes against ten separate Palestinian terrorist bases in Lebanon (Operation *'K'shichut'* or 'Rigidity 6'), later followed by extensive ground incursions (Operation *'Kalahat'* or 'Turmoil 4') against bases in southern Lebanon following Black September's failed attempt to assassinate Tzadok Ophir, an Israeli diplomat in Brussels. The blood and fire war of Black September against the State of Israel continued with a vengeance.

Less than two weeks after the Olympic Games murders Black September initiated its infamous 'postal offensive'. On 18 September agents in Amsterdam sent seventy letter bombs to Israel and Israeli representatives around the world. Although most of the explosive parcels were identified and neutralized, one succeeded in killing Doctor Ami Shachuri, the Agricultural Attaché at Israel's London embassy. On 4 October Black September operatives in Malaysia sent eleven letter bombs to Israeli and Jewish addresses throughout the world in such diverse target locations as Chile, Rhodesia and Jamaica. On 25 October the organization's sleeper agents in Israel audaciously mailed letter bombs to American President Nixon, Secretary of State Rogers, and Defense Secretary Laird in an attempt to bring the Arab-Israeli conflict to American shores. As will be seen later in this book, when relating the

Shin Bet's counter-intelligence and counter-terrorist efforts, these 'sleeper' agents turned out to be a mixed Palestinian-Jewish espionage group working on behalf of the Syrians and Black September whose leader, oddly and tragically enough, was Udi Adiv, a native born *sabra*, a *kibbutznik*, and an ex-paratrooper.[8]

October 1972 also saw the beginning of the anticipated attempts to free the surviving Palestinian Munich commandos from German custody. Three had survived the Fürstenfeldbruk mêlée, but as a Black September spokesman ominously warned, 'The sky is full of German airliners'. On the morning of 29 October a Lufthansa Boeing 727, on a routine flight from Beirut to Ankara, was hijacked by two Black September commandos (some reports identify the hijackers as belonging to Doctor Habash's PFLP). Hours later, the three tight-lipped Munich Olympics terrorists were led from their prison in Bavaria and ferried in a privately hired executive jet to the Libyan capital of Tripoli to a hero's welcome. The released men appeared on Libyan television offering little remorse and they promised that, if ordered to do so, they would carry out similar operations in the future. As Palestinian leaders basked in their glory, proclaiming that 'We are all Black September now', heads were bowed in shame in Israel. The perpetrators of one of the most ghastly terrorist outrages in recent memory had proved that crime did indeed pay.

Now victorious and cocky, Black September continued on its murderous path. The day after the release of the surviving Munich Three, Black September agents posted fifty letter bombs from Malaysia to Israeli and Jewish representative offices world-wide. Days later, Indian police, acting on an anonymous tip, seized 42 letter bombs intended for Jewish companies throughout western Europe. Other, more sinister, plots were uncovered, including a planned sea-jacking and subsequent massacre at Haifa by four Black September gunmen.

Perhaps fittingly, 1972 ended on a somewhat positive note for Israel. On 28 December two smarly dressed individuals approached the Israeli embassy in Bangkok, Thailand. The police officer standing guard over the facility in this most peaceful of countries was sure that the two men were diplomats returning from the investiture of Prince Vajiralongkorn as Crown Prince, and he allowed them in with a salute and a smile. Once inside the grounds, the two terrorists in full morning dress made it possible for two other heavily armed comrades to gain entrance to the grounds and within minutes they had seized the embassy and six very valuable hostages, including the Israeli Ambassador to Cambodia, Shimon Avimor. They threatened to destroy the building, together with its hostages, if 36 persons named on a list were not released from Israeli custody. The embassy was immediately surrounded by Thai police and military units. The Thai Chief of Staff, who coincidentally had been in Munich at the time of the massacre, courageously entered the embassy grounds unarmed and miraculously succeeded in.convincing the terrorists that Israel would never comply with their demands and that their efforts were futile. The Black September gunmen surrendered and were flown to Cairo together with the Egyptian Ambassador. After a short imprisonment in Egypt they were released to Syrian custody where, according to *Al-Ghoumhuriya*, they faced a secret Palestinian court-martial for failing in their mission.[9]

Black September's Far Eastern fiasco ended an extremely bloody year on a considerably peaceful note. It was the first, and last, Israeli embassy seized by terrorists. Symbolically, the Bangkok incident was a sad portrait of the bitter struggle waged by Palestinian terrorists against Israel in the four corners of the earth. It was the largest single successful year ever for Palestinian terrorist operations against Israel, but one which would soon be avenged.

'Call in the Spooks'
The Mossad's War Against Black September

The threat which Black September's reign of terror posed to the State of Israel was both dire and immediate. Traditionally, Israel's response to an encroachment against her national security was simple and unrelenting: decisive military action. Yet unlike an el-Fatah training base in southern Lebanon, Black September was not a tangible target to be wiped out by a squadron of F-4E Phantoms conducting a surgical air strike, and unlike a Soviet surface-to-air radar system, Black September's infrastructure couldn't be plucked out of the desert by heliborne IDF paratroopers. Black September was a highly secret, extremely well-organized force trained for spectacular acts of terror. They were instructed by and modelled on the KGB and GRU, the recipients of technical and military assistance from the Cubans, Czechoslovaks, North Koreans, and East Germans. They were supported logistically and financially by the intelligence services of the Arab states. Most importantly, they were not revolutionaries hoping to change the world's political balance in an instant, but soldiers committed to total war against the State of Israel on a global battlefield. To defeat Black September, Israel would have to break tradition and respond in kind.

The Mossad or *Mossad Merkazi Le'mode'in Ve'tafkidim Meyuchadim* (Institution for Intelligence and Special Tasks) was Israel's youngest, although certainly its most flamboyant intelligence service, and the one most suited for an all-out war against Black September. It was not, however, an organization seeking or willing to kill; it was best described by Tzvi Zamir when he stated, 'What the Mossad looks for are men trained to kill but with a deep aversion to killing.'[10] In historic terms, Mossad was a cumulative amalgam formed out of two of pre-independence Palestine's intelligence organizations: the *Sha'i* or *Sherut Yediot* and the *Mossad L'Aliyah Bet*. The *Sha'i* (Information Service) was the *Haganah*'s ultra-secret intelligence arm and it also controlled the internal security unit *Sherut Bitachon* (Security Service) which was the forerunner of today's *Sherut Bitachon Haklali* known as the *Sha'ba'k* or Shin Bet for short. The *Mossad L'Aliyah Bet* was the Jewish Agency's intelligence network which assisted Jewish refugees in post-Holocaust Europe to reach Palestine by *any means possible*. The network of agents, smugglers, operatives, and safe-houses which the *Mossad L'Aliyah Bet* established in post-war Europe remained intact following the declaration of Israeli independence, and the transition from a refugee smuggling organization into a national foreign intelligence service was smooth and natural. Like any government agency struggling for the spotlight and attention, *Sha'i*, Shin Bet and the Mossad *L'Aliyah Bet* were professional, highly political and extremely competitive.

In April 1951, Israel's Prime Minister/Defence Minister, David Ben-Gurion, decided to unify and co-ordinate his nation's intelligence-gathering capabilities. The man who reformed and co-ordinated the Israeli intelligence community into the effective body of forces it is today was Reuven Shiloah, the chairman of the *Va'adat Rashai Hasherutim* (Service Commander Committee), the Israeli Government's principal intelligence and security agency, answerable to the Prime Minister's office. He ordered the integration of most of the specific military intelligence units from *Sha'i* into something controlled by the Israel Defence Forces. This meant the small though powerful Naval Intelligence component, the embryonic Air Force Intelligence Service, and the field intelligence units forming into what became known as IDF Military Intelligence (*Agaf Modei'in*, or as it is better known, *A'man*). *Sha'i*'s indigenous Political Intelligence Unit was made independent from the Ministry of Foreign Affairs, and the Secret Intelligence Service, to be known as the Mossad, was born.

In its formative years, Mossad developed a reputation second to none, due largely to its Controller (or *Memuneh*) Isser Harel, who assumed command on 16 September 1952. A former counter-intelligence officer and Shin Bet chief, Isser Harel was fiercely honest, straightforward and intrinsically gifted enough to run a spy organization. In the days when the Mossad consisted of a few small rooms in a Tel Aviv office complex, and with a staff of dozens, Harel told Ben-Gurion that, 'A political intelligence organization without proper funding, government support and resources would humiliate and one day haunt the State of Israel.'[11] Indeed, the Russian-born spymaster had been proven right: the Shin Bet was rocked by several espionage cases involving trusted aides to Ben-Gurion acting on behalf of the Russians, and Military Intelligence was involved in the disastrous Operation 'Suzannah' or 'Lavon Affair' in Egypt. Not only did Mossad keep its nose relatively clean, but it upstaged its counterparts the world over.

Mossad's first true *coup*, helping to propel it towards world renown, was that of being the first Western intelligence agency to obtain a copy of Soviet Premier Nikita Khrushchev's historic speech given to the 25 February 1956 meeting of the Soviet Communist Party Congress during which he denounced Stalin's policies. The Khrushchev speech was obtained by a lone Mossad maverick, and the operation came to personify the unique, loyal and extremely egalitarian Mossad *esprit de corps*.

During the next ten years, Mossad succeeded in pulling off two of the most dramatic intelligence operations of the post-war era. The first was the kidnapping of Nazi war criminal Adolph Eichmann from his lair in Buenos Aires in 1960 to stand trial in Jerusalem. The second, and perhaps most important militarily, was the masterful one-man intelligence sensation of Eli Cohen, Mossad's spy in Damascus. Cohen, an Egyptian Jew, managed an elaborate identity and political masquerade where he elevated himself from the obscurity of a wealthy 'Syrian' businessman in Argentina to trusted confidant of the Ba'ath Party and designate for the post of Defence Minister. Before his capture, attributed by many to his over-zealousness, Cohen provided his handlers in Tel Aviv with an accurate, almost intimate, portrait of the Syrian military and, most importantly, their elaborate defences along the Golan Heights. The information he gathered was of monumental importance to the IDF capture of the Golan plateau on 9 June 1967.

Another successful Mossad *coup*, instrumental in Israel's striking 1967 War victory, was in convincing a religiously persecuted Iraqi pilot to defect to Israel with his MiG-21, giving the Israel Air Force's fighter-pilots an even greater edge in aerial combat thanks to what they learned from their acquisition.

Although Mossad succeeded in carrying out its ordained task of political action and foreign intelligence-collection in the years prior to June 1967, the post-1967 era brought it increased responsibility with the task of counter-terrorism in a global arena. The sweeping Israeli military victory in the 1967 War brought greater regional involvement from the superpowers. The Soviets took the lead by re-building the Arab armies with massive arms shipments and by bolstering the budding Palestinian liberation movement with KGB assistance and control. This development contributed enormously to the growing co-operation between the various international terrorist outfits, from both the left and the right of the political spectrum. Since the majority of terrorist attacks at the time were directed by the Palestinians against Israeli and Jewish targets, it was this development which most worried the already over-taxed resources of Mossad.

Initially, Mossad and Shin Bet scored impressive victories against Palestinian terrorists and their European comrades. As will be seen later, Shin Bet's inspired security efforts helped make El Al virtually hijack-proof, while Mossad, headed by its Controller, Major-General Meir Amit, had its agents arduously track and undermine Palestinian terrorist capabilities throughout the Middle East and Europe. Major-General Amit took control of Mossad in 1963 and greatly increased espionage activity against the Arab states and the then fledgling Palestinian liberation movements. Amit was a 'soldier's soldier' in the Israeli tradition, and remarkably would be the only man at the time of this book's writing to have headed both Military Intelligence and Mossad. Meir Amit also understood the international dimensions of Palestinian terrorism, and appreciated that Israel would have to act internationally in order to defeat it.

According to foreign sources, Meir Amit dispatched Mossad agents to El Al offices world-wide to supervise the security interrogation of suspicious travellers purchasing tickets at the last moment for flights to Israel. As indicated in *The Spymasters of Israel*, Stewart Steven's masterful examination of Israel's intelligence services, the tactic was extremely successful. On several occasions, would-be hijackers and saboteurs were identified, fingerprinted and photographed, thus terminating their careers as terrorists.

Most of the European intelligence services regarded the Palestinian offensive as strictly an Israeli problem. They forced Mossad into unilateral initiatives which would eventually enlighten the Europeans as to the activities and training of their own, indigenous, urban terrorist groups. The operations of a half-Jewish, neo-Marxist West German professor working on behalf of Mossad in the early 1970s not only succeeded in uncovering dozens of planned PFLP operations, but helped the West Germans unravel the intricate labyrinth of the Baader-Meinhoff gang. The PFLP's ties to international groups such as the Provisional IRA and the Japanese Red Army were uncovered and dealt with through their nation's respective internal security services.[12]

Perhaps Mossad's greatest success in the early days of this campaign was the tenacious activity of Baruch Cohen, their station chief in Brussels. Historically, Paris was the hotbed of Palestinian activity in Europe and therefore it was also the centre of Israel's intelligence efforts on the continent. De Gaulle's pro-Arab policies and his arms embargo against Israel, however, critically limited Mossad's freedom of movement and its co-operation with France's counter-intelligence service, the *Service de Documentation Extérieure de Contre-Espionnage* (SDECE). As a result, Mossad's European operations were split among Amsterdam and Brussels, and the 35-year-old Cohen, working under the alias of Moshe Hanan Yishai, undertook enormous responsibilities in taking on the Palestinians. His efforts provided invaluable intelligence on the PFLP's penchant for the recruitment of unsuspecting European females for terrorist deeds, including the capture of two French Moroccan sisters as they patiently stood in line at passport control at Lod Airport planning to deliver explosives to Israel. Cohen's investigations also led to the uncovering of the identity of the PFLP's European master of terrorist operations: an Algerian, and owner of the prestigious Parisian *Théâtre de l'Ouest*, named Mohammed Boudia. Both Boudia's and Cohen's names would appear in the headlines in the months to come.

Even with all the intelligence Mossad had gathered on the Palestinian groups, their operatives continued to function against Israeli or Jewish targets in Europe. The intelligence offensive also failed to answer the most pressing tactical question facing Israeli planners: What to do with the terrorists?

Many high-ranking Israeli military and political leaders openly advocated the assassination of the top Palestinian terrorist leadership as the most effective deterrent to anti-Israeli terrorist activity. The Officer Commanding (OC) IDF Southern Command at the time, the ever-controversial Major-General Ariel 'Arik' Sharon, even went so far as to advocate the formation of a special *military* command under General Staff control to eradicate Palestinian terrorism world-wide once and for all. Sharon's previous successes against Palestinian insurgency while commander of 'Unit 101', and then against Palestinian terrorism in Gaza during his tenure as OC Southern Command, proved that violent, unorthodox military means was a viable option. Assassination, on the other hand, had always been a very sensitive topic in Israel's intelligence circles, and was not looked upon favourably by those who feared that open murder by Mossad, Shin Bet and *A'man* (IDF Military Intelligence) would forever lower their standards of morality. When Mossad embarked on its murderous letter bomb campaign against German scientists working on ballistic missiles capable of delivering chemical and biological payloads for the Egyptians in the early 1960s, its controversial political overtones caused such a rift between Prime Minister David Ben-Gurion and his Controller, super spymaster Isser Harel, that the latter resigned in anger.

Assassination as a tool of counter-terrorism policy had, however, been successful in the past. The July 1956 assassinations of Colonels Hafaz and Mustafa, Egyptian Military Intelligence's controlling officers of the Palestinian Fedayeen in Egypt and Jordan, by Israeli agents was a brilliant success. The parcel bomb explosions not only ended the lives of two very influential Egyptian intelligence officers, but it curbed the Fedayeen, and any serious Palestinian military threat, for more than a decade. If the policy of killing leaders were to be re-established, it would have to comply with the IDF's strict adherence to *Tohar Haneshek* or 'Purity of Arms': the moral code which dictates and limits the use of deadly force. The new logic declared it a policy of direct deterrence rather than one of indiscriminate revenge. While the notion remained a hot topic of debate, it would be the massacre of Christian pilgrims at Lod Airport by the Japanese Red Army on behalf of the PFLP that would set the machine in motion.

As the blood was still being cleansed from the baggage claim hall at Lod Airport, Mossad agents in Beirut, acting under the direct orders of Tzvi Zamir, booby-trapped the car of Ghassan Kanafani, a poet, novelist and intellectual. He was also a member of the PFLP's Central Command and one of the planners of the Lod Airport massacre. He was killed, tragically with his 17-year-old niece, in a fiery explosion of twisted metal. Six weeks later, Kanafani's obvious successor, 29-year-old Bassam Abu Sharrif, an articulate PFLP information officer, was severely injured when a book bomb addressed to his Beirut office exploded in his face.* Such attacks were not declared as official Israeli policy, but they served as effective reminders to the PFLP that they were not immune from the long arm of Israeli justice.

The tragedy at Munich hit Israeli Prime Minister Golda Meir hard. She had a well-earned reputation as Israel's 'iron woman'; but she also prided herself on being a 'national grandmother', a leader who had a maternal care for the well-being of her people and who could conduct top secret government meetings in her kitchen over tea and home-made cake. She had been ecstatic when the initial Press reports described the German police rescue operation as a brilliant success, only to be shattered by a telephone call from Mossad chief Zamir in Munich describing the horror he had witnessed. Mrs Meir symbolically viewed the athletes as her children and no matter how much of an Israeli disaster Munich was, it was a personal tragedy as well. Prime Minister Meir was quick to blame it on her intelligence services, and on the Mossad in particular. Why hadn't they been able to infiltrate Black September properly in order to gain information and disrupt the Munich operation? Why hadn't Shin Bet painstakingly researched the nationalities of the foreign workers at the Olympics Village, and why hadn't more stringent security measures been applied to such an *obvious* terrorist target as the Israeli Olympics team?

Inevitably, heads would roll and on 16 September 1972 the 'iron woman' wielded her axe. As a result of the official government Koeppel Report's findings into the Munich Massacre, Prime Minister Meir ordered three high-ranking Shin Bet and Mossad officers to resign. They were a Shin Bet officer assigned to the Bonn embassy, a Mossad analyst long since due for retirement, and a clerk in the Foreign Ministry, the Mossad's close ally (*see* chart). The impetus for an all-out intelligence offensive against Black September had been given and Prime Minister Meir gave the go-ahead.

On 10 September 1972, with the flags at Israeli installations still flying at half mast in honour of her eleven slain Olympians fallen in Munich, Black September struck once again in a foiled attempt to assassinate an Israeli diplomat in Brussels. The target was Tzadok Ophir, an apparently low level employee at the Israeli Embassy, who was in fact an undercover Mossad agent in charge of, among other things, infiltrating the Palestinian terror networks. Some little while earlier, Mohammed Rabah, a known Moroccan *emigré* who had offered to work for the Israelis in the past, telephoned Ophir and offered some valuable information on future Black September operations in Europe. The temptation was too great at a time when agents were desperate to

* Today, a partially blinded Abu Sharrif is seen on network news shows throughout the world in his capacity as PLO information officer.

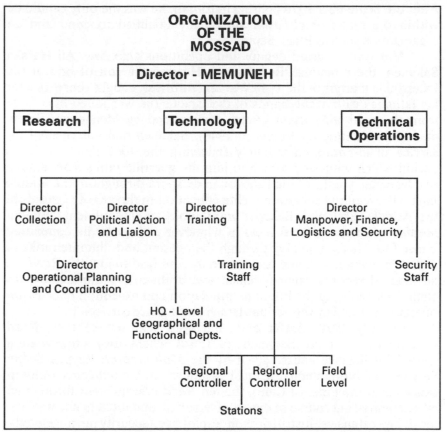

ORGANIZATION
OF THE
MOSSAD

Director - MEMUNEH

Research   Technology   Technical
Operations

Director
Collection

Director
Political Action
and Liaison

Director
Training

Director
Manpower, Finance,
Logistics and Security

Director
Operational Planning
and Coordination

Training
Staff

Security
Staff

HQ - Level
Geographical and
Functional Depts.

Regional
Controller

Regional
Controller

Field
Level

Stations

get any possible leads that could bring the perpetrators of Munich to justice, and Ophir would value any morsel of information, even if it were a *nom de guerre*, a telephone number, or a face! The experienced Mossad agent went against the normal operation protocols and agreed to meet Rabah at a secluded café. During the meeting, Rabah pumped four 9mm bullets into Ophir, who miraculously survived the attack.[13]

A few weeks later, three terrorists burst into the apartment of Khader Kanou, a Syrian radio reporter in Paris, and shot him dead. According to numerous accounts, Kanou was a Mossad informer and the gunmen were identified as Black September commandos.

Black September's attacks against the Mossad agents only days after the Munich fiasco was a clear indication as to their effectiveness and intentions. It should have come as no surprise to the Israelis.

Black September's leaders were all extreme hard-liners who had deep historic and family ties with their native Palestine. Saleh Khalef, known by his *nom de guerre* of Abu Iyad, was a native of Jaffa and one of the founders of *el-Fatah* together with Yasir Arafat. His cunning and ruthless style brought him to the command of *el-Fatah*'s *Jihaz el-Razd*, the organization's much feared intelligence and reconnaissance section.

After the September 1970 fighting in Jordan, he was the only candidate within the ranks of *el-Fatah* sufficiently qualified to command an organization such as Black September.

Abu Iyad's trusted deputy and operations chief was Ali Hassan Salameh, the infamous 'Red Prince'. He was the son of one of the Palestinian martyrs of the 1948 War and ruthlessly sought vengeance for his father's death at the hands of the Israelis (he was killed by a force from the right-wing Irgun group, commanded by Menachem Begin, during the fighting for Ramla in 1948). Salameh had volunteered for service in *el-Fatah* immediately following the 1967 Arab defeat, a period which witnessed a rush to join the guerrilla ranks from among the desperate youths of the Palestinian diaspora throughout the Middle East. His wealthy background, élite education in the private schools of the Middle East and Europe, good looks, and confident, affluent *machismo* made him a success in whatever endeavour he committed himself to. He rose quickly through the peasant and illiterate ranks of *el-Fatah*, eventually being summoned by Abu Iyad to join the *Razd*. As an internal security agent Salameh was brilliant and unrelenting, his claim to fame being the brutal manipulation and execution of *el-Fatah* operatives turned by the various Israeli intelligence services.†

In early 1970, Arafat and Abu Iyad sent ten of their *Razd* lieutenants, including Salameh, to Cairo where they underwent a special intelligence course given by the *Mukhabarat*, Egypt's Secret Service and undoubtedly the most advanced Arab intelligence outfit in existence at the time. In Cairo, the ten *Razd* officers went through an all-encompassing course in the art of terrorism and intelligence warfare, receiving extensive instruction in espionage, security arrangements, cold-killing, and explosives from KGB and GRU trained agents. The ten would soon form the nucleus of Black September and would provide the State of Israel with its most challenging adversary yet.

As noted earlier, the standard Israeli reaction to a terrorist incident was an act of military retribution against an identifiable target. For example, in retaliation for the 1968 El Al hijacking to Algiers, IDF paratroopers under the command of Colonel 'Raful' Eitan conducted a daring commando raid against Beirut International Airport (Operation 'Tshura', or 'Gift'), destroying thirteen Middle East Airlines (MEA) aircraft in the process. Such retaliatory raids and air-strikes were a more difficult proposition when dealing with Black September and it was decided that more covert initiatives were appropriate. Such a step was made possible by two very unique individuals: Mossad chief Major-General Tzvi Zamir and Military Intelligence commander Major-General Aharon Yariv. Both were the antithesis of the stereo-typical cocky and gung-ho Israeli generals, and in many ways an unlikely duo to command such a violent operation.

† Years later the rumour, now believed to be fact, stated that the 'Red Prince' was himself turned, becoming one of the CIA's most valuable sources of intelligence in the Arab world.

Tzvi Zamir was born in Poland in 1924, and whisked to Palestine by his Zionist parents that same year. He volunteered for the *Pal'mach* (the *Haganah*'s élite, British-sponsored guerrilla strike force) in 1942, but after the war was imprisoned by the British for his work on behalf of illegal Jewish immigrants to Palestine. In 1948 Zamir commanded the *Pal'mach*'s 6th Battalion during the brutal fighting in and around Jerusalem. He would rise up the IDF command ladder to hold a variety of posts, ranging from *Giva'ati* Infantry Brigade commander and commanding officer of the infantry school to OC Southern Command during the peaceful era of the early 1960s. In 1966 he was appointed the IDF's Military Attaché in London and as a result didn't participate in the 1967 War, which did not go down well with all sections of the IDF. He was, however, considered a brilliant and tireless worker who had the very amiable personality of a 'boss' able both to instruct and learn. He was given the title of Controller in 1969 when Prime Minister Levi Eshkol, under intense political pressure to appoint a general to the Mossad helm, satisfied his critics with Major-General Tzvi Zamir. Although Zamir's ascension stifled the military and outraged hardline Mossad professionals, the new Controller won over his critics with his industrious methods. Most importantly, Prime Minister Meir had the utmost confidence in him, although she held another man in even greater regard.

Major-General Aharon Yariv was born in Moscow in 1920. He emigrated to Palestine, joined the *Haganah* in 1939 and, like many other Palestinian Jews, served in the British Army in the fight against Hitler. An infantry commander in the defunct Alexandroni Brigade in 1948, Yariv also rose quickly in the IDF chain of command, serving as IDF Military Attaché in Washington and commanding the Golani Infantry Brigade before entering the intelligence world. He was appointed Military Intelligence chief in 1963 and served in that post brilliantly for nine years. His leadership and innovative approach to intelligence-gathering and analysis efforts were considered instrumental in Israel's lightning Six Day War victory, and the cutting edge in directing the IDF's special operations initiative during the subsequent War of Attrition. He was about to assume a government post assisting Defence Minister Moshe Dayan when Prime Minister Meir offered him the unique and hitherto unprecedented post of 'Special Adviser for Terrorist Matters'.

Zamir and Yariv quickly established a developed, though sometimes uneasy partnership in directing their nation's new course of action. Although Yariv's appointment undermined the office of the Controller, the decision for all-out war against Black September did have one very immediate effect on Mossad; its operating budget was doubled overnight.

The largest question looming over the heads of Zamir and Yariv was, who to hit? It was unanimously decided not to pursue the top political leadership of the PLO, but to extinguish the careers of the operational planning geniuses. It was these men who most threatened Israel and who offered the prospect of further carnage. Yet if Palestinians were to be killed, they had to be the right Palestinians. They would have to be men who were proved to be guilty of heinous crimes by the exhaustive intelligence dossiers compiled by Mossad agents and analysts. Clearly world opinion would shed few tears for the deaths of the planners of the Lod and Munich massacres, but should anything go wrong operationally and damage Israel's interests, the murders of murderers had to be untraceable – those being deterred would know who had acted. In the end, Zamir and Yariv's newly created 'Joint Task Force against Terrorism' chose the most guilty; some of these men were protected by bodyguards, others by the diplomatic immunity of Arab embassies, and yet others by their own anonymity in the labyrinth of western Europe's terrorist underworld – or so they thought.[14]

One point, however, is crucial to this change in Israeli policy. The authorization Prime Minister Meir gave Zamir and Yariv to find and kill the leaders of Black September was not a *carte blanche*; Mossad and the intelligence and security services were under strict governmental restrictions. According to certain foreign sources, Mossad was required to obtain the personal go-ahead from Prime Minister Meir before any attempt was made on the life of a Black September leader and, according to other foreign sources, the authorization for every operation was obtained from a secret tribunal chaired by Meir, Defence Minister Moshe Dayan and Foreign Minister Yigal Allon.

There have been dozens of accounts written about the 'hit teams' or 'assassination squads' which roamed Europe and the Middle East in search of the Black September executives. They range from the fictitious stories of a singular unit of 'commandos and spooks' roaming Paris, London and Rome, to more believable, though less spectacular, versions of different intelligence teams operating against different targets. The hit teams have been the recipients of dozens of emotive names, such as Black June, Wrath of God (WOG), The Avengers, and Squad 101. The Israelis remain characteristically tight-lipped about their war against Black September. Although it may take a decade before the true, archival record of Israel's European War emerges, enough is known to give us a clear picture of the operational organization, then and now, and the activities of the unit concerned.

It is highly doubtful that a hit team was assembled and specially trained as assassins for this one specific task. A more likely occurrence, in the author's opinion and in the opinion of foreign intelligence officials and reports, is that each Palestinian terrorist target was encountered by a separate team of agents, expert in the country in which they had to operate. In addition, the squads were probably composed of a mixture of specialists from separate intelligence, security and military units including Shin Bet and the IDF General Staff Reconnaissance Unit *Sayeret Mat'kal*. Edgar O'Ballance, in *Language of Violence: The*

Blood Politics of Terrorism, believes that the teams operated in two distinct sections: an Aleph or 'A' Team would commit the assassination, while a BET or 'B' Team would create diversions and facilitate an escape. Israeli embassies, El Al airline and Zim shipping offices would provide safe cover, refuge, and arms caches when needed.

Whatever the true disposition and identity of the Israeli intelligence operatives who were dispatched to Europe, their deeds cannot be overlooked. Their first target was Wael Zwaiter, a low-key, quiet man who loved literature and worked as a translator at the Libyan Embassy in Rome. He was also a former high-ranking officer in the *Razd*, Black September's operations chief in Italy, and believed to be the mastermind behind several unsuccessful attempts to blow up El Al airliners in mid-air.

On 16 October 1972 two unobtrusive men standing in the lobby of his block of flats, pumped twelve rounds of gunfire into Zwaiter as he returned home from an evening out. The weapon used was a .22 calibre Beretta automatic, using half-powder rounds which were still deadly at close range, but which detonated with less noise. The success of this deployment was complete, as none of Zwaiter's neighbours heard the shots over the showing of Fellini's *8½ Weeks* on TV. The two gunmen were seen fleeing into the night in a red Fiat 125 driven by a blonde 'female'.§

No group contacted Reuters or UPI to claim responsibility for the murder, as is normal operating terrorist procedure, and this, when coupled with the low-velocity .22 weaponry used – the same employed by El Al Skymarshals – made Israel a likely suspect. That the assassins had got the right man was confirmed the next day by a Black September obituary in a Beirut newspaper which referred to Zwaiter as, 'one of our best combatants'.

The next man to die was Doctor Mahmud Hamshari, the PLO's official representative in France. A balding and bespectacled intellectual, Hamshari was Black September's second in command in Paris. What made him extremely dangerous to Israel was his close-knit involvement with the PFLP; he was tied to an abortive 1969 attempt on the life of Ben-Gurion, as well as the pro-Syrian Popular Front for the Liberation of Palestine-General Command (PFLP-GC) led by an ex-Syrian Army officer, Ahmed Jibril (the PFLP-GC had bombed a Swissair flight to Tel Aviv, killing 47 people).

Unlike Wael Zwaiter, Hamshari was not an easy target. As the official representative of his people's liberation movement, he was a public figure aware of the threat of assassination and he never travelled without a well-armed escort of PLO bodyguards. The Israelis wished to avoid, at all costs, any gangster-style shootouts in the streets of Paris

---

§ Although a female was reported, the Israelis have been known to use male soldiers or agents in drag to divert attention: for instance, during Operation 'Spring of Youth' (*Aviv Ne'urim*) a joint Mossad-IDF commando raid against Black September, in Beirut in April 1973, the General Staff Reconnaissance Unit commander, Lieutenant-Colonel Ehud Barak, was disguised as a woman.

and therefore another method of eliminating Hamshari was required. According to foreign sources, the hit team commander, named 'Mike' or 'Micha', came up with an ingenious method of killing, ensuring no risk to innocent bystanders and with a twist of macabre irony: the telephone would be the fatal instrument, the same machinery with which Hamshari had arranged the Munich operation.

In early December 1972, 'plumbers' working on the pipes at Hamshari's block of flats 'accidentally' damaged the telephone wires leading to Hamshari's apartment. Responding to his angry complaints to the exchange, a technician arrived and, under the watchful gaze of Hamshari and his bodyguards, fixed the telephone. Unknown to them, he had placed a potent supply of explosives in the telephone's base. The powerful device was to be activated by a high-pitched electronic signal and armed only when the answering voice identified itself as Hamshari's. On the morning of 16 December 1972, Hamshari impatiently awaited a call from an 'Italian journalist' promising to arrange an interview. When the telephone rang, Hamshari raced to answer it. 'Is this Doctor Hamshari?' the caller asked. His affirmative reply was followed by a deafening explosion. He would live long enough to tell the French investigators that he heard a high-pitched buzz before the destructive blast. He died on 9 January 1973.[15]

Less than two weeks after Hamshari's death, two Mossad agents¶ landed in Nicosia; since the 1967 War Cyprus had become the centre of the underground intelligence battle – the 'War of Spooks' – between Israel and her Arab enemies. Only one hour's flight from Beirut, Cairo, or Tel Aviv, strife-torn Cyprus was a natural staging-point for both Arab and Israeli agents to begin covert actions, command dead letter drops, and run operatives. Because of its proximity to Europe and the Arab-Israeli conflict, Cyprus also became the centre of KGB operations, and KGB co-ordination of Palestinian terrorism.

As the two Israeli agents arrived in the Cypriot capital, a nervous middle-aged Palestinian checked into the Olympic Hotel. He was Abd el Hir, Black September station chief in Cyprus and an extremely

¶ According to Israeli authors Michael Bar-Zohar and Eitan Haber in their excellent book *The Quest for the Red Prince*, the identities of the two agents were 'Jonathan Ingleby and the famous "Mike".' Oddly enough, new revelations of the Mossad's 'alleged' hit teams have come to light as a result of the 1989 ousting, through force and folly, of Panamanian dictator General Manuel Antonio Noriega. General Noriega's chief adviser was a 62-year-old Israeli named Mike Harari; the man it has now been disclosed who was the infamous 'Mike' of the 1972–3 hit teams in Europe.

The once shadowy Mike Harari was born in Tel Aviv, in 1928. According to foreign sources, he volunteered for service in the Haganah at the age of 18 in 1945, and quickly rose through the ranks of the underground militia, eventually serving the *Mossad Le'Alliyah Bet* in Rome helping to smuggle Jewish refugees to Palestine. His flair for covert operations proved impeccable and, following the 1948, began a career in Mossad as a counter-intelligence specialist. According to legend, the Israeli Prime Minister, Golda Meir, personally ordered Harari to lead two hit teams in Europe, choosing him because of his cool leadership, intimacy with Europe and reputation as a flawless intelligence officer. His shining star status faded, however, when his team murdered the Moroccan waiter, Ahmad Bouchiki, in Lillehammer, in Norway, in July 1973. Following this débâcle which had a resounding impact on the Israeli intelligence community, resulting, many have argued, in the epic *Michdal*. Harari laid low and returned to the shadows where, according to foreign reports, he helped stage and plan the 4 July 1976 Operation 'Thunderball' rescue of 103 Israeli and Jewish hostages at Entebbe, in Uganda. Harari was later dispatched to the Mossad's Mexico City station where he met the Panamanian strongman; he soon retired from Mossad and became Noriega's chief consul in Tel Aviv.

effective KGB agent. He directed operations and recruited likely talent for the KGB schools in the Crimea, and for eventual ideological training at Patrice Lumumba University. On the night of 24 January 1973, Abd el Hir returned to his hotel room; the moment he switched off the light by his bed, a Mossad agent pressed the button on his ultra-sonic radio transmitter, detonating an explosive device hidden under the mattress. The fatal blast was so destructive that an Israeli couple honeymooning in a nearby room thought that *they* were the target of a Palestinian terrorist attack.

Abd el Hir's comrades were quick to avenge his murder. On 26 January 1973, Mossad station chief in Madrid, Baruch Cohen, using the alias Moshe Hanan Yishai, walked into the 'Morrison Pub' snack bar on calle Jose Antonio in the city. He was to meet a member of his network of Palestinian students which he had assembled in Madrid; they provided him with accurate information on Black September, but the *Razd* had managed to infiltrate the network, and turn the tables on Cohen. As he walked into the popular student café to meet his contact, two men emerged, firing three shots from a silenced automatic into Cohen's chest. He died later that evening and it was rumoured that a list of all Mossad agents in Europe had been found on Cohen's body.

The murder of Baruch Cohen was a serious setback for Israel's counter-terrorist efforts, and a personal loss for the Mossad. He was eulogized as a master spy, and a tribute was paid to him by an official government spokesman, which was unusual in the Mossad world of supreme secrecy. The hunters were now becoming the hunted. As if to emphasize their own ability to inflict casualties in this shadowy war, Black September struck again in Cyprus on 12 March, when they shot Simia Glizer, a senior Mossad officer and former member of Menachem Begin's *Irgun*. One can only speculate that after Israel's killing of their link man, Abd el Hir, the KGB had retaliated by providing the *Razd* with valuable intelligence regarding Mossad personnel.

The cycle of violence continued, moving once again to France. The next Mossad target was Professor Basil Al-Kubaissi, one of Black September's more ambitious leaders. His responsibilities included maintaining a proper state of preparedness of the organization's vast arsenal, overseeing communications, and supervising safe houses. The Iraqi-born Al-Kubaissi had been a life-long revolutionary, attempting to assassinate King Feisal of Iraq in 1956 with a failed explosive device. He escaped to New York, and it was there, on 16 March 1973, that he masterminded three car bombs in an elaborate attempt to assassinate Prime Minister Golda Meir, on a state visit to the city. The first two bombs, one placed in a parked car outside the Israel Discount Bank and one placed in a parked car outside First Israel Bank and Trust Company, failed to explode due to technical failures. The third, parked outside the bustling El Al terminal at John F. Kennedy International Airport, was discovered and defuzed seconds before it would have exploded and killed scores of innocents.

On the night of 6 April 1973, two men confronted Al-Kubaissi in Paris. Realizing what was transpiring, he shouted '*Non! Ne faites pas cela!*' only to be fatally wounded by nine .22 calibre bullets fired by silenced Berettas. Al-Kubaissi did not travel with bodyguards nor did he hide in safe houses. He believed his connections with the intelligentsia of the Parisian academic world would shield him from suspicion.

Three days later Israel struck at the very heart of the Black September Organization with her boldest move to date against a terrorist target, when a combined force attacked the international headquarters of Palestinian terrorism – Beirut. Operation 'Spring of Youth' signalled to Black September that there was no longer anywhere on earth safe for them to hide. This highly successful combined Mossad-IDF operation would be repeated fifteen years later with equally devastating effects.

According to foreign reports, on 1 April 1973, four Mossad agents posing as Europeans had arrived separately in the Lebanese capital. They checked into fashionable seaside hotels, rented vehicles, and seemed extremely interested in the coast-line and weather forecasts. They were never seen together and aroused no suspicion.

On the night of 9 April, an armada of IDF/Navy *Dabur* ('Bee') patrol craft and missile boats assembled off the Beirut coast. The ships carried a task force of Naval Commandos, the General Staff Reconnaissance commandos from *Sayeret Mat'kal*, and reconnaissance paratroopers from *Sayeret Tzanhanim*, the IDF's conscript Paratroop Brigade's élite recon force. The men had four primary objectives which included the destruction of the headquarters of the Democratic Front for the Liberation of Palestine (DFLP) and the *el-Fatah* office responsible for operations in Israel proper. The principal targets, however, were three top Black September officers: Mohamed Najer (also known as Abu Yusef), the *el-Fatah* and Black September operations and intelligence genius behind most of their terrorist attacks world-wide, including the assassination of Jordanian Prime Minister Tal, the Munich massacre and the Bangkok fiasco; Kamal A'dwan, a senior *el-Fatah* officer responsible for running terrorist cells in the West Bank and the Gaza Strip; and Kamal Nasser, the official spokesman for the Palestine Liberation Organization and a high-ranking Black September officer. Luckily for the Israelis, all three lived in two adjacent blocks of flats on Rue Verdun in West Beirut's fashionable Ramlat el-Bida district.

Their deaths were entrusted to the General Staff Recon commandos, led by such famous special forces personalities as Lieutenant-Colonel Ehud Barak (one of the most decorated soldiers in IDF history and, at the time of this book's writing, the deputy Chief of Staff), Major Yonatan 'Yoni' Netanyahu (the commander and lone IDF fatality of the Entebbe rescue), and Major 'Muki' Botzer.

The commandos were ferried to Beirut's Dove Beach by a force of naval commandos and met by the Mossad agents in hired cars. Dressed in a combination of civilian clothing, female drag, and hippie garb of the

Woodstock generation, the commandos succeeded in silencing the terrorists guarding the blocks of flats and proceeded to eliminate the three men on their list. In a vain attempt to resist, Abu Yusef tried to reach his bedside AK-47 before being cut down in a hail of gunfire, while A'dwan succeeded in wounding one of the commandos with his Kalashnikov before he too was killed. Although the commandos were met and engaged by a Lebanese Gendarme Land-Rover, the whole operation was completed without serious incident in just 29 minutes. They were ferried back to the waiting missile boats with a gold-mine of documents taken from their victims' apartments. The operation's other objectives were also fulfilled and it appeared, at least for the moment, that Israel was winning its covert war.

The 'Michdal'

Operation 'Spring of Youth' was a bitter defeat for Black September; in just half an hour the IDF had eliminated the concentrated terrorist threat which had plagued Israel's installations, borders and citizens for almost two years. The Israelis were absolutely triumphant following the raid, with Golda Meir proudly saying, 'We killed the murderers who planned to murder again.'[16] By terminating three of the organization's top minds, Israel critically curtailed Black September's capabilities to mount further terrorist attacks and, perhaps more importantly, it was a giant boost to IDF morale which had sagged since the army had become bogged down in the four-border War of Attrition. The Beirut raid was also an intelligence *coup* of unimaginable proportions. Kamal A'dwan for example, was also involved with *el-Fatah*'s *Razd*. Files captured in his flat not only gave the Israelis details of operations, future plans and lists of agents inside Israel and the Occupied Territories, but the codes for communicating with them as well. According to Edgar O'Ballance, the intelligence gained in that one Beirut flat averted a rash of attacks which were intended to coincide with the twenty-fifth anniversary of the founding of the State of Israel.[17]

Beyond the glory and the self-satisfaction, the Israelis knew that their acction would surely be avenged by one Palestinian group or another. Ali Hassan Salameh was still at large and further attacks somewhere, sometime were inevitable. Operation 'Spring of Youth' was the zenith of Israel's intelligence offensive thus far, but the war would continue in true and bloody fashion. This time, however, the mission had been pre-emptive, rather than retaliatory.

Realizing that Salameh was planning a major operation in Cyprus, in response to the mistaken Israeli downing of a Libyan passenger aircraft on 21 February 1973, Mossad decided to draw first blood. In the early hours of 12 April 1973, Moussa Abu Zaiad, a senior Black

September terrorist, was killed by an incendiary device in his hotel room in Athens. Originally the Greek investigators believed the explosion to be a result of one of Zaiad's poorly assembled devices, but according to foreign sources the Israelis hinted that it was indeed a Mossad operation.

On 1 March 1973, Black September gunmen committed one of their worst atrocities ever when they took over a diplomatic reception at the Saudi Arabian Embassy in Khartoum, subsequently murdering in cold blood the American Ambassador, his soon to be appointed successor, and the Belgian chargé d'affaires. Following the attack, many leaders of the PLO passionately tried to dissociate themselves from the event, and from Black September. The Khartoum massacre was in fact the *raison d'être* which set Yasir Arafat on a more moderate public path. The PLO now began to work on diplomacy as much as anything else. Salameh, however, would have none of the public relations game and, according to intelligence sources, he ordered the planning of several 'spectacular' European operations.

The man entrusted with Salameh's plans was Mohammed Boudia whom the Beirut documents, now with the IDF, indicated was the principal figure in the Palestinian's European network. Although he was technically attached to Doctor Habash's PFLP, Boudia had intimate ties with Black September as well as with the KGB. It was the fact that Salameh had appointed Boudia as Black September operations chief in Europe which ultimately signed his death warrant.

Boudia was a difficult man to find and a harder one to kill. Elusive and cunning, he remained an enigma even though the French supposedly had him under constant watch. A superbly trained intelligence agent, Boudia changed his routine daily – frequently changing trains on the Paris Metro, never driving a route two days running and often employing make-up to alter his appearance. In May 1973, however, a group of 'foreigners' entered the French capital in search of the legendary Algerian theatre-owner; they nicknamed him 'Blue Beard' because of his prowess with the ladies, and hoped to bring the curtain down on his reign of terror once and for all. Late on the night of 28 June 1973, after weeks of detective work and exhaustive surveillance, the Mossad team made its move while Boudia was spending the early morning hours in the company of a lady in the Latin Quarter. He came out of the house at 11 a.m., and carefully examined his automobile for the tell-tale signs of sabotage. Satisfied, Boudia climbed in unaware that a radio-controlled explosive device had been placed under the car seat. It would arm itself like a land-mine when pressure was applied, and could then be detonated by a radio signal. The powerful blast killed Boudia instantly.

The Israelis had in fact been aware of Boudia a long time before the Beirut raid. In March 1973, two members of his Paris cell, Talab al-Jabari and Adib Sadat Salem Hussein, were arrested in Como with information the Italian police had received from Mossad relating to a planned attack on the El Al office in Milan. A day later, French police in Lyons arrested two Arabs in possession of plastic explosives; they also implicated Boudia following a less than pleasant DST interrogation. Although Doctor Habash and the KGB would immediately replace Boudia with 'Carlos the Jackal' as their European chief of 'Terror International', the Algerian's passing would not go unavenged. On 1 July 1973, black militant gunmen working for Black September shot and killed Colonel Yosef Alon, the Israel Air Force attaché in Washington, DC, as he left his home for work.

Colonel Alon's murder was the beginning of a very bad month for Israel's covert intelligence efforts against the Palestinians. In historic terms, it was a period known simply as 'the *Michdal*', the nebulous Hebrew word for non-performance and neglect. The *Michdal* was a far-reaching deterioration of all of Israel's security services, including Mossad and Military Intelligence, and was as much an error of tactics as a national mood of invincibility and over-confidence. This total failure in Israel's intelligence capabilities ended on the charred battlefields of the Golan heights and Sinai Desert in the Yom Kippur War. It began, however, in the small, hitherto unknown Norwegian village of Lillenhammer.

With most of Black September's lieutenants now dead, maimed, or too frightened to rear their heads in public, only the enigmatic Salameh remained unscathed. In July 1973, however, Mossad received word that he was in Scandinavia planning a major terrorist spectacle involving an airline hijacking. At the time, Stockholm was the bustling centre of international terrorism, serving as a peaceful pit stop for the revolutionaries of the Palestinian, Japanese, and western European underground armies to spring into action. As a result, Sweden received much of Mossad's Scandinavian efforts. When reports filtered in to Mossad HQ in Tel Aviv that an Algerian-born officer in Black September's European operation named Kamal Benamane was bound for Scandinavia to meet Ali Hassan Salameh to co-ordinate the next terrorist attack, Sweden, Denmark, and Norway became extensions of the Arab-Israeli battlefield.

The 'Lillenhammer débâcle' as it became known has been the subject of several books. Although little could be gained by repeating the story in detailed fashion here, a minimum synopsis is necessary. Understandably, the Israeli intelligence community remains tight-lipped to this day about their fiasco and folly in Norway, and most information has come from the trials of the captured Mossad agents in Oslo.

Benamane was tracked by more than twenty Mossad agents from his home base in Geneva until his arrival in Norway via Copenhagen Airport. Meanwhile, Zamir ordered his operations chief, 'Mike', quickly to assemble an Aleph and Bet team for immediate deployment. The large group was composed of Israeli nationals and European Jews, either from Scandinavia or knowledgeable in the Scandinavian languages, in what can be considered an *ad hoc* intelligence squad. Kamal Benamane's final destination was Lillenhammer, a small and sleepy summer resort town in central Norway. The Israeli agents kept track of him and as soon as he met Salameh it was reported to Prime Minister Golda Meir who dispatched Tzvi Zamir to Oslo using an Israeli passport under the name of Tal Sarig, in order for him to control the government-sanctioned assassination.[18]

Over-confidence, over-zealousness and operating in virgin territory have been given as reasons for the amateurish method with which the tracking and planned hit of Salameh was undertaken. Although in an interview to the popular Lebanese weekly *As-Sayad* Salameh stated he was in Stockholm at the time of the Mossad operation, other reports do place him in Lillenhammer. That inefficient surveillance, including misidentification, was the order of the day comes as no great surprise when one considers that British security agents argue that an efficient 24-hour surveillance involves as many as twenty well-trained agents *all of whom should be familiar with their area of operation!* In Rome or Paris, the tracking of a target could be achieved by hundreds of agents without raising the suspicions of a single citizen, while in Lillenhammer, where everyone knew just about everyone else, it was a most difficult undertaking.

When contact with Salameh was finally made it began a disastrous chain of events. Besides pumping fourteen .22 bullets into the wrong man, a Moroccan waiter named Ahmed Bouchiki, the fleeing team was careless, and a number of them were eventually caught. Their arrests by the Norwegian police and subsequent humiliation in public trials in an Oslo court focused world attention on the intricacies of Mossad's efforts against Black September. Israeli agents in a European gaol had been Prime Minister Meir's greatest nightmare when authorizing the killing; a bad dream turned national disgrace was now materializing before her very eyes. Six Mossad agents were convicted on counts ranging from espionage to complicity to commit murder, and an Israeli diplomat was thrown out of Norway. In Israel, a public outcry led to demands that both Prime Minister Meir and *Memuneh* Zamir resign at once.

Lillenhammer was an embarrassment for Mossad. In a brief year, they had come from the heights of glory and an aura of brilliant invincibility to a mood of self-defeatism and a reputation for ineptitude. It was, at the time, the worst disaster in Mossad history and it ended Mossad's war against Black September; anonymity could no longer protect Israel's covert efforts. A Palestinian hit by a speeding tram car in Zurich would now surely be blamed on Mossad, let alone one shot in the chest with a .22 Beretta. Europe could no longer be a battlefield for the Israelis; future engagements would have to be on Arab soil, which meant far greater danger and therefore less likelihood of an operation being ordered. The subsequent resignation of Aharon Yariv as Special Adviser for Terrorist Matters in order to run for political office in the 30

October 1973 elections – thwarted by the outbreak of war – was a convenient method of passing the assassination teams into Israeli folklore.

The events in Norway were symbolic of a deeper and more serious malaise affecting intelligence-gathering on the conventional Arab threat to Israel; the preoccupation with Black September had combined with over-confidence during the post-1967 era and led to a neglect of traditional and staple threat assessment work. Before Military Intelligence suffered the Egyptian–Syrian–Soviet inspired 'earthquake' of October 1973, she was given a warning of her vulnerability when an anti-terrorist operation again went humiliatingly wrong.

Israel had yet to assassinate a high-ranking political leader from the Black September Organization; most mysteriously of all perhaps, she had left Abu Iyad himself untouched. The PFLP's Doctor George Habash was another story. Israeli leaders had long maintained a personal vendetta against the Marxist Habash and non-confirmed reports have it that several Mossad staff meetings openly discussed his assassination.

On Friday, 10 August 1973 dozens of senior IDF and intelligence officers assembled at an IAF airfield in the north, expecting the arrival of a very special flight. Among the impatient group was Defence Minister Moshe Dayan, IDF Chief of Staff Lieutenant-General David 'Dado' Elazar, and OC Operations Major-General Yisrael 'Talik' Tal. While the rest of the nation gathered with their families for traditional Friday night *Shabbat* meals, Israel's military leaders were gathered to greet two very special visitors to the State of Israel: Doctor George Habash and his Operations chief, Wadi Haddad!

Military Intelligence had learned of the PFLP commander's plans to fly from Beirut to Baghdad – then the nerve centre of PFLP operations before Damascus assumed that dubious honour – and had opted for a daring kidnapping which would bring Israel its most valuable anti-terrorist victory to date. Only fifteen minutes after Iraqi Airlines Flight A.006 left Beirut for the quick hop to Baghdad, a group of IAF Mirage IIICs and F-4Es appeared, diverting the Caravelle aircraft and its 81 passengers into Israeli airspace. Upon landing at an anonymous airfield in northern Israel, the Caravelle was surrounded by floodlights and armoured cars. Heavily armed commandos entered the aircraft and examined each passenger in search of the two elusive PFLP leaders. They were not aboard the aircraft. Disgusted, embarrassed, and confused, Major-General Tal looked at his Defence Minister and Chief of Staff and angrily shouted, 'You must offer your resignations at once.'*

The IDF had tried, and failed, to take care of Habash on previous occasions. On 21 February 1973, an IDF assault force of paratroopers and Naval Commandos staged an attack on two Palestinian bases near Tripoli in northern Lebanon in which more than 40 terrorists were

---

* In 1986, a similar, unsuccessful attempt to kidnap Habash was made when IAF aircraft intercepted a Libyan Airlines Gulf-Stream jet *en route* to Damascus.

killed and almost a hundred wounded (Operation '*Bardas*' or 'Hood 54-55'). According to foreign reports, one of the main objectives of the raid was the selective elimination of Doctor Habash, whom intelligence sources had located as being in the base at the time on a routine inspection of his troops. The wily Habash is still alive today, the survivor of a civil war in Lebanon, incessant war with Israel and often bloody wars against his fellow Palestinians and brother Arabs.

On 6 October 1973, Israel's intelligence *Michdal* was completed when the combined military might of Egypt and Syria initiated a savage surprise attack against the State of Israel – the 1973 Yom Kippur War. Through luck, tenacity and what some like to think of as divine intervention, Israel saved itself from a severe military defeat and instead achieved a decisive military victory. Many factors were involved in the intelligence failure which allowed the Yom Kippur War to erupt, but, in this author's opinion, Israel's obsession with avenging Munich and the terrorist attacks of 1972 was a monumental contribution. It was an obsession, however, which refused to die, even though Israeli Prime Minister Yitzhak Rabin ordered the cessation of all Mossad assassination of Palestinian terrorists in September 1974.[19]

Following his close calls with death, and Mossad's virtual destruction of Black September, the 'Red Prince' entered the political hierarchy of the PLO's leadership. He was the commanding officer of the PLO's *Force 17,* the organization's élite guard and special operations force.† Salameh was so trusted by Arafat, that he was groomed as the PLO's next commander, being one of the two men chosen to accompany Arafat on his much vaunted visit to New York for the address at the United Nations on 13 November 1974. Salameh also went on state visits with Arafat to Moscow and the various Arab capitals for the obligatory hand-shaking photo session at summits.

When Lebanon disintegrated into civil war, Salameh was a key figure in the Palestinian's military effort against the Lebanese Christians and then against the intervening Syrians. He was, nevertheless, noted as a man in search of moderation, enjoying a special relationship with Christian Phalangist military warlord Bashir Gemayel, even rescuing other Christian leaders in dire situations. During the bitter fighting in Beirut, Salameh was also instrumental in safe-guarding the lives of American diplomats in the embattled capital. As already mentioned, unofficial rumours report him as being the CIA's man in the PLO, a source of invaluable intelligence who travelled to the United States, including Agency-paid vacations to the peaceful paradise of Hawaii.

On 8 June 1977 Salameh shed his playboy image when he took as his second wife Lebanon's former Miss Universe, Georgina Rizak.

---

† *Force 17* or the 'Security Command of the General Committee' was formed in the early 1970s by Ali Hassan Salameh, as an élite military wing directly answerable to Chairman Arafat. The name *Force 17* came from the office number in *el-Fatah*'s headquarters in Beirut's Farkhani district. *Force 17* fighters came traditionally from poor and desperate Palestinian families in the Lebanon refugee camps, whose hatred for Israel and loyalty to the PLO was absolute, unflinching and never to be compromised.

Marriage to one of the world's most beautiful women did not diminish Salameh's hatred for Israel, however, and his command of *Force 17* gave him many means of expressing his loathing, as evidenced by the bloody incident at Country Club Junction in March 1978 (*see* page 159).

The IDF responded to the incident just days later with an invasion of southern Lebanon (Operation 'Litani') whose objective was the rooting out and destruction of the PLO infra-structure along Israel's northern border. That kibbutz attack, one of the worst in Israel's history, also required specific retribution and, once again, the killing of the 'Red Prince' received enthusiastic Mossad attention.

By the late 1970s Mossad had undergone some fundamental changes as a result of its earlier fiascos. After Tzvi Zamir's resignation in September 1974, the new Controller appointed by Prime Minister Rabin was Major-General Yitzhak Hofi, a tough career paratroop officer. Hofi had been deeply affected by Israel's intelligence *Michdal* – as OC Northern Command, he had led the beleaguered and outnumbered armoured and infantry forces under his command to hard-won victory against a determined and sometimes overwhelming Syrian enemy. Just like the IDF, Mossad also burst out of its Yom Kippur War malaise after the brilliant 4 July 1976 rescue of 103 Israeli and Jewish hostages held by the PFLP at Entebbe, Uganda. Israel was a different nation as well: long controlled by the socialist Labour party, Israel was now governed by the right-wing *Likud* bloc, with ex-*Irgun* commander and devout hard-liner Menachem Begin as the nation's Prime Minister. With this change in national resolve, the Israeli Government decided to go ahead with an operation to eliminate Salameh once and for all.

A wanted man's worst enemy is routine. Once married, Salameh was to bring about his own downfall by developing a routine life-style which made him a relatively easy individual to find. He did still live in Beirut though, which was not Rome or Paris, and the chances of an Aleph or Bet team emptying a few magazines of .22 fire into him and escaping was remote at best! Killing Salameh would have to be fool-proof, safe and non-incriminating. When Mossad agents dispatched to Beirut concocted a plan to blow him up with an ingeniously produced bomb placed in the West Beirut health club he frequented, a leading government authority vetoed the idea because of the high risk to innocent civilians – another, safer method was needed.[20]

Erika Mary Chambers, or 'Penelope' as she was also known, was regarded as an eccentric though harmless Briton by her West Beirut neighbours. The dishevelled thirty-year-old spinster had lived in West Beirut since 1978; her flat was on Rue Verdun, within sight of the block attacked during Operation 'Spring of Youth' several years earlier. She loved cats and often fed the neighbourhood strays, but her main passion was art. She spent countless hours at her open window, palette in hand, painting the Beirut skyline. No one knew that her *real* interest was the daily Beirut traffic and most especially the times and schedules of a motorcade consisting of a tan Chevrolet station-wagon loaded with armed men, followed by a Land-Rover jeep carrying heavily armed *Force 17* commandos in camouflage fatigues. The motorcade belonged to Ali Hassan Salameh.[21]

On 17 January 1979, another British national named Peter Scriver had landed at Beirut International Airport on a direct flight from Zurich by Swissair. He made his way to the Hotel Méditerranée near the beach, and the next morning picked up a Volkswagen Golf from the Lenacar rental agency, which earlier he had arranged by telephone from Zurich. Later in the day, he rendezvoused with another tourist to the Lebanese capital, a Canadian named Ronald Kolberg who was travelling on business for his kitchenware firm in New York and who was staying in the Royal Garden Hotel. Earlier, Kolberg had rented a Simca-Chrysler, also from the Lenacar agency. On 18 January, an 'exhausted'-looking Erika Chambers walked through the doors of the Lenacar establishment to hire a Datsun for a holiday to the Shouf Mountains. She drove the car away, filled up with petrol but parked it only a few blocks from her flat.

On 21 January, Peter Scriver checked out of the Hotel Méditerranée and, instead of driving his Golf to Amman, as he had told the bellboy he would, drove around for about half an hour, eventually parking on Rue Verdun just outside Miss Chambers' window. He later hailed a cab for the airport and took a Cyprus Airways flight to Nicosia. Early the next morning, Kolberg checked out of the Royal Garden Hotel and, following a quick drive past the home of Ali and Georgina Salamch on Rue Verdun, where he observed the complement of well-armed *Force 17* guards outside, made his way north through the Christian sector of the city towards the port of Jounieh. There he rented a room in the Montmartre Hotel looking over the sea, where the blurred grey silhouettes of unidentified ships lurked in the distance.[22]

On the same day, Ali Hassan Salameh was to make a routine drive from his home in Beirut to a convening of the Palestine National Council (PNC) in Damascus. After parting from Georgina, who was five months' pregnant, he headed in typically routine fashion along a route which took him past Miss Chambers' home on Rue Verdun. He used the route twice a day, and through her coded scribblings which were well-hidden between her paintings and cats, 'Penelope' was able to determine, almost to the minute, when Salameh's entourage would drive by.

As Salameh's tan Chevrolet station-wagon and accompanying Land-Rover headed down Rue Verdun towards the intersection at Rue Madam Curie, Penelope eagerly pressed her face to the wall and counted down. When Salameh passed by the Volkswagen Golf Peter Scriver had parked a day earlier she flipped a switch to a radio-controlled device which turned the Beirut street into a hellish inferno, engulfed in a chaotic mess of metal and fire. After seven years, Mossad had finally killed Salameh.

Later that night, two figures on the beach near Jounieh, boarded a Zodiac rubber dinghy and headed towards a distant outline on the calm sea. The following morning, Lebanese police found a Simca-Chrysler and a Datsun rented from Lenacar. 'Ronald Kolberg' and 'Erika Chambers' were never seen again. Although by 1979 Mossad had established close ties with Bashir Gemayel's Christian Phalangist militia, there is no evidence available, despite intense speculation, to link the Phalange with the assassination of Salameh, although it remains a source of intense conjecture.

The message on 22 January 1979 from Mossad HQ to the Prime Minister's office was simple and concise: 'Munich has been avenged!'[23]

As will be seen later, Ali Hassan Salameh would not be the last top PLO operations genius to die a violent death.

Infiltration, Manipulation, Proxy and a Never-ending Intelligence War

If the assassination of the 'Red Prince' accomplished any grand objective, it was the end of the existence of Black September as a potent terrorist phenomenon;* this, in turn, meant the end of Mossad's secret war against them. But other Palestinian terrorist groups were still operating world-wide with virtual impunity, conducting further attacks against Israeli targets and, starting with Yasir Arafat's November 1974 speech to the United Nations General Assembly, gaining political influence and acceptance.

Despite this, the late 1970s was generally a period of defeat and turbulence for the varied forces which composed the Palestine Liberation Organization. First there was the disastrous hijacking to Entebbe in June 1976 which not only served the PFLP its most humiliating defeat ever, but catalyzed the State of Israel to break out of its 1973 War trauma. Secondly, it can be described as the period when Arab fought Arab and, more specifically, Palestinian fought Palestinian. In Lebanon, the goal of a Palestinian state was overshadowed by the PLO's desire to dominate the country; the bitter fighting in the Civil War not only resulted in the deaths of thousands of Palestinians – by 'conservative' estimates approximately 30,000 killed, and more than had ever been killed by the Israelis and Jordanians *combined* – but it tore asunder a once secure base of military operations against Israel's northern frontier.

* The last grand Black September operation was a foiled attempt on the life of Morocco's King Hassan II, because of his faithful protection of the minority Jewish population.

One unforeseen by-product of the Lebanese Civil War was an intense inter-Palestinian rivalry which periodically erupted into internecine warfare. New, even uniquely anti-Arab, Palestinian terrorist groups were formed; these ranged from the inconsequential, such as 'Black September II', to the more menacing 'Abu Nidal Faction', named after the alias of its founder, Sabri al-Banna. This situation was further exacerbated by the Camp David peace negotiations between Israel and Egypt in 1977. Although space limits a comprehensive listing of all Palestinian terrorist attacks against Palestinian and Arab targets, the more notable ones were: the murders of PLO representatives in Kuwait, London, Paris and Islamabad by Abu Nidal gunmen in 1978–9; attacks against Iraqi diplomats (the sponsors of the Abu Nidal faction) in Libya, Paris, and Brussels by *el-Fatah* operatives; and even unclaimed attacks against Syrian diplomats. Throughout this Cain and Abel period in the Palestinian revolution, Israel remained the ultimate target: Israeli oranges were poisoned throughout western Europe (26 January 1978); the PFLP attacked El Al passengers in Paris's Orly Airport (20 May 1978); and the Syrian-sponsored *Saiqa* was behind the 5 April 1979 bomb explosion inside the Israeli embassy in Nicosia.

As evidenced by its actions during the years 1979 to 1989, Mossad's anti-terrorist objectives were threefold: infiltration, manipulation and, if necessary, elimination. Mossad's operations over this period, just like its earlier hit-team activities, have only become public knowledge as a result of spectacular victory or crushing defeat. As will be seen throughout this chapter, Mossad would share in both the agony and the ecstasy. Their zones of interest, and hence activity, were now greatly expanded as well, continuing to cover the old haunts such as Germany, Great Britain, and Cyprus, but now including the United States of America too.

The international nature of the PFLP, further revealed by its make-up during the Entebbe incident, also served public notice to the internal security agencies and foreign intelligence services of the European community as to the dimension and realities of Palestinian/west European terrorist forces operating in Europe: it was now no longer just an Israeli problem. Israel's intelligence bodies began to develop a close-knit working relationship with their European counterparts, forming what became a united front against terror. Nowhere was this relationship more significant, more historical and yet more jaded than with the Federal Republic of Germany.

There had been an obvious need for Germany to maintain more than friendly relations with Israel; the Germans and Jews had shared much of the tragic history of this century together, albeit under very different circumstances. The Holocaust, and the establishment of a Jewish nation from the ashes of the Nazi death camps, was obviously the main reason for West Germany's support of the State of Israel. Many saw German friendship towards Israel as a moral obligation, a repayment to a people for the crimes committed against humanity. By the same token, the 1972 Munich Olympics was an event which it was hoped would project a new Germany's return into the family of civilized nations. The deaths of eleven Israeli athletes was a cruel blow to this aspiration and it provoked Germany into active participation, alongside Israel, in the war against terrorism. The Germans set out to destroy the infra-structure of their own internal terrorist army, the Baader Meinhoff Gang, as well as the countless other hidden 'liberation' and 'revolutionary' underground armies. Most notably, an élite Border Guard anti-terrorist unit called GSG-9 was formed as a response force; it soon proved itself highly effective in action with the rescue of 90 hostages on a Lufthansa flight held by Baader-Meinhoff and Wadi Haddad Faction Palestinian terrorists at Somalia's Mogadishu Airport on 17 October 1977.[24]

Yet behind the public assurances of anti-terrorist resolve, the Federal Republic of Germany also maintained covert diplomatic ties with the PLO and hoped, through political means, to avoid further bloody incidents on German soil such as the 1972 Munich Massacre. As part of the bargain, the Germans would not compromise or bother known Palestinian operatives in the FRG. The marriage was consummated in late 1978 by the West German Minister of Interior's meeting with the Libyan leader and terrorist sponsor, Muammar Qaddafi, followed by agreements between Abu Iyad and senior West German intelligence and security service officials.

The pact worked well, as evidenced by the fact that no anti-Israel PLO attacks† took place in Germany until April 1979 when Mossad successfully conspired to destroy it. The revelations of what is now known as the 'Bavarian Incident' were generally ignored by the international Press at the time, but publicized months later in the reputable Israeli daily *Ha'aretz*. The insight which this latest chapter in the 'War of the Spooks' offers the student into trickery, innovation, and sheer brilliance is impressive, and deserving of its due course.

On 26 April 1979, only four months after the death of the 'Red Prince', four Palestinian men in their mid-twenties were arrested in West Berlin by heavily armed policemen from the city's Criminal Investigations Unit. The four had been under intense surveillance for days and were apprehended while sitting in their red Mercedes whose trunk held the group's weapons cache consisting of hundreds of pounds of high-explosives and several automatic rifles. Three of the captured men were identified as low-level operatives allied to Yasir Arafat's *el-Fatah*; they had entered West Berlin in typical fashion through the eastern half of the city. The apparent leader was a 27-year-old Palestinian, a West Berlin resident named Hassan al-Harti. The cell's plans

---

† Attacks by anti-Arafat groups such as the Abu Nidal Faction and the pro-Syrian *As-Saiqa* continued, however, with the 15 October 1978 abortive attempt to destroy the city's Jewish Community Centre and a Jewish shop in West Berlin.

called for dozens of bomb attacks on targets which included the head of the dwindling Jewish community in West Berlin, Heinz Gelinski, a survivor of *five* previous Palestinian assassination attempts.[25]

That same day, West German Border Guards (including members of GSG-9) arrested another car-load of Palestinian terrorists belonging to *el-Fatah* as it attempted to enter West Germany near the town of Pasau on the Austrian border. Three days later, Border Guards (and again GSG-9), arrested another car-load of *el-Fatah* terrorists at the town of Eltan near the Dutch border. In their possession were 110 kilograms of high-explosives, detonators and 7.62mm AK-47 assault rifles. Their planned campaign had been thwarted by advance warning from Mossad, and subsequent close-knit co-operation between Israeli intelligence and the B.N.D., the West German intelligence service. Yet what makes this rather routine incident so amazing is what was to follow.

While in the custody of the Bavarian authorities, Mossad agents were given unlimited access to four of the Palestinian terrorists, a fact unprecedented in West German judicial history. This included an intense Mossad interrogation administered completely in Arabic so that the Bavarian officials looking on curiously could not understand what was being asked, and more importantly, what was being answered. Klaus Kinkel, one of the heads of the B.N.D., argued that the behaviour of Mossad's agents in the Bavarian gaol, as if they were operating in an Israeli prison, violated German law. His suspicions raised further questions and speculations, including an apparently bizarre West German theory that all of the Palestinian operations had been covertly masterminded by none other than Mossad in an attempt to prove that the PLO could not operate freely in Germany without the knowledge and eventual intervention of Israel. Needless to say, the public outcry stemming from the Mossad interrogation was meant to destroy West Germany's gentleman's agreement with Libya and the PLO. The Mossad action was both innovative and devious. According to one West German intelligence source, 'A small team of Mossad agents could achieve the results of one thousand West German spies.'[26]

It is on public record that both the French and Italians entertained secret agreements by the Libyans and the PLO to cease Palestinian terrorist activity on their sovereign territories. It nevertheless remains a mystery as to whether the Mossad attempted to destroy these pacts of appeasement as they had done in Germany.

The controversy was exacerbated by the mysterious situation of the *el-Fatah* ringleader, Hassan al-Harti. Not only had the West Berlin Police allowed al-Harti bail (unheard of for somebody caught with explosives, weapons and maps of Jewish targets) on condition that he report to the authorities once a week, but they had delivered his travel documents to him by special police courier when he requested permission to visit a sick relative in Stuttgart! These papers included one of the two suspect Lebanese passports which were found in his possession and, needless to say, al-Harti was never seen again. At the trial of the other Palestinians, one of the captured men told prosecutors that he had seen an Israeli passport in al-Harti's home in Kliest Strasse 5. Other reports indicated that al-Harti had previously been arrested in Lebanon for spying on behalf of Israel, and his mother and sister were Israeli citizens.[27]

The PLO spokesman in Beirut, Abdallah Franjieh, shed further insight, and another dose of mystery, into this incident when he stated that the Palestinians caught in West Germany and interrogated by the Mossad in Bavaria had indeed been dispatched as part of a 'Beirut Avenger Squad' sent to Europe in search of the female Mossad agent responsible for the assassination of Ali Hassan Salameh months earlier. The *Razd* had learned that the woman, believed to be none other than 'Penelope', was in Germany and *el-Fatah* was determined to get her. If it had succeeded it would not have been the PLO's first retaliatory strike at Mossad; in July 1974 a 22-year-old Israeli tourist, Ya'akov Tugendreich, mysteriously disappeared while visiting Norway. He was never heard of again. An ex-parachutist jump master in the IDF, Tugendreich was said to have been a member of an 'unidentified' élite reconnaissance unit; this claim was made in an anonymous telephone call to Tugendreich's relatives in Israel in 1975, linking his secret military service with his disappearance. European Press reports connected Tugendreich's disappearance with the failed Mossad hit on Ali Hassan Salameh in Lillenhammer.[28]

Mossad is a politically sophisticated organization and its working brief includes the exploitation of diplomatic situations which will work in Israel's favour; one such instance was their exposure of a secret meeting between the PLO's UN representative, Doctor Terzi, and the US Ambassador, Andrew Young, on 26 July 1979. Such contact was expressly forbidden in a 1975 agreement negotiated between the United States and the State of Israel, whereby US Government officials were forbidden by law to meet representatives of the Palestine Liberation Organization until that organization abandoned the use of terrorism and agreed to recognize the existence of Israel. The news that Mossad conducted surveillance of the UN's PLO ambassador did not disturb American intelligence officials, but the fact that the US Ambassador was also worthy of Mossad's attention intensely angered many in Washington, although it didn't surprise any seasoned intelligence veterans. The Mossad leak, channelled through *Newsweek*'s Jerusalem correspondent, Milan Kuebek, eventually forced Ambassador Andrew Young to resign in disgrace, and torpedoed the US–PLO dialogue just as Mossad knew it would. Mossad Controller Major-General (Res.) Yitzhak Hofi was severely criticized for publicizing the Young–Terzi meeting since it also exposed Mossad's capabilities and objectives in the United States. Hofi's tactics were successful, however, and as will be seen, would not be the last time Israeli intelligence would be caught and severely criticized, whether by will or by misfortune, for its intelligence-gathering operations there.

In 1981 alleged Mossad anti-terror operations akin to the hit teams of the early 1970s were once again being undertaken in Europe. This active role was welcomed by Israeli agents disillusioned with 'white collar' sideline operations such as the Bavarian and Andrew Young incidents.

The place was Rome, site of the first alleged Mossad hit team victim, Wael Zwaiter, the date 9 October 1981 and the target was Maghd Abu Shrar – the PLO Information Minister. Abu Shrar was one of the PLO's most popular figures in Beirut, and had been responsible for conducting numerous pro-Palestinian intellectual symposiums in European capitals which were hoped to achieve as much newspaper and television coverage as possible. One city he hated visiting, however, was Rome, as he considered it a haven for Mossad's European activities. He sensed that his coming trip to publicize Israeli injustices against Arabs was a dangerous one and he often commented that he would be a marked man in the Italian capital. He believed the Italian intelligence community was extremely pro-Israeli and anti-Palestinian. Even though an Italian-PLO pact existed which immunized Italian territory from PLO attacks, Italian intelligence chief, General Maliti, was known in PLO circles as a lover of Israel. Some credence is given to Abu Shrar's fears by a recent article in the popular Israeli daily *Yediot Aharonot* which disclosed that Italian authorities have opened an investigation into several high-ranking Italian intelligence officers who are accused of assisting Mossad to blow up an Italian Air Force C-47 Dakota over Venetian waters, *en route* from Italy to Tripoli in Libya. Prior to this, all that was known was that the aircraft had mysteriously disappeared. On board the doomed flight were five Palestinian terrorists working for the PFLP who had been arrested in Rome in April 1973 for attempting to shoot an El Al airliner out of the Italian skies with SAM-7 'Strella' hand-held surface-to-air missiles. According to reports in the Italian weekly *Panorama*, the then head of the Italian secret service, General Ambrogo Viviani, helped Mossad carry out the sabotage and later assisted in the cover-up.[29]

In keeping with the very strict PLO rules of security for officials travelling outside the 'safe' confines of Beirut, Abu Shrar was met at Rome's Leonardo da Vinci Airport by Nimer Hamad, the PLO 'ambassador' to Rome, in an armoured-plated limousine. He was booked into two Rome hotels and even offered a complement of heavily armed *Force 17* bodyguards which he refused, accepting instead a licensed Browning 9mm automatic belonging to the PLO's Rome office. Ominously, Abu Shrar gave a speech later that evening *threatening* traitors to the Arab cause. He chose as an example the case of Egyptian President Anwar es-Sadat, killed just three days earlier. At the end of the lecture, Abu Shrar went back to Room No. 319 at the Flora Hotel; a

few hours later, a tremendous explosion rocked Room No. 319, killing
its occupant instantly.

Italian investigators determined that the fatal explosion was
caused by three kilograms of high-explosives. They dismissed Abu
Shrar's assassination as the 'typical results of an inter-Palestinian
rivalry', even though speculation and certain strong facts do implicate
Mossad: a mysterious and uncharacteristic delivery of an extra pillow
was made to his room even though Abu Shrar always slept with only a
blanket. Despite such evidence a full-scale investigation was never
conducted.

The PLO was appalled by the lack of Italian tenacity in pursuing
the killers of Abu Shrar, and officers in their Rome office planned a
large-scale demonstration on 6 June 1982 to pass outside the headquarters of the Italian Security Services. The two masterminds of the
demonstration were Kamal Hussein and Nazea Matar, two *Force 17*
soldiers attached to *Commando 18* – an élite sub-unit of *Force 17*
which undertook the most difficult assassination directives – working
out of the Rome office. That same day, the IDF launched Operation
'Peace for Galilee' and invaded Lebanon to destroy the PLO; meanwhile, later that evening, 'anonymous gunmen' killed Hussein and
Matar.

Israel's long expected invasion of Lebanon was the climax of a
nation's frustration over an intolerable military threat long looming
over its northern frontier. It was also the tragic outcome of an Israeli,
and Mossad, decision to fight the Palestinians through proxy.

Israel's relationship with Lebanon's Christians was forged out of
the military realities of the Lebanese Civil War. In 1975 the various
Christians' militias, most notably the Chamoun family's 'Tigers' and the
extremely well-organized Phalangists of the Gemayel clan (also known
as the Lebanese Forces), turned to the Israelis in desperation in order to
thwart the dire threat which the combined Muslim–Palestinian force
posed to two thousand years of Christian hegemony in Lebanon. With
casualties growing and the traditional family-run arms suppliers asking
a hefty price for badly needed weaponry, the Christians turned to
Mossad for help. The files on them in Mossad and Military Intelligence
archives were thin, and not very enlightening, although the general
consensus in Tel Aviv was that as long as they were fighting the
Palestinians, they warranted greater interest and some support.

At the beginning of 1976, the first official Mossad contingent made
its way to the port of Jounieh and Christian East Beirut. According to
numerous accounts stemming from the Lebanon War, the first formal
contacts between Mossad and the Christians took place in Jounieh with
representatives of the Chamouns and Gemayels. The meetings were
very clandestine: Israeli intelligence officers were ferried to beach
rendezvous by a rubber Zodiac craft launched from an IDF/Navy
Missile Boat.[30] At first they were polite, diplomatic, and sometimes
shocking, as battle-hardened Israeli military and intelligence officers

were dumbfounded by the brutality of the fighting. In due course this Israeli reticence was overcome and a special relationship would develop between the Israelis and the Lebanese Christians; Mossad, in particular, enjoyed the potential establishment of a united Jewish-Christian front against the Muslim Arab world. Through a gradual process of weapons sales, military training and eventual political guidance, Mossad helped drag Israel into its Lebanon quagmire and into what many consider their *Michdal*, similar to the Military Intelligence-inspired failures which allowed the 1973 War to take place.

Space affords only the briefest of mentions for this first Mossad failure of the 1980s. Mossad had indeed developed close ties with the Lebanese Christians, but their dealings were mainly with the Christians' élite and this led the Israelis to overestimate their potential. According to foreign intelligence sources, the temptation of creating a new political order in the Levant – termed by many as the Pax Israel – was too great for Mossad, and they seriously misjudged the tragic military shortcomings of the Lebanese Forces. In contrast, Military Intelligence chief Major-General Yehoshua Saguy understood the complex tribal mentality of the Lebanese religious factions only too well, and strongly disagreed with Israel's reliance on the Lebanese Forces as integral partners in Israel's Lebanese military strategy. He strongly pleaded for restraint and no commitment to the Lebanese Forces, but to no avail. On 6 June 1982, Israel invaded Lebanon and pushed all the way to Beirut, as a result of the assurances from Bashir Gemayel – the doomed Lebanese President-elect – that the Lebanese Forces would handle the Palestinians in the Lebanese capital. During the true battle for Lebanon in the summer of 1982, the only time the spartan Lebanese Forces used their Israeli-supplied weapons in anger was when they were allowed into Beirut's Sabra and Shatilla refugee camps, where they massacred hundreds of Palestinian men, women and children. This butchery, news of which reverberated around the world, underscored the tragic futility of Israel's Lebanon adventure. Major-General Yehoshua Saguy was scapegoated and removed from his post as head of IDF Military Intelligence, as recommended by the resultant report of the Kahan Commission, and two other senior officers were upbraided for 'a breach of the duty incumbent upon them'.[31] The culpability of Mossad was difficult to establish, but the entire affair was a matter of national shame for Israel and, by default or not, Mossad was labelled with a negative reputation which was not restored until the assassination of PLO No. 2 man, Khalil al-Wazir, the infamous Abu Jihad (to be covered in a later chapter).

According to foreign reports, the Mossad achieved perhaps its greatest level of international counter-terrorist co-operation when in 1985 a new level of 'understanding' was reached between Israel and the United States under the guidance of rogue Lieutenant-Colonel Oliver North.

At 0910 hours on 14 June 1985, TWA Flight 847 from Athens to Rome was seized by Lebanese Shi'ite gunmen and diverted to Algiers. For the next two days, the flight crisscrossed the Mediterranean, refuelling both in Beirut and Algiers while a cautious US Government dispatched its élite Delta Force commandos to the Mediterranean. On the second day of the crisis, having landed in the Lebanon, the Shi'ite gunmen, who had been conducting a reign of terror against several American servicemen on board the aircraft, brutally murdered a US Navy diver, 23-year-old Robert Stethem. Although several hostages had been released, the 39 remaining captives were split into several groups, to hamper any attempted rescue operations, and dispersed throughout the urban labyrinth of Muslim West Beirut. The United States immediately contacted the Syrians, Iranians, and *Amal* leader Nabih Berri with a request that the 'crisis be resolved quickly'; but the most important asset at the United State's disposal was the State of Israel.

During the TWA crisis, the close political, military and intelligence relationship between the United States and Israel reached its zenith. A secret and direct channel between the US National Security Council (NSC) and an Israeli team (according to reports, to have consisted of Defence Minister Yitzhak Rabin, the Prime Minister's adviser on counter-terrorism Amiram Nir, former Mossad official David Kimche, IDF Chief of Staff Lieutenant-General Moshe Levy, Military Intelligence Chief Major-General Ehud Barak and the IDF Military Attaché in the Washington embassy, Major-General Uri Simhoni – a former commander of the IDF's Northern Command reconnaissance battalion known as *Sayeret Egoz*) was established. Together, and in unprecedented co-operation, the NSC staff and their Israeli counterparts scrutinized all military options available to secure the release of the hostages.[32]

After several weeks of tense negotiations and unrealized threats of massive US military action, the 39 hostages were released by their Shi'ite captors – but not before Israel freed from Atlit military prison more than 700 Lebanese Shi'ite prisoners the IDF had captured in southern Lebanon.

Accordingly, the next US–Israeli intelligence joint venture was the quest for Immad Mughniye, the operations chief of *Hizbollah* in Lebanon. A most cunning, ruthless and ingenious terrorist, there was no mystery as to why Mughniye was wanted by both the Americans and the Israelis. He was responsible for the 1983 bombings of the US embassy (an act which virtually destroyed the CIA station in Lebanon) and the Marine and French peace-keeping barracks, as well as the 16 March 1984 kidnapping and eventual murder of CIA station chief William Buckley. Mughniye was also behind the 4 November 1983 suicide-bombing of the Israeli Border Guards headquarters in Tyre (*see* page 126), the Shi'ite operation which almost eliminated Israel's counter-terrorist capabilities in southern Lebanon and resulted in increased Shi'ite terrorist operations against Israeli military and security forces.[33]

While the capture or termination of Mughniye was obviously on the minds of the operational planners in the Israeli intelligence community, to the Americans it was an obsession. When Mughniye was located in the South of France, apparently as a result of Mossad's monitoring of *Hizbollah* communications in Lebanon, he was placed under immediate Mossad surveillance and a joint CIA/NSC–Mossad plan to abduct him was set in motion. Mughniye was in France in order to prepare the groundwork for terrorist operations which would secure the release of George Ibrahim Abdallah, the notorious figure implicated in the 1982 Paris assassinations of US Deputy Military Attaché Charles Ray and Israeli diplomat Ya'akov Barsimantov, the chief of Mossad's France station.‡ The French were to have also kept vigilant coverage of Mughniye's movements, but the DST is said to have secretly taken him to the airport and placed him aboard a flight to the Middle East – later claiming that the Americans and Israelis had been monitoring the 'wrong man'.[34]

Although the plans to end Mughniye's terrorist career ended in frustration, the new counter-terrorist partnership would flourish for the next few years – especially under the guidance of Lieutenant-Colonel Oliver North, the man responsible for what has been termed the 'Israelization' of US anti-terrorism strategy – culminating in Israel's assistance in bringing the *Achille Lauro* incident to a favourable conclusion. The 'marriage of convenience' would end, however, in a mire of controversy when the massive espionage efforts of Israeli spy Jonathan Jay Pollard became public knowledge and when Israel's, and Mossad's in particular, role in the Iran-Contra Affair was uncovered. Nevertheless, in the period following the débâcle in Lebanon, Mossad's relationship with the US intelligence community was a short-lived blessing.

Although post-Lebanon War intelligence operations were generally more subtle than 'active', they did continue and included an unsuccessful campaign to locate and assassinate Abu Nidal. Although Mossad operations against terrorism remain highly classified to this day, one series of operations which could not remain secret were their recent actions in that most favoured of terrorist haunts – Cyprus.

The cause for action stemmed out of the December 1987 Palestinian uprising, or *Intifadah*, an expression of frustration against the stagnant campaign for a Palestinian state. The *Intifadah* had truly begun on 25 November when a hang-glider crossed into northern Israel on the south Lebanese winds, carrying a PFLP-GC terrorist who

‡ In an interesting development to Israel's covert war against *Hizbollah* and Islamic Jihad, French police have commenced an investigation into claims by Islamic Jihad that in October 1989 Mossad agents kidnapped a key Islamic Jihad operative in Paris and were holding him in the Paris embassy, awaiting the chance to whisk him back to Israel for trial. Although Jerusalem has vehemently denied this allegation as 'absurd', French airport security officials were ordered to look out for passengers boarding flights to Israel who appeared to be travelling against their will.

proceeded to kill six soldiers from a *Na'ha'l* unit (Hebrew acronym for *No'ar Halutzei Lohem* or Pioneer Fighting Youth) at their base at Beit Hillel near Kiryat Shmoneh. As a result of the Palestinians' first major assault on an Israeli military target for quite some time, the once invincible aura of the Israeli soldier was destroyed. The local youths used stones, Molotov cocktails, and burning tyres in their attacks on soldiers in the Occupied West Bank and Gaza Strip, scenes which inevitably became a part of the landscape.

For the Palestinians, and the Palestine Liberation Organization in particular, the *Intifadah* was a public relations bonanza. The once merciless Palestinians were viewed by the world's media as a tenacious 'David' fighting the giant IDF; the once moral guardians of the Middle East were now looked on as brutal 'Goliaths'. Hoping to turn the tables on a sacred part of Zionist history, the PLO cleverly planned to exploit this unexpected media attention by staging a symbolic re-enactment of the *Haganah*'s refugee ship *Exodus*, but with a ship full of their own returnees who had been deported by the Israeli authorities for their participation in hostile terrorist activity (HTA). The proposed sailing, as intended, struck a raw nerve with the Israeli Government which, according to foreign accounts, immediately set in motions plans to sabotage it.

The Palestinian ship intended to sail from Cyprus to Haifa, not expecting to be able to dock but to be turned back just as the British had done to the Jews. Cyprus was the obvious embarkation point for the Palestinian operation since the PLO had a well-established intelligence network there. The Cypriots had been more than friendly to the benevolent Palestinians and a PLO ferry service, oddly enough run by the Christian Phalangists, which ran between Limmasol and Beirut was successful and prosperous. The sailing date was set for the end of February and a run-down ferry, the *Sol Phryne*, was purchased by three PLO officers from *el-Fatah*'s 'Western Office', a body responsible for terrorist operations in Israel and the Occupied Territories. With much pomp and ceremony, the PLO renamed the ship *el-Awda* – 'the Return'.

On 27 February 1988, the three *el-Fatah* officers, Mahmed Tamimi, Marwan Qiali, and Mahmad Bahias – all sporting the rank of colonel in *el-Fatah* and the reputation of fearless fighters – were killed by a car bomb placed in their grey Volkswagen Golf. The PLO spokesman, Bassam Abu Shariff, a man intimate with the capabilities of Israeli intelligence, blamed Mossad for the assassinations, although Israel vehemently denied any participation in the bombing which was claimed by an unknown Arab group. Eighteen hours after the triple killing, a magnetic mine attached below the waterline of *el-Awda* detonated, leaving a 3-foot by 2-foot gash which postponed the Palestinian homecoming 'indefinitely'. The Palestinians and many foreign intelligence officials blamed Mossad for this explosion too, claiming that IDF Naval Commandos assisted in the operation. Once again Israel publicly denied any involvement, although it was obvious that the events only served Israel's interests.

One Mossad operation which was compromised and publicly exposed was the fascinating case of Ismail Hassan Sawan, a double agent, infiltrator, and suspected by many of being one of Mossad's most valuable agents inside the PLO. The 'Sawan incident' exploded into an international affair between Israel and Great Britain after a large weapons cache was found in his London flat by detectives from Scotland Yard. His tale of intrigue, terrorism, and espionage can, however, be traced to the Lebanese capital, Beirut.

In late 1977, Ismail Hassan Sawan left his native Jerusalem for West Beirut, to study at the American University. The PLO had long used the American University as a draft hall for new recruits to their cause; this was especially the case following the bloodbath of the Lebanese Civil War, when the PLO was licking its wounds and counting its severe losses. When PLO officers learned of Sawan's Jerusalem background he was immediately recruited with a monthly salary of 100 Lebanese Pounds. When summer vacation came around, Sawan packed his belongings and made the lengthy bus trip from Beirut to Jerusalem, via Damascus, Amman, and the Allenby Bridge crossing. Upon his return home, Sawan's brother immediately grabbed him and explained that the 'Jewish Shin Bet' knew he had been recruited and that if he did not want to be arrested he must 'co-operate'. Co-operation means intelligence work, and in a Shin Bet apartment in Jerusalem, near Mount Herzl – where Israel buries its dignitaries and war dead – Sawan met his contacts: 'Captain Alias' and 'Major Yunis'.[35]

Captain Alias was brief and direct with Sawan. He told the frightened Palestinian the exact date he had joined el-Fatah and the address and telephone number of his Beirut flat. Alias did not force Sawan to become an operative, but he did explain that if he did not co-operate he could never return to Jerusalem. There and then, Ismail Hassan Sawan became a double-agent.

Back in Lebanon, Sawan underwent the obligatory terrorist course at a PLO training camp in southern Lebanon. He became proficient in the use of the AK-47, the art of grenade-throwing, and plastic explosives. Upon graduation he was ordered to return to 'Occupied Palestine', where he would receive a weapon and instructions from a senior el-Fatah man in the PLO hotbed of Nablus. Needless to say, the contact in Nablus was arrested by Shin Bet and Sawan was paid a hefty bonus with which he planned to study engineering in Europe. This revelation did not bother his handlers at all. Sawan's files were duly transferred to a Mossad man code-named 'Morris'.

Sawan first made his way to Paris and then to an engineering school in London, all the time subsidized handsomely by Mossad. In London, Sawan had a new handler named Albert, a salary of £600 per month, and was given one primary mission: find Major Abd al-Rahim

Mustafa, the *Force 17* commander in London, and infiltrate his organization by blending into the ever-growing Palestinian community there. Sawan eventually reached and gained the trust of Major al-Rahim Mustafa, who had been dispatched to London following the Lebanon War under the personal orders of Yasir Arafat in order to establish a network of deep cover sleeper-agents.§ The Major was provided with substantial funds to operate his clandestine force and he laundered them through PLO-owned businesses throughout the London metropolitan area which were staffed solely by PLO personnel. These employees included another Mossad double-agent named Bashar Smarah, a Druze from the Golan Heights town of Majdel Shams, who would eventually be expelled from Britain after informing British police of his double-agent status.

Sawan was a Mossad agent for four years. He succeeded in his studies, and took a British wife. He met Albert frequently in the hotels of London's West End and provided a gold-mine of information on PLO activities in London, as well as on Syrian agents operating on behalf of the rejectionist front Palestinian terror groups. Much of this information was passed to the British, no doubt assisting MI5, MI6, and Scotland Yard's Special Branch. It was for this reason that Sawan felt little danger when he was arrested in his Hull flat following a return trip to Israel on 17 August 1987. A large arms cache had been found, left there by Major al-Rahim Mustafa.

British police were investigating the execution of Palestinian cartoonist Nadji el-Ali al-A'adami, killed by a hit team thought to be from Major al-Rahim Mustafa's *Force 17* commandos. The murder followed the publication of a caricature unfavourable to Chairman Arafat in a Kuwaiti paper. Nadji el-Ali al-A'adami was a famous cartoonist from the very militant refugee camp of Ein el-Hilweh near Sidon. During the Israeli invasion, when all Palestinian males were interrogated by Israeli military intelligence, a high-ranking IDF officer recognized al-A'adami as being the famous artist he was, shook his hand with great respect, and ordered the 'celebrity's' *immediate* release. Recognizing the plight of his brethren living in the squalour of refugee camps, al-A'adami often wrote articles and drew cartoons ridiculing PLO officials living in five star European hotels with unlimited expense accounts while other Palestinians were starving near Beirut. Needless to say his work angered the PLO, a fact not lost on investigating detectives who had suspected the PLO anyway. They followed all leads, including the London commander of *Force 17*, and when Major al-Rahim Mustafa's personal diary was discovered – ironically, in an Arab restaurant in the predominantly Jewish district of Golders Green – its decoded notations led the police to Sawan's flat.

§ Other noted notches on Major al-Rahim Mustafa's belt included personal participation in a 1978 machine-gun attack on El Al passengers in Munich, and being the one-time commander of *Commando 18*. After an unsuccessful 'tour of duty' in Beirut in 1985 he was captured and tortured by the Shi'ite *Amal* militia for four months.

Sawan felt the British would know everything about his, and Mossad's, activities in Britain and naturally told his inquisitors all they wanted to hear. This sent shock waves through the British intelligence community, who were appalled by the sheer volume of Israeli intelligence work taking place on their sovereign territory. On 17 June 1988, the British ordered the expulsion of Arieh Regev, Mossad's liaison officer with British intelligence, and the PLO's representative to Britain. Eventually five Israeli diplomats, claimed by the British to be Mossad agents, were expelled, virtually closing down Mossad's UK station. The incident was a bitter blow for Mossad, especially coming from the government of Prime Minister Margaret Thatcher who was highly respected for her stance on terrorism and who must certainly have appreciated the efforts of Shin Bet and Mossad in 'the struggle'.

The British had good reason to be hostile; according to the Arab weekly magazine *Ad-Dastur*, Israel's London embassy was one of five Israeli embassies (the others being in Washington DC, Canada, West Germany, and Australia) which ran Mossad agents. In Britain, MI6 had said it would not interfere with Mossad's operations on British soil as long as it did not compromise British authority, and all information gathered on terrorism was duly passed on to MI5. However, British tolerance was slowly destroyed by Mossad's complicity in several kidnapping operations, including a Nigerian government official, Omaru Diku, and an Israeli nuclear technician, Mordechai Vanunu; forged British passports discovered by immigration officers; and finally by the Smarah and Sawan affairs. The incident thus developed into the British version of the Pollard scandal in the United States, a disaster which Isser Harel, Shin Bet's legendary first commander and Mossad master Controller, referred to as 'the worst bungled affair in Israeli history'.[36] Sawan was sentenced to eleven years in prison following a trial at the Old Bailey.

The series of Mossad intelligence failures came to a boil in the most public manner. In January 1989, a Tel Aviv Superior Court ruled that the IDF Military Censor's Office could not censor 38 sections from an article in the Tel Aviv local newspaper *Ha'ir* which severely criticized the current Mossad Controller, later identified as Nachum Admoni, for his lack of imagination in highly sensitive intelligence matters, and told of his imminent resignation. He was described as plodding and not liking initiative, and among the examples cited from the never-ending Mossad *Michdal* were: the negligent loss of a package of British passports intended for use by Mossad operatives but left in a phone booth in Germany; the Pollard spy mess; Israeli involvement in 'Iran-gate'; the arrest of an 'alleged' Mossad agent in Greece on 28 April 1988 after a foiled murder attempt on a PLO diplomat in Athens; and, finally, the Sawan Affair. Unfortunately, successful operations against terror, such as Mossad's role in the Abu Jihad assassination, had to remain classified and closed to public scrutiny. Prime Minister Yitzhak

Shamir, an ex-Stern Gang member and Mossad officer, loyally stood by his Controller and refused to name Admoni's successor.

This chapter on Mossad's war against terrorism has a pertinent footnote. Twenty years after the KGB helped bring about the explosion of the Palestinians' international terrorism campaign, *Glasnost* came to the Arab-Israeli intelligence war. In an interview on Russian Radio, KGB deputy commander General Vitali Ponomorov said the KGB was willing to co-operate with the Mossad in anti-terror operations. There was no official reply from Tel Aviv.

2. The Shin Bet

El Al and the Shin Bet's War Abroad

On 21 December 1988, Pan American Flight No. 103 made its routine holiday flight from Frankfurt to New York and Detroit via London's Heathrow Airport. After the stop-over in London, during which some passengers disembarked and others boarded, the Boeing 747 continued its trans-Atlantic journey in earnest. The 'No-Smoking' lights had just been extinguished as the aircraft reached an altitude of 31,000 feet, when an explosion in Cargo Bay 41 ripped through the thin fuselage, causing the Jumbo jet to disintegrate and plummet into the scenic Scottish countryside in and around the town of Lockerbie. In all, 259 passengers and crew members were killed, as were eleven Lockerbie citizens, their lives cut short when the debris of the broken aircraft descended upon them in a blazing inferno.

Early suspicions of metal fatigue were ruled out and the theory slowly took hold that the plane had been blown out of the sky by a terrorist bomb. Emerging evidence tended to corroborate the beliefs of those who said that a sophisticated barometric and timer detonation device had set off a charge of Czech Semtex explosive at a pre-determined time or altitude. British investigators painstakingly reconstructed the destroyed aircraft, inevitably coming to the conclusion that the bomb had been smuggled on board in Frankfurt, possibly by a terrorist working on the tarmac, in a radio cassette recorder which could hold approximately half a kilogram of the deadly explosive. The perpetrators of the barbaric act had been clever, but were eventually uncovered by the ritual delays of congested air traffic. Had the flight not been held up for 25 minutes on the Heathrow runway it would have exploded over the ocean, with little hope of ever recovering any possible evidence.

While the initial list of suspects varied from an obscure Palestinian group called 'May 15', the forever militant PFLP, and even the radical Shi'ite *Hizbollah*, the eventual, and most probable, suspect became Colonel Ahmed Jibril's Popular Front for the Liberation of Palestine General Command (PFLP-GC). The PFLP-GC, a Syrian-controlled anti-Arafat faction of the PLO, is believed to have blown up the aircraft with Syrian and Libyan logistical assistance (and with Iranian funding – $10 million in exchange for revenge against the USS *Vincennes'* mistaken downing of an Iranian airbus over the Persian Gulf) in order to avenge the 1986 US bombing of Tripoli, and to destroy Yasir Arafat's new quasi-diplomatic stance which accepted the right of the State of Israel to exist. Although Jibril, an ex-Syrian Army intelligence officer, vehemently denied responsibility for the Pan Am bombing, the evidence clearly points to his group. In October 1988, West German anti-terrorist police had arrested fourteen PFLP-GC terrorists in a Frankfurt flat, including a senior officer named Hafaz Kassam Dalkamoni. A large arms cache was seized together with several Toshiba 'Boombeat' radio barometer bombs identical with the one which later brought Pan Am 103 out of the sky. (In 1970, the PFLP-GC used a similar explosive device to destroy a Swissair Zurich–Tel Aviv flight, in which 47 passengers were killed.)

According to the Israeli newspaper *Ma'ariv*, Mossad had learned of an intended plan by an unidentified Middle Eastern terrorist group to bring down an airliner during the peak holiday period. As a result of this tip-off, Mossad had even warned Britain's MI6 through its liaison in London, but, tragically, the warning prompted little action. Adding to the mystery and anger was the fact that early in December, an anonymous telephone caller had contacted the American embassy in Helsinki and warned that a Pan Am flight out of Frankfurt would be attacked by 'Palestinian' terrorists – possibly by Abu Nidal's 'Black June' faction. Although the warning was passed on to the airline and US diplomats abroad, who discreetly stayed clear of Pan Am flights for their trek home for Christmas, the travelling public was left in the dark.*

As a result of the indiscriminate slaughter, public uproar centred around the lack of tangible security Pan Am had provided for its passengers, given the warnings, as well as the negligent security displayed at many of the world's hundreds of international airports.† Why weren't the doomed travellers warned of the impending danger? Why wasn't the check-in baggage X-rayed and hand-searched? Why weren't all travellers questioned? Overshadowing the natural human need for answers and rationalization following such a ghastly tragedy was the fact that secure international air travel is unquestionably the hardest thing in the world to guarantee; with countless millions of passengers flying annually, and millions more servicing the travellers, it is virtually impossible. While the inquisitive Press was lambasting Pan Am for ineffective security, no one bothered to question who was handling the luggage at Frankfurt Airport or who provided the catering services for the Pan Am flight in Heathrow? Also lost in this quest for the negligent

---

* In September 1989 the United States Federal Aviation Administration, the FAA, fined Pan Am $630,000 in civil penalties for security lapses found after the bombing of Pan Am 103.
† Ironically enough, Pan Am sacked an Israeli security firm it had hired to examine its security *because* it had issued a stinging report criticizing the lack of effective anti-terrorist defences at Pan Am buildings world-wide.

and the guilty was the fact that the terrorists were well trained and undoubtedly supported by the intelligence services of Iran, Libya and Syria. With the chilling possibility that a combined government intelligence service/international terrorist command was jeopardizing civilian travel, the world looked to one source for an example, a precedent, and a hopeful solution: El Al, Israel National Airlines, and in particular the organization responsible for the world-wide security of El Al – the mysterious, elusive, and always tenacious Shin Bet.

Much like Mossad, Israel's *Sherut Bitachon Haklali* or General Security Services (known today by the acronym *Sha'ba'k*, or Shin Bet for short) has played an instrumental role in safeguarding the nation against threats to her existence. Similarly, the majority of Shin Bet's operations must remain highly classified; however, unlike Mossad's shadowy warriors, Shin Bet maintains a vigil against enemies both at home and abroad, their campaigns more often than not remaining unsung except to a few select individuals. In their full-scale war against terrorism, they have fought in the *casbah*s of Hebron and Nablus, as well as in the olive groves and seaside promenades of the Israeli landscape. Yet their preventive, sometimes undisciplined style of counter-terrorism has served as an international role model and stands as a measure of Israel's national resolve to fight terrorism. The Shin Bet has had little choice in its course of action; from 1968 to 1987, Palestinian terrorists committed more than 600 acts of murder, sabotage, and mayhem outside Israel in which 552 people died and more than 2,000 were seriously wounded. Of that total, only 55 were Israelis and 39 Jewish.[1] A testament no doubt, in the author's opinion, to the efforts of Shin Bet.

The *Sherut Bitachon* was initially an integral department of the *Haganah*'s *Sherut Yediot* or 'Information Service'. Responsible for counter-intelligence and internal security during the struggle for Israeli independence, they were at the vanguard of the struggle, often overwhelmed in their task by having to keep tabs on the British, the Arabs and the rival Jewish 'liberation' movements such as Menachem Begin's *Irgun* – a task they achieved with sometimes brutal ferocity. Following the decree of Israeli independence, the newly named *Sherut Bitachon Haklali* (General Security Services) focused its efforts on Arab and KGB counter-intelligence infiltration, as well as engaging for a time in positive intelligence-gathering of its own, mainly against the Balkan states. Shin Bet's first commander was also considered its best, the famous Isser Harel – a man whose intelligence genius helped shape the organization's character and innovative make-up, who inspired those who joined to engage in the tireless pursuit of Israel's hidden enemies.

Today, Shin Bet can best be described as Israel's equivalent to the American Federal Bureau of Investigation (FBI), and Britain's MI5. Under a government mandate, it is responsible for counter-espionage, internal security and what has developed into its most public venture, counter-terrorism. Besides being responsible for the personal security of

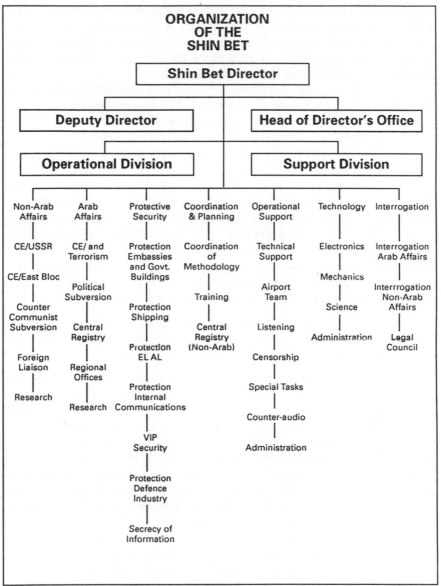

the Israeli President, Prime Minister, Foreign and Defence Ministers, it is divided into eight distinctive departments each with a specific task (*see* chart). The 'Protective Security' and 'Non-Arab Affairs' sections are entrusted with Shin Bet's liaison with foreign counter-intelligence services and are responsible for the protection of Israeli embassies, consulates and offices, high-ranking government personalities travelling abroad, and of course El Al and Zim (Israel's national shipping line) craft and facilities. Although Mossad is responsible for unilateral operations and liaison on intelligence matters, and Military Intelligence controls the attaché system and military liaison, Shin Bet handles unilateral 'protective security' and liaison with the local security services in order to safeguard Israeli personnel and installations. For example, there is a regional Protective Security field office in Paris, mainly tasked with the security of El Al and Zim.

This joint security arrangement between El Al and Shin Bet is most interesting and most successful. Although El Al is responsible for paying and providing for the personnel who maintain the airline's ever-vigilant security (mainly Israeli college students who have completed military service with distinction), their recruitment, training, arming, and control is singularly a Shin Bet mandate.

Security for El Al is divided into two distinctive components: airport and aircraft; both are attended to with equal resolve. At all El Al points of departure, travellers checking into an El Al flight are subjected to a two-hour check-in procedure, step one of which results in long lines: baggage search and a polite interrogation. While the bags are opened and searched, and any suspicious object thoroughly examined, travellers are asked a litany of pre-rehearsed questions intended to bring about unrehearsed responses. These questions include:

> 'Are these bags yours? – Did you pack them yourselves? – Have the packed items of luggage left your possession at any time? – Has anyone given you anything, a parcel, a letter, or a gift, to give to anyone in Israel?'

If the interrogation is uneventful, as are most, the security officer glances once more at the holder's passport in search of any deviation which might prompt suspicion, puts his signature to a coloured security sticker (changed daily and applied to every item of checked-in luggage) and *orders* the passenger 'not to accept anything from anyone and to have a pleasant and safe flight'. Arab passengers, nervous travellers and those just deemed suspicious, can expect to have their suitcases rifled and even ripped apart. If complete security is still not guaranteed, the unfortunate passenger or potential terrorist can expect to be strip-searched and even denied access to the aircraft.

The routine instigated by El Al and emulated by few other international carriers, personifies Israel's reliance on human ability over the much-vaunted multi-million dollar technological security devices available today. While a metal detector can indicate if a passenger is carrying a gun, and an X-ray machine can detect a hidden gun or hand-grenade in a travel bag, and while new expensive machines can detect the odour and chemical signature of plastic explosives, they do have very real limitations. Only a specially trained individual can detect the nervous sweat of a man carrying a pistol, grenade, or a sophisticated bomb. A machine can not scour a crowd for that *one* suspicious individual carrying a WZ.63 submachine-gun, nor can a machine question, reason and rely on experience and human intuition.

To complement this first stage of the security institution at El Al airport ground facilities, intimidating-looking individuals, who are assumed to be Shin Bet, provide the additional layer of defence. They wear mirrored sunglasses, communications earpieces, and either hold their trigger fingers on Beretta 9mm automatics or carry 'travel bags' which, according to legend, contain a loaded Uzi and magazines. They maintain a constant, though restrained vigil around the terminal area.

Realizing that the personnel servicing the aircraft can pose as great a threat to the safety of an El Al flight as a passenger carrying a grenade, only the cleaning crews and catering services, having undergone a full Shin Bet security check, can work *near* an El Al aircraft. On the ground, heavily armed El Al security officers protect the aircraft at all times and at take-offs and landings the aircraft receives an escorting motorcade. This escort varies from an unmarked vehicle, at a 'safe' airport such as New York's John F. Kennedy, to an armoured car at a more volatile location such as Rome or Munich. Complementing this effort in many El Al stations are the local police and para-military forces, such as officers armed with Heckler & Koch 9mm submachine-guns who patrol El Al locations at Heathrow in London.

Once on board, the security only increases. While El Al is naturally tight-lipped about its on-board security precautions, foreign sources have indicated an extensive array of aircraft defences. These include armoured-plated reinforcement of the fuselage and all cargo areas, intended to secure the pressurized aircraft from an explosion or a mid-air shootout (it is thought that this saved the El Al Rome to Tel Aviv flight which the PFLP-GC tried to blast out of the sky in 1972 in much the same fashion as the later Pan Am 103). Also used are electronic infra-red deflectors to thwart heat-seeking surface-to-air missiles such as the SAM-7; internal aircraft surveillance cameras; and, of course, the much vaunted El Al 'Skymarshals', actually Shin Bet agents, equipped with their favourite Beretta .22 with its half-load charges. According to *Time* magazine, El Al Skymarshals pose as innocent passengers and carry Uzi submachine guns.

These security tactics have clearly worked. Even though the lengthy security checks have bred such sarcastic jokes as El Al stands for 'Every Landing Always Late', the methods have saved countless lives. In addition, ever since the first PFLP hijacking of an El Al flight to Algeria in 1968, not a single El Al airliner has been successfully abducted.

The massive security which Israel has applied to El Al might be considered extreme, but the measures are justified. Palestinian and other terrorists have long made international air travel an extension of the bloody Arab-Israeli battlefield and one of their prime targets has been the facilities of El Al. According to a report on international terror by the IDF Spokesman's Office, since 1968 El Al has found itself the target of the terrorist attacks listed on page 208.

This litany of terrorist attacks against El Al does not include an equally long list of attacks against Israeli diplomats and diplomatic facilities as well as against Zim offices, Israeli trade fairs, and other miscellaneous targets. Nor the dozens of Palestinian terrorist attacks against foreign air carriers flying to Israel, such as the PFLP-GC's destruction of a Swissair flight in February 1970 in which 47 were killed; the ANYLP attack on 20 July 1973 in Athens on TWA passengers coming from Israel in which four were killed; and the 27 June 1976 hijacking of an Air France Airbus to Entebbe, Uganda, by the Wadi Haddad Faction/PFLP. Nevertheless, this long list of terrorist attempts to disrupt and destroy El Al and other air traffic to Israel serves to illustrate the wide variety of groups with which Shin Bet must contend, as well as the tactics used to accomplish these objectives. Two recent attacks against El Al, however, are worthy of further examination for they not only accentuate the blood-chilling war between Palestinian air terrorists and Shin Bet but, in the light of Pan Am 103, stress what can be done to defeat attacks against airline offices, passenger terminals, and flights filled to capacity.

His true name is Sabri al-Banna and he is considered the world's most dangerous terrorist. The Jaffa-born individual with the cunning eyes who would take on the *nom de guerre* of Abu Nidal, broke from the mainstream PLO in 1973 because of the group's softened position on Israel. He formed an extremely violent and fanatical anti-Arafat, anti-Western terrorist movement which has been supported at one time or another by Iraq, Syria and Libya. It has operated under a variety of names, such as the Abu Nidal Faction, Black June, Revolutionary Organization of Socialist Moslems (ROSM), Black September, Arab Revolutionary Brigades and Egyptian Revolution. Their first attacks were bold and directed against *el-Fatah* PLO loyalists and moderate Arab states, such as the attack on the Intercontinental Hotel in Amman on 17 November 1976 and the assassinations of PLO officials in Paris, London, Brussels, and Islamabad. But Israeli and Jewish targets were not to be neglected either: Abu Nidal gunmen murdered the Chairman of the Austrian-Israeli Friendship Association in Vienna on 1 May 1981 and perpetrated a murderous attack on a Vienna synagogue on 29 August 1981. On 3 June 1982, deep-cover Abu Nidal gunmen in London critically wounded Israel's Ambassador to the Court of St James's, Shlomoh Argov, literally sparking off the 1982 Lebanon War and advertising the murderous objectives of Sabri al-Banna to an international audience. Other heinous attacks were to follow, including the August 1982 attack against a Jewish restaurant in Paris in which six were killed, the April 1983 assassination of PLO leader Doctor Issam Sartawi in Portugal and a bloody hijacking of an Egyptair flight to Malta in which 68 passengers and crewmen were killed in the chaos of a failed rescue attempt by Egyptian commandos after the terrorists had begun to execute several Israeli passengers. It would, however, be a precision attack against two European cities that would put Abu Nidal on the map.

The Christmas decorations lavishly displayed at Rome's Leonardo da Vinci Airport were as beautiful as they were deceiving. Behind the glittering ornaments, made festive by the thousands of travellers heading home for holidays, the airport was tense and nervous. In early December, the Paris-based anti-crime organization, Interpol, had received a warning (from Mossad it has been rumoured), that terrorists of Arab origin would strike a European airport in 'spectacular' fashion during the heavy Christmas travel period. As a result, several preventive precautions were taken, including the closing of a balcony overlooking ticket counters in Rome, and heavily armed undercover Special Branch officers infiltrating crowds near the check-in counters at Heathrow. But when the terror came on 27 December 1985, the beefed-up security was to no avail.

At 0903 hours, four Middle Easterners, dressed in a variety of expensive Western dress, who were milling about at the Leonardo da Vinci check-in area, sprang into action. After glancing at one another in one last sinister moment of co-ordination, the four placed scarves over smiling faces and pulled out AK-47 7.62mm assault rifles and thirteen Russian and Chinese anti-personnel grenades from their travel bags and began their murderous mêlée. To announce their arrival, grenades were thrown first at a coffee bar, where General Donato Miranda Acosta, the Mexican military attaché, and his secretary were killed. Then, the grenades and gunsights were directed against the El Al counter where passengers were preparing to board the daily flight to Israel. The bursts of automatic fire and grenade detonations were deadly and, according to one witness, 'people were falling down all over the place'. But the El Al security guards acted quickly, and in the manner in which they were thoroughly trained. They pulled their 9mm and .22 calibre automatics out of the holsters placed conveniently in the curve of the back, and crouched in the well-rehearsed firing position. By the time the Italian police arrived, the El Al security guards had killed three of the terrorists and critically wounded the fourth. In the five minutes of gunfire and ricocheting shrapnel, fifteen people died and 74 were wounded. The terrorists had been high on amphetamines, the signature of Abu Nidal attacks, which explained how they continued their murderous rampage even after being wounded by the El Al security guards.

The overhead photograph of dead victims, tagged by police for identification, horrified most of the civilized world. According to one Italian security official, had the El Al guards not taken hold of the situation the body count of dead could have been in the hundreds.

Moments after the shooting stopped in Rome, three men in dirty jeans and combat jackets attacked the second-floor departure area at Vienna's Schwechat Airport. Their target was the El Al ticket counter and the passengers waiting to check in for Flight 364 to Israel. In the confused fire-fight, Austrian policemen and El Al security guards returned fire, but could not prevent the terrorists from getting to within 30 feet of the counter and hurling the F-1 anti-personnel grenades like balls with subsequent murderous effects (once again, the Vienna attackers had been high on amphetamines). Two minutes after the first shots were fired, the terrorists – some wounded by the returned gunfire – fled, commandeering an airport automobile. In an ensuing gun battle and car chase for two miles, the terrorists were stopped by the police. The toll in Vienna was two dead, and 47 wounded.

The Abu Nidal Faction claimed responsibility for the massacres. They proudly justified them as a military attack in retaliation for Israel's 1 October bombing of PLO headquarters in Tunis, although this claim seems ridiculous considering that Abu Nidal has specialized in killing PLO officials for years.

Within ten minutes, the world was reminded of the awesome scourge Israel had been combating for years. None of the surviving Rome or Vienna attackers carried identification, but investigators were able to identify them as Palestinians from West Beirut's refugee labyrinth who had been recruited by an Abu Nidal officer as part of a ten-man squad called the 'Martyrs of Palestine'. They had planned to seize hostages at the Rome and Vienna airports as a prelude to the more ambitious and surely suicidal commandeering of El Al jets to Israel. In a benign show of their nation will to combat terrorism, both the Italians and Austrians issued an international arrest warrant for the master terrorist, al-Banna.

If the Rome and Vienna massacres illustrated the devastating dangers a mad terrorist leader can pose to innocent people, a foiled attack against El Al four months later would not only show the guilty hand of a sovereign government in the perpetration of international terrorism, but how the El Al Shin Bet-inspired security effort saved the lives of more than 400 passengers.

El Al Flight 016 is the routine flight between New York and Tel Aviv via London's Heathrow Airport. As is the usual case on flights to Israel, the aircraft was filled to capacity with first-time travellers to the Holy Land, Orthodox Jews, and homeward-bound Israelis laden with tons of electronic goods bought at the hundreds of discount outlets in New York catering to such tourists. The stop-over in London afforded a brief glimpse of the British capital, as well a last-minute opportunity to purchase the much coveted foreign cigarettes and perfumes at the enormous Heathrow duty-free shops. On 17 April 1986, pleasant routine almost gave way to destruction.

Security at Heathrow on that cloudy Thursday morning had been tight but normal. Passengers boarding Flight 016 had been subjected to the typical two-hour check-in and the inquisitive baggage and passport scrutiny. After passing through passport control, the obligatory X-ray machine and metal-detector examinations, passengers proceeded to the gate and one final El Al security check.

One passenger that day was a 20-year-old pregnant Irish woman named Ann-Marie Murphy. As she stood in a small booth enclosed by a curtain, an El Al security agent questioned Murphy as to the reason for her trip to Israel. Not being a Jew, travelling alone and being clearly pregnant, Murphy aroused great suspicion in the Shin Bet-trained security agent. After admitting that the baby's father was a 32-year-old Jordanian-born Palestinian named Nezar Hindawi, who wanted to avoid El Al because he was a Palestinian and because of the airlines security, her ominous answers prompted a more thorough check. Upon searching her bag, given to the unknowing Miss Murphy by her Palestinian lover, the agent discovered a false bottom in her handbag and 1.5 kilograms of Semtex attached to a sophisticated detonating device. Quietly, the frightened Irish woman was whisked away for questioning by anti-terrorist policemen from Scotland Yard. The other passengers were to learn of their close brush with death only upon landing at Israel's Ben-Gurion International Airport.

Hindawi was a known terrorist – a member of the Abu Nidal Faction, whose brother Ahmed Hazi Hindawi was the confessed bomber of the 'La Belle' Nightclub in West Berlin. He had brought Miss Murphy to Heathrow Airport, and in a hired car driven by a Syrian diplomat who was an agent for Syrian Air Force Intelligence, the country's premier espionage service; he returned afterwards to the Syrian embassy. If someone in Damascus did indeed unilaterally order the El Al bombing, many Western intelligence experts believe it stemmed from the February 1986 Israel Air Force interception of a Libyan airliner in another failed attempt to capture Doctor George Habash. Instead of finding the elusive PFLP chief, the Israelis once again found a startled group of passengers including seven Syrian politicians and the assistant secretary general of the ruling Ba'ath Party. Western analysts believe it is possible that extremists in Syrian Air Force Intelligence, commanded by Brigadier-General Mohammed Khouli, sanctioned the bombing to initiate a war between Israel and Syria. According to sketchy reports, General Khouli was imprisoned following the failed bombing.[2]

A day after Flight 016 was supposed to have exploded somewhere over Europe, Nezar Hindawi was arrested after the Syrians refused to facilitate his escape. Under interrogation, the connection between Hindawi, Abu Nidal, and the Syrian Government was fully exposed.‡ Hindawi admitted to having been ordered to make romantic contact with a 'European-looking' woman, to promise to marry her and then send her off to Israel, and her death as a human time-bomb on an El Al flight. There must also be, in the author's opinion, some credence to speculative accounts connecting the failed Hindawi bombing to the PFLP-GC. Jibril's PFLP-GC enjoys close ties with Syrian Air Force Intelligence, it has been the principal terror group engaging in airline bombings and, perhaps most importantly, frequently orders its agents to recruit innocents to become 'human time-bombs'. In light of the Pan Am 103 incident, this theory must be given serious consideration.

Oddly, and perhaps foolishly, the Syrians allowed Hindawi to live after his role in the operation was complete. When a particularly vicious

‡ As a result of the findings in Hindawi's subsequent trial and conviction in London, Britain broke diplomatic relations with President Assad's Syria in an act Israel described as courageous.

terrorist attack is being planned, measures for eliminating possible surviving terrorists are attended to with great care. This happened in another Abu Nidal/Syrian act of terror – the 5 September 1986 attack on Sabbath eve prayers at Istanbul's *Neve-Shalom* Synagogue in which 22 were killed – when the terrorists were issued with several grenades armed with 0-second fuzes to ensure that no police interrogations ensued!

The efforts of that nameless El Al security guard not only saved the lives of the 400 passengers, but clearly helped avert a major Middle East military confrontation with world-wide repercussions. Had the El Al aircraft been blasted out of the sky, and the Syrian connection made, it is safe to assume that Israel would have gone to war.

Averting one tragedy did not of course ensure the cessation of attacks on El Al. Another soon followed on 26 June 1986 when an agent discovered a booby-trapped suitcase at the check-in desk at Madrid. It exploded, injuring the guard and thirteen others, having been set up by Abu Musa's renegade faction of *el-Fatah*. While it did inflict casualties it also proved that such terrorist attacks could be foiled by effective human intelligence (HUMINT) and deterrence such as displayed by Shin Bet. This message bore heavy tones of hindsight following the destruction of Pan Am 103 two years later.

Today, Shin Bet remains vigilant in its duties, securing Israel's installations and facilities abroad. Yet the neat little war outside Israeli embassies and El Al terminals is but a small element of the total Shin Bet offensive against terrorism. Its true war is fought daily on the streets of Israel; in the minds of courageous agents, in the paranoid personas of double agents, the secretive pasts of informants and, as is often the case, in an all too brutal a fashion.

The Watchful Eyes from Within
The Shin Bet Counter-terrorist Campaign at Home

For the various Palestinian liberation movements, no prize is greater than striking inside the boundaries of Israel. Blowing up an airliner over the European skies might place the 'plight of the Palestinians' on the network news, but attacking a target in the Zionist heartland is the true justification for their existence as a movement. Such attacks also serve notice to the Israelis themselves that they cannot continue to ignore the refugee problem while resting securely behind the might of the Israel Defence Forces. Terrorism, in its most basic form of secretive cells and arms caches, is not in fact a military threat that can be defeated by battalions of élite infantrymen stationed along the frontier; nor is it solely a criminal matter to be neutralized by the detective capabilities of a police force used to combating thefts. It is a covert intelligence war of nerves aimed at destroying a society's internal stability and confidence; as a result it must be tackled by the unique talents of a nation's internal security force. In Israel, this most difficult task is allotted to the experienced counter-intelligence officers of Shin Bet.

In this task the 500-man-strong Shin Bet (according to foreign sources) is hopelessly outnumbered. From 1965, the first year of *el-Fatah* attacks against Israel, until May 1987 there were 8,000 Palestinian terrorist attacks *inside* Israel. As a result of the violence during this period, 405 Israeli civilians were killed and 2,815 seriously wounded.[3] It is safe to assume that were it not for the diligent efforts of Shin Bet the toll of casualties would have been much higher.

The task of internal security has always been a demanding, though historically manageable task. During the years 1948–67, the principal non-military threat to the State of Israel was the vast, and sometimes exorbitant, number of foreign intelligence agents operating within the nation's boundaries. In its truly formative years the intelligence service scored numerous, and sometimes quite impressive, counter-espionage victories. On 31 March 1961, Shin Bet agents and Israeli Police Special Tasks Division officers arrested Lieutenant-Colonel Yisrael Be'er, an IDF officer who served on the General Staff and was a self-appointed historical archivist close to the office of Prime Minister David Ben-Gurion. He was, in fact, a seasoned KGB agent who for years had been passing bits of information to the Eastern bloc. Another spy captured by them was Professor Kurt Sita, a German-born physicist teaching at Haifa's prestigious Technion University, who had been an agent for the Czechoslovak Intelligence Service. There were other, more secretive captures of enemy agents, such as the 1956 arrest of former SS Leutnant Ullrich Schonhaft, who escaped from Germany to Palestine after purchasing the identity papers of Gabriel Sussman, a Jewish survivor of the Holocaust. The new 'Sussman' made a life in Israel, eventually blending into Israeli society and even joining the Israel Defence Forces where he reached the rank of First Lieutenant in the Artillery Corps. He was arrested in a joint Military Intelligence/Shin Bet sting operation after his intense dealings with Egyptian Military Intelligence were uncovered.

Basically, Shin Bet's first two decades of internal security passed quietly. Israeli citizens were generally not susceptible to recruitment by foreign espionage services because Israel's severe military predicament had created a unique national *esprit de corps*. According to Isser Harel, Arab intelligence efforts were minimal, ineffective, and largely restricted to terrorist activity. Even the severe threat fedayeen guerrillas and other Arab infiltrators posed were largely restricted to Israel's frontiers, and never managed to infiltrate into the Israeli heartland or compromise sensitive security, government, or political installations. In fact, these fedayeen attacks were largely para-military in nature, and terrorist outrages, such as the placing of bombs on buses, were not common-place yet. The aftermath of the Six Day War would change everything.

The lightning Israeli military victory in the 1967 Six Day War altered the geo-political map of the Middle East. For Shin Bet, Israel's acquisition of the Golan Heights, the West Bank and the Gaza Strip increased their areas of responsibility four-fold. For the Palestinians, Israel's capture of the West Bank and Gaza, filled with refugees from the earlier wars, served as a call to arms for dozens of highly political and revolutionary Palestinian liberation organizations which emerged out of the Arab defeat. This included the creation of the PFLP and *As-Saiqa* on 11 December 1967 and the formation of Ahmed Jibril's PFLP-GC on 24 April 1968. These new groups naturally prompted a huge increase in Palestinian terrorist activity abroad and in Israel. For Shin Bet, 1967 signalled the beginning of a newly expanded war against terrorism, not an end.

During the eighteen months following the Six Day War, there were hundreds of terrorist attacks inside Israel which originated from what became known as the Occupied Territories. These included the planting of land-mines, such as the one which a school bus detonated near Be'er Orah, and which killed two and injured 28 students on 18 March 1968; the detonation of an explosive device in Tel Aviv's Central Bus Station on 4 September 1968, which killed two and injured sixty; and the explosion of a PFLP car-bomb in Jerusalem's Machane Yehuda market on 22 November 1968 in which twelve civilians were killed and 68 seriously wounded. The murderous attacks from territories no longer separated by barbed wire and minefields proved as serious a threat to Israeli security as the combined, though badly beaten, Arab convention-al military forces. The IDF, the Border Guards, and the National Police were dispatched into the once foreign domains of Nablus, Hebron, Bethlehem, and of course, the most volatile hotbed of Palestinian nationalism, the Gaza Strip; but their armoured cars, foot patrols and weapons were of little use without intelligence. In the 'territories', that meant Shin Bet.

As mentioned earlier, Shin Bet is divided into eight different departments or sections: (a) Arab Affairs; (b) Non-Arab Affairs; (c) Protective Security; (d) Operational Support; (e) Technology; (f) Inter-rogation and Legal Council; (g) Co-ordination and Planning; and (h) Administration. Much like the Israel Defence Forces, it is sub-divided into regional commands, with a southern command office in the city of Ashqelon responsible for the Gaza area; the north of Israel including the Golan Heights is controlled by the Haifa 'command' office, and the West Bank is controlled by an office in Jerusalem. The remainder of Israel is controlled by the Tel Aviv field office, which in turn is a part of the Shin Bet national headquarters. Of all these departments, it is the Arab Affairs, Operations Support, and Interrogation and Legal Council which are most directly involved in countering terrorism.[4]

Arab Affairs is responsible for directing all Shin Bet's counter-espionage, counter-intelligence, and counter-terrorism operations against Arab-inspired sources; these range from tracking agents of the Syrian *Mouchabarat* to infiltrating a PLO cell in the Old City of Jerusalem. Its agents, according to foreign sources, are mainly Arabic-speaking veterans of the IDF's élite units or Intelligence Corps (*Heyl Mode'in*) who undergo extensive counter-intelligence and legal training. Unlike their counterparts in the American FBI, or the Eastern bloc internal security forces, Shin Bet officers do not have the power of arrest. In fact, their role is not that of an investigative force, but rather an intelligence-gathering body which works in a co-ordinated effort with the national police and the IDF. When an arrest is required, a Shin Bet officer submits a detailed report on the case together with a request for an arrest warrant to the Ministry of Justice, which in turn contacts the Police Special Tasks Division (similar to the British Police Special Branch) in order to apprehend the 'unfortunate' suspect.

Shin Bet's efforts against the budding and already established Palestinian terrorist cells in the West Bank and Gaza Strip were of monumental proportions. Luckily for the Israelis, the Jordanians had maintained an often repressive policy aimed at curbing Palestinian nationalist aspirations on its sovereign soil. They achieved this by threatening and imprisoning suspected leaders and by establishing an effective intelligence network. When the IDF captured the West Bank from the Royal Jordanian Army, it also captured the Jordanian *Mouchabarat* files on known *el-Fatah* and *Razd* members. This gift enabled a potential threat to be quickly neutralized. Gaza, however, was another story; here, the Egyptian *Mouchabarat* had for years armed and manipulated the organized Palestinian liberation outfits into a guerilla entity to strike out against Israel. When the Egyptians were forced to depart Gaza in a rather hasty fashion, their discarded arms found new, and quite enthusiastic, owners in the embittered Palestinians who had been made refugees for a second time in twenty years. Within weeks of the Israeli victory, Gaza erupted into a bitter battlefield.

As an 'occupied territory' under Israeli rule, law and order in Gaza was entrusted to a combination of civil and military administration (the latter courtesy of IDF and Border Guard units). For the Israel Defence Forces, a conquering army having just won a remarkable military victory few could ever have envisaged, garrison duty in the squalor of Gaza was dramatically different from the lightning *Blitzkrieg* method of warfare it had just faithfully mastered. At first the attacks against the curious Israeli soldiers, who naïvely viewed a tour in Gaza as a tourist expedition, were few and far between; the odd Molotov cocktail thrown at a command car and a pistol shot at a patrol commander. But as the newly formed Palestinian groups in Jordan, Syria, and Lebanon began establishing cells in the Strip, the attacks grew bolder. Through their very effective use of radio propaganda, they turned anger into rage and rage into fanaticism. Soon the attacks were against IDF troops patrolling the narrow alleys of Gaza City and along the thoroughfares of the refugee camps of Shati, Nutzirat, Burj, Mo'uzi, Dir el-Balach, Khan Yunis, Rafiah, and Jabalya; they became extremely bloody and increasingly effective. Pistols were replaced by AK-47s and Port Said 9mm submachine-guns (the Egyptian copy of the Swedish Carl Gustav submachine-gun), and petrol bombs by Russian-made anti-personnel grenades. The murders, bombings and arson attacks soon expanded to include Israeli civilian settlements near Gaza, and the poverty, hopelessness and sheer hatred for Israel prompted a host of terrorist attacks inside Israel proper as well.

By 1969, law and order had virtually ceased to exist in the Strip; it literally became an autonomous territory brutally controlled by the various and often feuding Palestinian liberation movements. By 1970, when 42 terrorists were killed and more than 300 captured, dozens of Israeli civilians and countless Palestinians who had collaborated had been murdered; those killed as traitors very often had their mutilated bodies displayed in the town squares as an effective public warning. The situation was so chaotic that Israeli Defence Minister Moshe Dayan even went so far as to remove the IDF from the thick of it, positioning the Israeli forces along the Gaza Strip's road arteries, entrances and exits – all far away from the violence. A thick, impassable barbed wire fence was built around the Strip and severe restrictions were placed on travel inside Israel. Nevertheless, the terrorism continued and the need for the nameless men of Shin Bet to act grew ever more urgent if things were not to get completely out of control.

Gathering intelligence in Gaza was a demanding task for those officers assigned to Shin Bet's Arab Affairs department. Finding a reliable and sympathetic individual willing to be an informant for the Israelis was a difficult quest indeed, and as a result they often had to turn to the intelligence agent's best sources of information: criminals, profiteers, drug dealers and addicts, pimps and prostitutes. These individuals cared little about their national revolution, concentrating instead on the means, financial or security-wise, to ensure their personal well-being and ultimate survival. When the IDF 'evacuated' Gaza, the informants or *bishtril* (Arabic for traitor) were Shin Bet's eyes and ears and its principal source of intelligence. This practice, however, was very costly; in one instance, in 1970, Palestinian terrorists believed to be loyal to the Marxist PFLP murdered eleven Gaza prostitutes, who were considered to be Shin Bet operatives, in a single night of bloodshed. One of the women who was pregnant, was shot at point-blank range after a known terrorist was arrested by heavily armed Shin Bet plainclothesmen as he left her home. Other informants had phosphorus grenades thrown into their homes and their throats slit open in the marketplace.[5]

Although the decision to pull the IDF out of the Gaza refugee camps did save the lives of Israeli soldiers, it thus resulted in the deaths of countless Palestinians and it placed an overwhelming amount of pressure on Shin Bet which was unable to stem *all* the terrorist activity directed against Israeli targets. The situation was fuelled by public anger in Israel when, in January 1971, two Israeli children and their mother were killed by a grenade thrown into their car during a drive near the Strip. The murders horrified the Israeli public, already brutalized after almost four years of incessant hostilities, and enormous political pressure was placed on Prime Minister Golda Meir to resolve the Gaza troubles. Israel's 'Iron Lady' convened an emergency cabinet meeting and ordered law and order to be brought back to Gaza immediately. Companies of Border Guards stationed in the West Bank were rushed into the fray to intimidate the local Gazans into acquiescence; resultant beatings led to complaints and an official IDF inquiry, but the methods worked and, for a few months at least, terrorism in the Strip ceased. In the late spring, however, the AK-47s and grenades returned to Gaza and, with little recourse remaining, IDF Chief of Staff Lieutenant-General Haim Bar-Lev allowed his OC Southern Command to handle the situation in his own unique manner. That man was Major-General Ariel 'Arik' Sharon, the boisterous, controversial and highly effective officer who knew exactly what was needed to turn Gaza into a model of obedience, and he placed Shin Bet in the vanguard.

Shin Bet began in systematic fashion: they used the long list of 'suspected' terrorists to make wholesale arrests and, once in custody, the prompt and effective interrogations which followed usually provided a bonanza of information. With a firm list of terrorists in his hand, Major-General Sharon opted to administer his very unique brand of counter-terrorism. He *conscripted* the IDF's most élite units, such as Southern Command's *Sayeret Shaked* ('Almond Recon'), the Paratroop Brigade's *Sayeret Tzanhanim* ('Paratroop Recon'), the Golani Brigade's *Sayeret Golani* ('Golani Recon') and, according to foreign sources, *Sayeret Mat'kal* ('GHQ Recon'), to enter the Strip and patrol the camps on foot, initiating thorough searches of homes and persons in the hopes of rooting out the terrorists. This close-contact approach would eventually result in numerous fire-fights and hand-to-hand engagements. Sharon considered it a crusade and he enlisted the help of some of his old cronies from his 1950s anti-guerrilla force *Unit 101*. In typical fashion, the husky Major-General grabbed his own AK-47, and led many of the patrols personally.[6]

The IDF élite units operated in teams of four to five soldiers and subjected a targeted area to tireless patrols followed by long reconnaissance and intelligence-gathering forays. By having the soldiers operate on foot and concentrating on a particular location, the soldiers would learn to distinguish between the norm of everyday life and suspicious activity involving terrorists. In many instances the reconnaissance troops, guided by Bedouin trackers and Arabic-speaking soldiers, wore local garb and even attempted to infiltrate the ranks of the local terrorist groups. By late 1971, the combined IDF/Shin Bet offensive had driven most of the terrorists from the safety of the refugee camps into the bushes, caves and citrus groves surrounding Gaza. This new method of neutralizing Gaza was termed 'guerrilla versus guerrilla', although the IDF's operational success was made possible only by the intelligence Shin Bet liaison provided.

The rather overt, even pre-meditatively violent campaign initiated by these units achieved its intended objectives very early on: the terrorists were pushed underground where they would make mistakes and eventually compromise themselves. This clearing of the ground, in turn allowed Shin Bet to flourish. Many of Gaza's coffee-house owners, cab drivers, street cleaners, pimps and prostitutes were now once again placed on a hefty Shin Bet payroll and pressed into service. In its efforts to remove the terrorist grip of control in Gaza, Shin Bet surveillance squads were of invaluable importance. They occupied abandoned buildings, conducted stake-outs and, most importantly, relayed their information to the IDF forces in the area. They demonstrated a fine working relationship with the IDF and with military intelligence units in particular. In one such instance, Shin Bet surveillance officers uncovered a terrorist-controlled cave which smelled of cheap after-shave and talcum powder. After failing to find any bottles of perfume or other toiletries, the Shin Bet officers decided to stake-out the local Gazan barber shops. After a few days of 24-hour surveillance, they saw a sight which would amaze them. Outside a small, dishevelled barber's stall was a long line of AK-47-toting men patiently awaiting to have a haircut and shave. The agents called in the reconnaissance paratroopers and, after a brief show of force, the guerrillas were arrested.[7] One of the most dynamic investigators to emerge from the fray was a young officer named Yossi Ginausor, a man Sharon and, as will be seen later, most Israelis would never forget.

By December 1971, the Gaza Strip had been pacified and this state of affairs was to last for sixteen years. The terrorist wanted list dropped from 165 in September to a mere 55. Terrorist attacks against Israel and Israeli targets originating from the Gaza Strip, which in 1970 numbered in the hundreds, were reduced to a single attack. For Shin Bet and the IDF it was a monumental victory. Their luck would also continue in the year to come as the long list of West Bank and Gaza terrorists was uncovered by the IDF in Operation 'Spring of Youth' and their names duly passed to agents in the field.

If Gaza can be considered one of Shin Bet's most overt successes in the fight against terrorism during the post-1967 era, it was also one of its very few operations to be made public. In 1972, a massive Syrian espionage ring which had supported Palestinian terrorist attacks was uncovered by Shin Bet and made public; most shockingly, those arrested included a number of prominent Israelis. Another publicized incident was the 1980 murder of Shin Bet officer Moshe Golan, killed by a Palestinian double-agent he had been 'controlling'. Even in the aftermath of Israel's militarily successful though politically disastrous invasion of Lebanon, where according to foreign reports Shin Bet operated against those remaining Palestinians and the new Shi'ite enemy, they were still an enigma shrouded in a shield of secrecy. The shield, however, would soon be pierced, revealing the organization as never before.

The Dirty Secrets of a Dirty War

The Shin Bet v. Palestinian Terrorism, 1984–9

One of the more visible aspects of the Israeli landscape since the 1967 War are the thousands of Arab workers who trek daily from their homes in the West Bank and Gaza Strip into Israel for low-paid menial employment. As a result of stringent security checkpoints leading into Israel proper, these labourers are forced to depart their homes extremely early in the morning, and head back towards the 'territories' before nightfall, crowding taxis and buses for the protracted journey back across the Green Line. On 12 April 1984, four such Arab workers appeared to be heading back to the Gaza Strip after a day's work in Tel Aviv. They looked shabby, dirty and tired, and like many Arab labourers carried their belongings in a beaten-up suitcase and plastic shopping bags. As they boarded the No. 300 bus to Ashqelon at Tel Aviv's Central Bus Station, the four Arabs aroused little if any suspicion as Ashqelon was but a stop on the journey to another part of the world called Gaza.

It is reported that several of the passengers on that doomed bus ride were suspicious of the four since an Arab with a suitcase on any bus always brought its fair share of scepticism and fear. One of the passengers even confided his fears to an army officer sitting next to him, but the exhausted lieutenant was more interested in being left alone than by the four young Arabs sweating nervously nearby. Half an hour out of Tel Aviv, near the Ashdod Junction, the four Arabs suddenly acted, commandeering the bus by placing a butcher's sharp knife at the neck of the driver and threatening to blow up the vehicle with grenades and the suitcase, booby-trapped with a PG-7 grenade. A pregnant passenger anxiously pleaded to be released, but her anguish was ignored by the terrorists. After a brief scuffle, the angered bus driver managed to swing his front door open long enough to push her out and frantically order her to get help! She succeeded in flagging down a truck, whose driver raced to a roadside garage and contacted the police. A seemingly average spring day in Israel began to unfold into one of the most bizarre and controversial episodes in Israeli history.

A few miles outside Ashqelon, the bus encountered its first crudely assembled roadblock – a few police vehicles and snake's teeth spikes laid across the now isolated thoroughfare were meant to slow down the speeding vehicle. With the knife still pressed firmly at his jugular, the driver followed the orders of his captors and swerved around the obstacles to continue south towards the Gaza Strip. Seven kilometres down the highway, they met their second and final police roadblock at the Dir el-Balach Junction. Sharpshooters from the *Ya'ma'm*, the National Police Border Guard's élite anti-terrorist unit, shot out the tyres of the Mercedes bus, resulting in a chaotic few seconds during which the bus driver managed to help several passengers escape through kicked-out windows. The terrorists, however, quickly regained control of the situation and forced most of those on board to become hostages in a tense game of nerves. While twilight brought an eerie calm aboard the bus, legions of Border Guard and IDF units took up siege positions around the vehicle.

Hostage negotiators and senior-ranking military officers were rushed to the scene by helicopters and speeding Command Cars to begin talking with the four Gazans, who were demanding the release of 500 convicted Palestinian terrorists from Israeli prisons and wanted to see local International Red Cross representatives. What was immediately obvious to the officers was the fact that the men were all amateurs! They carried no automatic weapons, did not appear to be fanatical ideologues and had not distributed propaganda material of any specific terrorist organization. Most importantly, however, they did not appear to have taken precautions against a rescue attempt. Within hours of the hijacking the senior officers of the Israeli defence establishment had also arrived on the scene, including hardline Defence Minister Moshe Arens, Chief of Staff Lieutenant-General Moshe Levy, head of Military Intelligence Major-General Ehud Barak, OC Southern Command Major-General Moshe Bar-Kochba, and the Chief Paratroop and Infantry Officer Brigadier-General Yitzhak Mordechai. Mordechai was a veteran *Tzanhanim* officer who was decorated in the 1973 War during the bitter fighting at the Chinese Farm and who commanded the IDF's vanguard division which seized Beirut in 1982. He knew that his government would not be striking a deal with the four and, together with his field commanders, he prepared a contingency rescue plan. Also in attendance, but remaining quietly behind the scenes, was Avraham Shalom, the Shin Bet Controller, with his deputy, the experienced Reuven Hazak. Both names would feature prominently in the years to come.

According to foreign reports, a tense tug-of-war developed between Brigadier-General Mordechai and a senior Border Guard commander as to which unit – the Border Guard's *Ya'ma'm* or an IDF élite unit thought to be the General Staff Reconnaissance Unit but possibly a conscript paratroop force – should be given the honour of rescuing the hostages. Although Israel's 1974 Internal Security ruling, penned into policy following the Ma'alot débâcle, dictated the use of Border Guard and Police units in such scenarios, in the end the IDF force was given the task. According to interpretations of the logic used, it was felt that while the Border Guards might have more experience and training in hostage rescue attempts, the IDF conscripts were younger, with fewer family responsibilities to cloud their minds during the lightning strike.[8]

At about 0400 on 13 April, an empty Mercedes bus identical with the hijacked vehicle was brought to a nearby field allowing the soldiers to run a practice drill and perfect their assault skills to split-second perfection. While the incident was unfolding, and the military commanders prepared their units for the rescue operation, a small group of reporters had managed to slip through the police barricades and take up a curious surveillance around the hijacked bus. The sight of the Press caused little concern among the IDF and police officials, who knew every journalist would have to submit his written piece and photographs to the IDF Military Censor's Office for review of security breaches. In addition, the Israeli Press, although very independent and harshly critical, had never hampered military operations before; they fully appreciated that security matters came before sensational headlines. Nevertheless, journalists at the scene would eventually embroil Israel in one of its most bitter incidents, a web of lies woven by security officials which led to a severe crisis of faith in the IDF, and Shin Bet in particular.

At 0443, the commandos struck. In perfect synchronization, they stormed the bus with weapons ablaze. The first terrorist killed was sitting unsuspectingly by the steering wheel – the photograph of his bloodied corpse slumped against a windshield riddled by bullets was used by the papers to illustrate the success of the rescue attempt. A second terrorist was killed in the rear of the bus, holding his suitcase and booby-trapped PG grenade, while a female IDF soldier on the bus, Corporal Irit Portugez, was tragically killed by a burst of automatic fire as she rose from her seat while attempting to escape the mêleé. A minute later, the other hostages were free, two terrorists were dead and two terrorists had been captured unharmed. The rescue should have entered the history books as one of the many thousands of terrorist incidents perpetrated against Israeli civilians since 1948. It was to be remembered for something more far-reaching than that.

The two captured terrorists, Majdi Abu Shma'a and his cousin, Subhi Abu Shma'a, were first confronted by an outraged Brigadier-General Mordechai who dragged them aside and took it upon himself to beat up one of them in an impromptu interrogation, while the second prisoner received similar treatment at the hands of Shin Bet officers summoned to the scene. A few reporters and photographers witnessed what transpired, even noting that one of the Arabs had wet his trousers in fear. After this severe questioning, the two were held in the custody of the commandos, whose self-control in the light of the death of Corporal Portugez was admirable. Within minutes, other Shin Bet officers had arrived. All were identifiable by their civilian clothing, IDF-issue olive winter parkas, and 9mm Berettas tucked neatly into trouser holsters. When the Shin Bet agents dragged the two hapless cousins away for 'further questioning', dozens of camera shutters managed to capture it on film. At 0630 hours, Defence Minister Moshe Arens convened a press conference where he announced that two of the terrorists had been killed in the assault and that two others had died *en route* to hospital. The seeds of a conspiracy had been sewn.

Contrary to the statements, the two surviving terrorists had been taken to a citrus grove a few miles from where the hijacked bus had been stormed and literally beaten to death with sharp and heavy blows to the chest and skull with blunt objects. In a typically Israeli form of retribution, the terrorists' homes in the refugee camp of Dir el-Balach were also destroyed. Were it not for the presence of the fourth estate, the deaths of the terrorists and the destruction of their homes would have closed a chapter on the hijacking saga; instead, there now began a process which provided the opening glimpse into Shin Bet's workings and led to an uncontrollable unravelling of its labyrinth of secrecy.

Arens' statement was flatly contradicted by many eye-witnesses who said they had seen the two captives taken away bearing no sign of such injuries. Those who challenged the government version did not do so out of sympathy for the terrorists, but rather because they were outraged that the public, they felt, was being told blatant lies. Public opinion in Israel was naturally hostile to such Palestinian acts and was fully used to, and supportive of, stern measures being taken to stop them, but such sentiments stopped short of demands for summary executions (except of course among a minority fringe). Israel regarded itself, proudly, as a democracy and as such the rule of law and the concept of a fair trial was supported – how could Israel claim moral superiority over those it branded 'terrorists' if they acted in a brutal and deceitful manner? Many were determined that the truth be told.

As hints of an official cover-up began to emerge, Defence Minister Arens, with the blessing of Prime Minister Yitzhak Shamir's office, attempted to head off such accusations by organizing an investigatory committee under the legal guidelines of 'Clause No. 537 of the Military Jurisdiction Law' to determine the truthful cause of the deaths of the terrorists. The committee was headed by Major-General (Res.) Meir Zorea, a highly experienced and well-respected intelligence officer; it included, at Avraham Shalom's behest, a representative known to the Press only by the mysterious code-name of *Gimel* – the third letter of the Hebrew alphabet. *Gimel's* true identity was Yossi Ginausor (of Gaza–1971 fame) and, according to foreign reports, he ordered all Shin Bet officers testifying before the committee to provide false and misleading information so as to clear Shin Bet of any involvement in and responsibility for the deaths of the two cousins.[9]

The 'Zorea Committee' subpoened dozens of witnesses; these included the IDF commandos who stormed the bus, the Shin Bet officers at the scene and the National police pathologists who examined the bodies. On 20 May 1984, the committee's conclusions were published, with their findings:

■   The two terrorists taken alive were initially beaten by the assault force to prevent them from activating their booby-trapped briefcase and then beaten during the first interrogation they endured.

■   There was *no* official IDF or Shin Bet order calling for the execution of the two terrorists captured.

■   The pathologists determined that the terrorists were killed as a result of blows to the skull with a blunt and heavy instrument *before* they were removed from the scene by Shin Bet. The only officer identified by the 'Zorea Committee' as responsible for such violence was Chief Paratroop and Infantry Officer Brigadier-General Mordechai. His actions were considered questionable at best, and were to be investigated by the IDF Military Police Investigation Unit (*Me'tz'ach*, acronym for *Mishtera Tzvait Hokeret*).

The Zorea Committee findings, intended to 'answer' a host of questions and accusations, eventually opened a Shin Bet 'Pandora's box'!

On 29 May 1984, as a result of the committee's findings and in defiance of the objections of the censor's office, the Israeli daily *Hadashot* published a front page photograph which shocked the nation. It pictured a frightened man in handcuffs – Majdi Abu Shma'a – being led off to custody by two Shin Bet plainclothesmen (faces covered by self-imposed censorship) with the headline: 'This Is The Terrorist Beaten To Death At The Hands of The Security Forces'.[10] The censor's office shut down *Hadashot* for a few days in retaliation, but the damage was done: the publication of the photograph ruled out Arens' initial statements that the terrorists had died *en route* to hospital and the Zorea Committee's findings that the blows from Brigadier-General Mordechai were responsible for their deaths. It was now evident that a cover-up was being operated and that people had already conspired to hide the truth during the Zorea Committee's investigation. A second and more comprehensive investigation was warranted, and the earlier 'findings' were transferred to a Committee chaired by Attorney-General Yona Blatman which was tasked to determine whether there had been *criminal* misconduct by the security forces and if anyone in an official capacity merited criminal prosecution. The Blatman Commission consisted of representatives from the Justice Ministry, the IDF Advocacy Branch, the IDF Military Police Investigative Unit, and the Israeli National Police. While their investigation initially centred around Brigadier-General Mordechai as the likeliest perpetrator, it also moved on and concentrated on five mysterious Shin Bet officers who had assumed final custody of the hijackers following the incident. The commission began its work on 4 June 1984 and did not submit its findings until more than a year later, on 16 July 1985. The more striking conclusions were:

■   The two terrorists were taken to a 'nearby location' and were savagely beaten *en route*, and during the interrogation, with the butts of weapons, hand strikes, and harsh kicks.

■   Proof was found *suggesting* extreme violence was used by the five identified officers which caused the deaths of the two terrorists. Although definite violent strikes were personally issued by Mordechai, it was impossible to prove that their deaths can be attributed to him.

As a result of the findings, Professor Yitzhak Zamir, the government's legal adviser, suggested that Mordechai's case be given to the jurisdiction of the IDF's Advocacy Branch, and an internal disciplinary trial be administered to the five nameless Shin Bet officers cited, as well as three police officers also present at the scene (who would be exonerated at a later date).

Brigadier-General Mordechai's Military Tribunal began on 14 August 1985, and lasted a mere 10 minutes! The acting judge, Major-General (Res.) Haim Nadel, an ex-paratroop officer himself, exonerated Mordechai as acting perhaps incorrectly, though legally in the midst of a developing military operation.

The five Shin Bet officers were tried in an internal disciplinary tribunal and after pleading 'not guilty' were found 'not guilty'!

The No. 300 Bus incident had caused a bitter feud in the small and intimate Israeli defence community as Shin Bet attempted to 'save their own' by crudely and inefficiently attempting to pin a crime they knew he had not committed on Brigadier-General Mordechai. But the scandal, intrigue and tales of conspiracy seemed to have been buried. It would prove to be a tenacious scandal – one which refused to die until a complete purge of the security services, and the perpetrators of the seeds of conspiracy, had been achieved.

The incident refused to die because of two factors: the Press and the security services themselves. The Press were enraged at the steps taken to stop them exposing the cover-up; they were determined in this instance to act as a diligent public watchdog on the excesses of their government and to uncover how far the conspiracy reached into the political hierarchy. The security services were now engaged in a period of internal bloodletting. Many in positions of power were angry that competing agencies had tried to shift the blame to innocent parties and, of course, it provided an important opportunity to settle old personal scores.

The public airing of Shin Bet internal counter-terrorism policy led to a struggle between Avraham Shalom and his three top deputies who demanded his immediate resignation. Shalom had faithfully commanded the General Security Services since 1980 and had been a Shin Bet officer for more than half his life, participating in hundreds of counter-espionage operations including the capture of Adolph Eichmann in Buenos Aires. During the Lebanon War, Shalom was a tireless workaholic, often following the progress of his sleuths in a commandeered IAF helicopter and supervising the counter-intelligence activities of his agents in southern Lebanon. His three top deputies, second-in-command Reuven Hazak, No. 3 man Peleg Radai, and No. 4 Rafi Malca, wanted him to resign for the sake of the organization. They felt that only a change of leadership could allow the well-oiled Shin Bet machine to function smoothly once again. When the Blatman Commission's findings 'failed' decisively to implicate Avraham Shalom in the deaths of the two Arabs, his three deputies took it upon themselves to act, and in the words of one, 'prevent public damage to the organization'. Their efforts were supported by Professor Yitzhak Zamir, who urged the Prime Minister's office to replace Shalom as Shin Bet boss.

The command tug-of-war became known in the Israeli Press as the 'Senior Secretary Incident'; it was an inter-office power struggle of characteristically Middle Eastern ferocity. Hazak even went over Zamir's head and asked Prime Minister Shimon Peres to oust Shalom from his well-entrenched post, but the wily Peres chose to ignore Hazak's plea. When Yitzhak Shamir replaced Peres in October 1986 as part of a national unity government rotation scheme, Hazak knew his own days were numbered. In 1984, he was the pivotal commander of a top-secret Shin Bet investigation team which exposed, and brought to justice, an underground terrorist network of militant West Bank Jewish settlers who had attempted to murder West Bank mayors and killed and wounded Palestinian students at the Islamic College in Hebron. Infiltrating and exposing the ultra-secretive Jewish terrorists was a masterstroke for Hazak's team of intelligence officers, but it was politically embarrassing to the then ruling *Likud* government led by Shamir.[11]

The political implications of the Senior Secretary Incident are still considered controversial, unexplained, and its effects on and politicization of the Shin Bet hierarchy are as yet unforeseen.

Once in power, Shamir duly ousted the three mutinous Shin Bet rebels from their posts, and the five Shin Bet officers responsible for the entire affair in the first place – those guilty of the beating to death of the two Arabs – were granted full pardons from Israeli President Chaim Herzog. Although he attempted to keep his post, Avraham Shalom eventually resigned as head of Shin Bet.

One outcome of the fiasco caused by the April 1984 hijacking was tighter government monitoring of Shin Bet behaviour during counter-terrorist activity. This approach to an outfit once regarded as sacrosanct soon uncovered other dirty deeds in Shin Bet's log-book of anti-terrorist incidents. One of the most shocking and tragic was the case of a Circassian Moslem officer in an IDF infantry formation who was acclaimed for his courage under fire in Lebanon: First Lieutenant I'zat Nafsu.* The Circassians, together with the Druze and Bedouins, had been the only minorities in the Jewish State who openly volunteered for service in the Israel Defence Forces. The Circassians serve in a wide assortment of roles and units, although they have distinguished themselves in the 300th Infantry unit (a minority-composed unit) and as trackers attached to infantry and paratroop units garrisoned along Israel's volatile frontiers. Although they have been openly accepted

---

* The Circassians are a Muslim minority from the Caucusus Mountains of Russia who fled to the Ottoman Empire in the late 19th century. Many of them eventually settled in Palestine.

within the framework of what is a Jewish fighting force, with, it must be stressed, extreme care being given to safeguard their culture and sensitivities, the case of I'zat Nafsu proved that they would never be above suspicion by an internal intelligence service operating above the law and beyond the reach of reason.

I'zat Nafsu was arrested on 4 January 1980, charged with the grave crimes of espionage, treason and aiding the enemy during wartime. Nafsu, it was claimed, had supplied weapons and sensitive military information to Palestinian terrorists during his tour of duty in southern Lebanon while a serving officer attached to the IDF's Southern Lebanon Liaison Unit. Evidence against Nafsu consisted of shaky testimony from a Shin Bet informant whose credibility was suspect. (In fact, a Shin Bet officer went so far as to label the informer a 'dyed-in-the-wool liar'.) Nevertheless, Nafsu was pursued and purged by Shin Bet officers determined to uncover a PLO mole in the once untainted IDF. They seemed so determined that they would find one even if none existed. After brutal interrogations at the hands of Shin Bet officers, who included the subsequently discredited Yossi Ginausor, Nafsu gave way under the intense physical and psychological torture and signed a confession in a Shin Bet mini-trial.† During his military court-martial which would eventually sentence him to eighteen years in prison, Nafsu claimed that during the mini-trial, violent acts were committed against him – including the pulling of his hair, being badly shaken, thrown to a hard stone ground, kicked, slapped, beaten and insulted. He was stripped naked and paraded, ordered to shower with ice-cold water, and later told to stand in the cold for prolonged periods. Nafsu was also subjected to sleep and sensory deprivation and was told that if he did not sign his confession his mother and wife would be arrested and would suffer a similar fate to his own. The Military Court listened to Nafsu's claims of torture, but opted to believe the denials of Nafsu's interrogators rather than the pleas of the signatory to a legally obtained confession. He was convicted on 29 June 1982, and sentenced to eighteen years of harsh imprisonment.

The truth of the Nafsu case, labelled by many as Israel's Dreyfuss Affair, was only uncovered because Shin Bet was no longer so well-protected from public scrutiny after the Bus Affair. The case was made public by the media and explored in full depth by a government-appointed commission pressed into service to examine Shin Bet's counter-terrorism efforts, including the apparently standard use of torture against suspects.‡

† In the subsequent Israeli government examination by the 'Landau Commission' of the use of torture in extracting confessions from security prisoners and suspects, the General Security Service's use of mini-trials to obtain quick and expedient confessions and convictions was also severely criticized and ordered to cease.
‡ According to the Israeli Government Press release revealing the Landau Commission findings, Shin Bet mishandling of Arab suspects might have, oddly enough, hardened and brutalized many of the Arab prisoners, who are then ripe for recruitment by a terrorist organization behind the walls of Israeli prisons. Terrorist cells in the territories and points beyond command the smaller cells inside prison walls, to the point of executing prisoners suspected of collaborating with the Israeli authorities.

The Landau Commission (as it became known) was headed by former Israeli Supreme Court President, Justice Moshe Landau, and consisted of Judge Ya'akov Maltz, and former Mossad Controller Major-General (Res.) Yitzhak Hofi. The commission pried deep into Shin Bet history, and on 30 October 1987 their explosive findings were released, consisting of the following notations for future Shin Bet policy:[12]

1. For more than sixteen years, since 1971 [the peak of the Shin Bet offensive against Palestinian terrorism in the Gaza Strip], Shin Bet investigators *lied* to judges and legal officials when asked about the methods used to extract information from suspects. In addition, these lies were embedded into official Shin Bet policy by the service's three chiefs since 1971.

2. On the other hand, the commission 'recommends' that all criminal investigations against Shin Bet officers cease, in order to preserve the effectiveness of the organization, and its ability to combat the 'Hostile Terrorist Activity' (HTA) Israel will face in the future.

3. As a result of the findings, appeal trials by already convicted security prisoners will be expanded, and those *wrongly* convicted are fully entitled to monetary compensation from the Israeli Government.

4. Shin Bet investigators are permitted to hold an arrested suspect for eight days prior to an appearance before a judge, to subject the suspect to psychological pressure, use ruse and trick tactics to extract information, and to exert only the *required* amount of physical torture. [This ruling, in the light of the commission's findings on the widespread and 'traditional' use of often brutal Shin Bet methods of mental and physical torture, was most significant].

5. A suspect is to be held in administrational custody if abundant evidence against the individual is available, if he is caught in the midst of committing a HTA, or if he has been operating as an enemy intelligence agent for a hostile sovereign nation.

6. In addition, the commission recommends the improvement of interrogation facilities, which encompasses fitting rooms with reasonable lighting, and proper ventilation, and including the addition of daylight. Sanitation facilities must also be provided for suspects, including working, and clean toilets.

The second part of the report, dealing with improvements to be made in Shin Bet's use of interrogation, was classified and only issued to the Prime Minister's office. The public damage, however, had been done and, in the end, I'zat Nafsu was released from prison, awarded a four million Shekel (approximately £1.5 million) award for his suffering, and another painful chapter in Israeli security history was put to rest. Shin Bet was overhauled, redesigned from within, and badly shaken – the one time rock of Israel's survival had been dangerously dissected from 1984 on, perhaps never to be properly reconstituted. Israel's very precarious existence meant that Shin Bet did not have the luxury of regrouping from the sidelines; it would have to transform itself back into the vaunted intelligence service it once was while under fire, and 1986–8 would prove a most difficult period.

Even before the Palestinian *Intifadah* began, there were problems being posed for Shin Bet in the form of a noticeable increase in terrorist activity within Israel. This development was exacerbated by a new entrant on the scene – Islamic fundamentalism. With the Ayatollah Khomeini's Shi'ite revolution in Iran in 1979 serving as the vanguard for an Islamic call to arms throughout the world, Shi'ites in the region became more assertive and once moderate Muslims grew more extreme, brandishing the Koran and claiming it to be the answer to Western 'injustices'. In the Israeli context, Islamic fundamentalism was seen as an impatient successor to the then stagnant Palestinian leadership in exile. Nowhere was this more of a factor than in the Gaza Strip.

Shin Bet had succeeded in catching the *Jihad Al-Islami*'s (Islamic Holy War) Gazan network in October 1987, but one of their agents was murdered by four men who were themselves then killed in a shoot-out in the suburb of Shaj'ayia. This incident came just a few days after three other members of the organization had been shot outside the Boureij camp and a joint Shin Bet–IDF clampdown was ordered. In lightning pre-dawn raids, more than fifty of these Iranian-style revolutionaries were arrested and their vast and impressive arms caches confiscated. Among the terrorist cells captured was the one responsible for hurling a grenade at a *Giva'ati* Infantry Brigade swearing-in ceremony at the Wailing Wall in Jerusalem in which a father was killed, and dozens of spectators seriously wounded; they had also murdered an Israeli shop-keeper in 1986.

In addition to these successes, Shin Bet managed to foil a number of operations planned by countless terrorist networks loyal to Palestinian organizations based in Lebanon and Syria, and to capture the perpetrators of others. The IDF weekly magazine *Bamachane* noted that these included the October 1986 arrest of a PLO *el-Fatah* cell which had planted an explosive device on the No. 18 Jerusalem inter-city bus in 1983, killing six civilians and wounding scores of others; also the May 1987 seizure of a PLO cell in the Gaza Strip which had committed numerous acts of violence and murder there and in the Israeli cities of Ashqelon and Ramat Gan. The latter group were apparently seized only days before they planned a bold and bloody bombing spree in Tel Aviv. Thus, from October 1986 to May 1987 Shin Bet had managed to locate 108 terror cells, 58 of them prior to their carrying out their deeds.

The onset of the *Intifadah* presented Shin Bet with a new and puzzling challenge which was one exacerbated by the IDF's inability to quell the uprising. As opposed to the hard-line, expertly trained terrorists Shin Bet was used to facing, the *Intifadah* was run by hordes of teenagers armed with stones and a determination not to endure another 21 years of Israeli occupation. Even though the uprising was a popular effort of the local inhabitants of the Occupied Territories, it was run by a hardcore nationalist and religious leadership, headquartered principally in the Gaza Strip. With the Strip once again heading for anarchy, Shin Bet mobilized its legions of informants and went on the offensive.

The spontaneous *Intifadah* was different from the organized and co-ordinated terrorist-run disturbances in the Gaza Strip during the chaotic period of 1970–1, but the Shin Bet responses were similar and decisive. IDF units would patrol and attempt to keep the peace and civil order during the day, enforcing a strict curfew during the night hours. It was in the dark that Shin Bet went into action. When a Shin Bet officer in Gaza wants to meet an informant, they instruct an officer leading a patrol to paint a pre-arranged sign or symbol in a prominent place; it is then out in the open for everyone to see, but enjoys a unique significance to one very special, though nervous individual. Later that evening, a meeting will take place in great secrecy, and the next morning, if luck is in Shin Bet's favour, an arrest will be made or some useful surveillance will have been conducted.[13] This use of informants by Shin Bet was thought to be instrumental in staging a mid-summer's offensive against the *Intifadah* in 1988. According to foreign reports, two Shin Bet agents riding in an unmarked white Subaru sedan, abducted Mohamed Abu Hamam, believed to be a key *el-Fatah* leader of the uprising, as he strolled down the street of the West Bank town of Ramallah. As a result of his interrogation, which it has been alleged involved the use of torture, the names of a number of his confederates were obtained and 37 leaders of the popular council, the body of resistance leaders responsible for keeping the home fires of the Gaza *Intifadah* burning, were arrested.

Shin Bet did not allow itself to become pre-occupied with the *Intifadah* but continued to do what it did best – uncover plots. The year 1988 proved to be a good one for them: in February they foiled a PFLP plan to detonate a car loaded with high-explosives in the heart of downtown Jerusalem; in April they captured a PLO cell of *el-Fatah*'s élite *Force 17* who had set off bombs in several Israeli cities; and between October and November they uncovered some 93 terrorist cells, including an ultra-secret cell consisting of thirteen Israeli Bedouins, many of them IDF veterans, who had been involved in numerous attacks including throwing an anti-personnel grenade into a crowd of shoppers in Haifa. The fact that Bedouin IDF veterans were involved in such activity was a particularly disturbing development for the State of Israel. The Israeli Defence Ministry (*Misrad Habitachon*) claimed that most of the cells uncovered were engaged in petrol-bomb and explosives attacks against Israelis, and murderous attacks against Arabs believed to be co-operating with the Israeli security services. These 93 cells, which contained 610 people, could be broken down as follows: 62 were uncovered in the West Bank, 27 in the Gaza Strip, and four in Israel; 49 of the cells were indigenous to the *Intifadah*, 29 were affiliated to *el-Fatah*, five to the DFLP, three to the PFLP, five to an obscure Moslem fundamentalist group, three to *Jihad al-Islami*, and one to the notorious Abu Nidal faction.

This fine Shin Bet intelligence and security work, in light of the No. 300 bus and Nafsu scandals, was not lost on Defence Minister Yitzhak Rabin, who in December 1988 publicized a letter to the new and – for security reasons – anonymous head of the agency, in which he praised the 'unknown soldiers' of the General Security Services for the 'daring, determination, valour, sophistication and resourcefulness' they employed in the capture of murderers and terrorists.

A few months later, more praise of Shin Bet was offered by a very unlikely source. After IDF sappers had destroyed the homes of Gaza terrorists responsible for killing alleged informants, the IDF OC Southern Command, Major-General Yitzhak Mordechai,§ said that 'the security services have done an excellent job in the Strip'.[14] Even though their personalities might have clashed in a very ugly arena of violence and retribution, Major-General Mordechai realized that Israel's war against terrorism would be hopeless without the 'faceless warriors' of Shin Bet.

§ At the time of this book's writing, Major-General Mordechai was transferred to Central Command, where his expertise in quelling the *Intifadah* was needed.

Right: Major-General (Res.) Aharon Yariv, *c.* 1973. The mastermind of Israel's covert war against Black September during the 1970s. (United Nations/ Y. Nagata)

Right: The *El Al* flight, which was hijacked by the PFLP to Algiers on 23 July 1968, returns to Israel. The hijacking would prompt *Shin Bet*'s stringent security overhaul of the airline, and it would prove to be the last Israeli aircraft seized. (IGPO)

Right: Peering into an Arab village near the 'Triangle', a relaxed jeepborne Border Guard patrol searches for signs of Arab infiltration, *c.* 1960. (IGPO)

Left: Gaza 1971. Border Guard policemen handle several terrorist suspects in Israel's quiet, though bloody counter-terrorist campaign in the 'Strip'. (IDF Archives)

Left: Only days after Black September Organization terrorists hijacked a Sabena airliner to Lod Airport (9 May 1972), a heavily armed Border Guard ex-Egyptian Army *Whalid* armoured-car patrols the airport tarmac. (IGPO)

Right: Beleaguered-looking Border Guard policemen safeguard the claimed luggage section at Lod Airport only hours after three Japanese Red Army gunmen massacred 29 people, and wounded almost a hundred more on 30 May 1972. (IGPO)

Right: Commandos from an IDF 'élite unit' storm the Ma'alot schoolhouse, held by DFLP terrorists, 15 May 1974. The failed rescue attempt, and the ensuing massacre of more than twenty students led to an Israeli Government internal ruling which charged the police with the nation's internal security/anti-terrorist responsibility. (IGPO)

Right: Chief Inspector Gabi Last, *c.* 1985. At the time of Israel's Lebanon adventure, Last was the commander of the Border Guard's Northern Brigade, and was the architect of the Green Berets' presence in Lebanon. (Samuel M. Katz)

Left: Wearing a flak vest, and carrying the Israeli NCO's traditional CAR-15 5.56mm assault rifle, Yoel Baranas, the Border Guard 20th Company's company sergeant stands over a captured PLO arms cache in southern Lebanon. (Courtesy, Yoel Baranas)

Left: A blurry, personal photograph of three of the Border Guard 20th Company's sergeants sightseeing in Tyre, July 1982. They include the stout-hearted Yoel Baranas (right), and Haim Mader (left). Three months later, Haim Mader would be dead in the Border Guard's 'First Tyre Disaster'. (Courtesy, Yoel Baranas)

Left: IDF soldiers participate in the grim task of removing the dead and wounded from the Border Guard's Tyre headquarters, destroyed on 4 November 1983 by a Shiite suicide truck bomber. (IGPO)

Left, far left and below:
Heavily armed Border
Guard Command Cars
patrol a strip of the
volatile Lebanese–
Israeli frontier. (Samuel
M. Katz)

Right: Soldiers prepare
a display of Palestinian
and Shiite weapons
captured in Border
Guard operations in
southern Lebanon. Of
interest are the AK-47s
fitted with silencers,
and the 'close-kill'
Czech Vz.61 *Skorpion*
7.65mm machine-pistol
(IDF Spokesman)

Top left: An obviously 'relieved' National Police sapper, attached to the Border Guards, in Lebanon, jokes with comrades as he removes dozens of neatly packaged parcels of high-explosives from a once lethal car bomb in Sidon. (IDF Spokesman)

Above: A chain-smoking Border Guard platoon commander briefs his men prior to their setting out on a 'routine', though never routine patrol along the Lebanese border. (Samuel M. Katz)

Left: A smartly dressed Jerusalem police officer stands amid the rubble and devastation caused by the PFLP's 22 November 1968 car bombing of the city's bustling *Machane Yehuda* market. (IGPO)

Right: The West German motorized hang-glider used by a PFLP-GC terrorist to get into Israel and attack the *NA'HA'L* Infantry Brigade base at Beit Hillel, on 25 November 1987. The terrorist attack, one of the first ever directed against Israeli military forces, proved to be the spark which fired the *Intifadah.* (IDF)

Right: A Border Guard officer enters into delicate negotiations with an 'elder stateswoman' from the Jebalya refugee camp in the Gaza Strip, following an incident involving the throwing of a Molotov cocktail at an IDF jeep.(*Bamachane*)

Right: Police sappers inspect the charred remnant of a No. 18 Jerusalem bus blown up by Palestinian terrorists on 6 December 1983. The explosion killed four, and seriously injured 43. (IGPO)

Top left: A tin drum packed with explosives, and attached to a crude timing device, hidden in a crate of eggs. The device was planted in a crowded market by Palestinian terrorists, and discovered minutes before it would have killed dozens of people. (Samuel M. Katz)

Left: An Israeli police sapper team meticulously examines a 'suspicious object' in Tel Aviv's afluent Neot Afeka suburbs. (Samuel M. Katz)

BICYCLE BOMB

Left: An *el-Fatah* bicycle bomb, parked outside a Jerusalem cafe. The ingenious device had more than a kilogram of high-explosives packed in the seat, and metal frame. (Samuel M. Katz)

Left: A Wheelbarrow six-wheeled robot, being deployed from a police sapper vehicle. (Sigalit Katz)

Right: An Israeli police sapper using the ingeniously designed and produced 'Bambi' robot, responds to the sighting of a suspicious object near Bethlehem during the *Intifadah*. (Jonathan Torgovnik/ IDF Spokesman)

Right: Although robots are an essential element in the police war against terrorist bombings, the instincts and skill of the sapper is in the end the *deciding* factor between peace and mass carnage. Here, a sapper examines a photographer's bag, abandoned near a concrete 'security' pit in a Holon parking lot. (Samuel M. Katz)

Right: A police sapper and his bomb-sniffing German Shepherd search the Wailing Wall courtyard in the Old City of Jerusalem for explosive devices prior to Remembrance Day ceremonies (Samuel M. Katz)

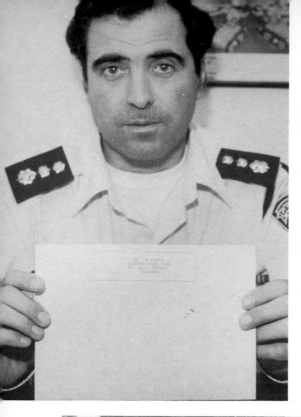

Top left: The commander of the National Police Bomb Disposal Squad, Chief Inspector Shlomoh Aharonishky, displays a Palestinian letter-bomb, postmarked in Turkey, and received, and intercepted, in Israel on 30 December 1987. (IGPO)

Left: A senior Border Guard officer brusquely strips the body of Dalal Mughrabi, female commander of the 'Kamal Adwan Commando' unit responsible for the Country Club Massacre. (IGPO)

Left: Border Guard anti-terrorist commandos make a slow, and cautious advance towards the Savoy Hotel in Tel Aviv, 6 March 1975 after it was seized by seaborne *el-Fatah* terrorists in one of the first, and most audacious Palestinian 'naval' attacks staged against Israel. (IGPO)

Right: The fiery hell of the 'bus of blood' burns at Tel Aviv's Country Club Junction, hijacked by eleven seaborne *el-Fatah* terrorists on 11 March 1978. Thirty-five people were killed, and more than 70 seriously injured. (IGPO)

Right: IDF paratroopers nervously search for escaped survivors of the 'Kamal Adwan Commando' unit in the sand dunes just outside the Tel Aviv suburb of Ramat Hasharon. (IGPO)

Right: Off the coast of Lebanon, a FN MAG 7.62mm light machine-gunner from the INS *Sufah* [or 'Storm'], a *Sa'ar* 3 missile-boat, aims his weapon at a merchant ship suspected of being a terrorist 'mother ship'. (IDF Spokesman)

Above: Armed with HARPOON, and GABRIEL SSMs, and capable of speeds in excess of 52 knots, an IDF/Navy Hydrofoil or *Snapirit* adds tremendous defensive range to Israel's campaign against seaborne infiltration. (Herzl Kunesari/IDF Spokesman)

Left: The jubilant crew of the IDF/Navy missile-boat responsible for sinking the terrorist 'mothership' SS *Attaviros* on 20 April 1985, pose for the cameras with a very special souvenir. (IDF Spokesman)

Right: A *Dabur* in the tranquil waters of the Gulf of Aqaba, with the plush palm forest of King Hussein's winter home just visible.

Right: A lightly armed, though potent *Yatush* patrols the Dead Sea. (IDF Spokesman)

Right: The *el-Fatah* ship SS *Doroti*, captured in the Mediterranean by the IDF/Navy on 2 August 1988. The ship was ferrying four high-ranking *el-Fatah* 'naval' officers, and two crewmen. (*Bamachane*)

Above: Major-General Ehud Barak (note *Skorpion* 7.65mm machine-pistol worn on holster), IDF Chief of Staff Lieutenant-General Dan Shomron (standing, and wearing sun glasses), and OC Southern Command Major-General Yitzhak Mordechai (lying on ground, and using walkie-talkie) observe, and command the Border Guard *Ya'ma'm* rescue operation of the *el-Fatah* hijacking of the Beersheba–Dimona bus, 7 March 1988. (IDF Spokesman)

Below: H-Hour! *Ya'ma'm* commandos storm the besieged Beersheba–Dimona bus, and kill the three terrorists. (IDF Spokesman)

Above: Two organizers of the *Intifadah* are escorted by heavily armed Military Policemen to 'no-man's land' in southern Lebanon, following deportation from Israel. (IDF Spokesman)

Below: A want ad for the *Ya'ma'm* placed in the IDF weekly magazine *Bamachane*, which says: Wanted: Officers and fighters! If you are a veteran of a combat unit, a graduate of a command course (squad leader and onwards), have a high-school education, are under 25 and in good health, we are offering interesting work in young teams, a good salary and working environment, and prime opportunities for advancement! (Author's Collection)

Below: Pro-Khomeini literature captured by Border Guard and IDF soldiers in southern Lebanon, January 1984. (IDF Spokesman)

Above: High-powered explosives masquerading as toys – captured by Border Guard forces in southern Lebanon, June 1982. (Israeli National Police)

Below: Israeli Prime Minister, Shimon Peres (right), meets South Lebanon Army commander, General Antoine Lahad to discuss joint-security arrangements along Israel's northern frontier. (IDF Spokesman)

3. The Border Guards and the Police Sappers

'The Men of Kfar Kasem'
Israel's Green Berets, 1950–82

They are the first to welcome a visitor to Israel. As a traveller walks down the mobile steps from his airliner on to the sun-parched tarmac at Ben-Gurion International Airport, the lone soldier keeping a proud vigil is both impressive and tell-tale. With his dark-green beret worn tightly, his sweater ironed to perfection and the American fatigue trousers pressed neatly, the soldier's smart appearance nearly obscures the reason for his presence. A further look reveals the seriousness of it all: the fully loaded *Galil* assault rifle, the pouches filled to capacity with magazines of 5.56mm ammunition, the grenades and other 'combat essentials'. As one of Israel's 'green berets', he is there to prevent the entrance of any terrorist into the country, as well as serving as a deterrent to those who would attack air travellers. Israel's green berets are, of course, their Border Guards and their role in Israel's war against terrorism has been a most remarkable one.

The *Ma'gav* (acronym for *Mishmar Hagvul*) or Border Guards are Israel's true 'guards without frontiers'. They are trained like combat infantrymen but under their command, and mandate, operate like policemen. Little is heard of them either inside or outside Israel; their contribution to the defence and security of their state has been largely unsung. Under the control of the Israeli National Police, but connected in mission and operational depth to the Israel Defence Forces, the Border Guards have always endured a separate and unequal identity from their brothers in arms in the IDF. Although the 'green berets' did not share in the glory of such military victories as the 1967 War, they were forced to fill the wide security gap such victories created, by serving in the unromantic and all too often dreaded role of policeman amid the hatred of the West Bank and Gaza Strip.

The Border Guards were created in 1950 as, it was to be hoped, a deterrent to the hundreds of Bedouin and Palestinian infiltrators who crossed the Lebanese, Syrian and Jordanian frontiers at will, committing acts of crime, nationalist-motivated terror and state-sponsored espionage (the Egyptian border was secured by an IDF, Bedouin-

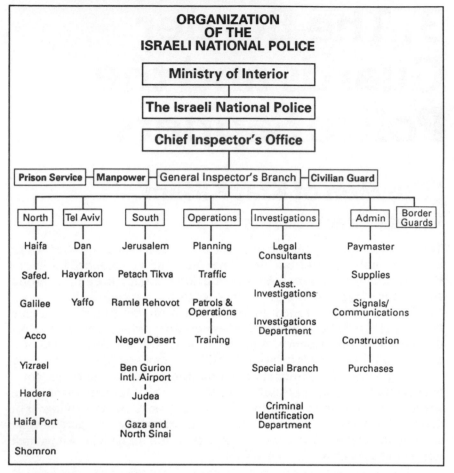

ORGANIZATION OF THE ISRAELI NATIONAL POLICE

Ministry of Interior

The Israeli National Police

Chief Inspector's Office

Prison Service — Manpower — General Inspector's Branch — Civilian Guard

North	Tel Aviv	South	Operations	Investigations	Admin	Border Guards
Haifa	Dan	Jerusalem	Planning	Legal Consultants	Paymaster	
Safed.	Hayarkon	Petach Tikva	Traffic	Asst. Investigations	Supplies	
Galilee	Yaffo	Ramle Rehovot	Patrols & Operations	Investigations Department	Signals/ Communications	
Acco		Negev Desert	Training		Construction	
Yizrael		Ben Gurion Intl. Airport		Special Branch	Purchases	
Hadera		Judea				
Haifa Port		Gaza and North Sinai		Criminal Identification Department		
Shomron						

dominated reconnaissance unit known as the *Sayeret Shaked* or 'Almond Recon'). The establishment by the United Nations of the State of Israel had resurrected a Jewish nation in the ancient land of the Bible, but it could not secure its territorial integrity. That task would fall to these ragged conscript policemen and soldiers, together with the IDF. The 'joint-security' arrangement they devised for border patrols continues, in one form or another, to this very day. The Border Guard's unit badge, in fact, symbolizes their joint-security objective best: a stone watchtower with a bright, vigilant searchlight.

Initially, the Border Guards were an integral element of the fledgling Israel Defence Forces, their first commander being the battle-experienced General David Shaltiel – commander of the Jerusalem front during the 1948 War. But the very nature of the Border Guards' principal responsibilities (safeguarding the outlying border settlements from infiltrator attack and closing the frontiers to smugglers and spies) resembled law enforcement objectives rather than military ones. Accordingly, they were transferred to National Police patronage in 1951. The dedicated unit soon became a police force of 'border mercenaries'; professional soldiers fighting for a salary as well as out of a sense of national duty. This separation from the Israel Defence Forces was a suitable move for the Border Guards as it was never meant to be a force committed to conventional military operations. Nevertheless, the Border Guards were modelled along para-military lines and divided into three, regional para-military companies: Northern, Central and Southern.

In 1953, the precarious situation along Israel's borders called for an expansion of manpower and its ranks swelled with ex-mandate period policemen who had extensive border experience with the British constabularies in Palestine. Policemen in the Border Guards, however, had to undergo rigorous infantry training, and service in its ranks was considered a fulfilment of the national military service obligation.

As befits a unit which could make full use of tracking and other nomadic skills, the Border Guards' ranks contained a high proportion of Israel's indigenous minorities: the Druze, Circassian Muslims, and the invaluable Bedouins. Although these people were full Israeli citizens, they were Muslims, spoke Arabic, and were initially considered too great a security risk for conventional military service. Patriotic to the end, however, they not only volunteered *en masse* into the ranks of the IDF, but would find a unique home in the Border Guards.* As opposed to service in the much larger IDF, the Border Guards offered Israel's minority soldiers the opportunity to work in much more secure, sensitive and intimate surroundings. Their close-knit and somewhat secretive communities favoured the Border Guards' smaller units and in the early, pre-industrial development days of the State of Israel, the Border Guards provided the minorities with steady, albeit dangerous, employment. Most importantly perhaps, they were openly welcomed and actively supported once inside; they were able to speak Arabic and understood the customs and personalities of the people they had to deal with on a daily basis and, with the Bedouins in particular, they enjoyed an invaluable inherent 'gift of the desert'.

The Border Guards' task of closing off a mountainous and desert border region to determined infiltrators was a very difficult undertaking. In the early 1950s, the heavily fortified fence now commonplace along the frontiers had yet to be built and the borders had to be secured with the help of this new, mobile, lightly armed force of jeep-borne police-men. Their secret weapon was the Bedouin tracker, a professional soldier trained in a combination of cultural and native skills to interpret footprints and marks in the desert. Prior to the advent of electronic sensory devices, the Border Guards' only means of detecting a border crossing was the eagle eye of a patrol's Bedouin tracker. Once a footprint or mark had been discovered, a high-speed pursuit would commence, not ending until the perpetrators, be they hashish smugglers

* In 1955, Druze elders demanded that their 18-year-old men be conscripted into the IDF, and the Circassians successfully demanded the same distinction a year later.

or Palestinian guerrillas, were found. The Border Guard patrols were never equipped with anything larger than vehicle-mounted .50 calibre machine-guns and, as a result, their effectiveness as a unit was dependent on speed, skill and cohesive deployment both on and off the field.

Although the Border Guards were instrumental in sealing off their assigned frontiers, they received very little recognition. The Israeli public, in fact, knew very little of their existence and contribution, concentrating more on the IDF and the spectacular headlines made by Major Sharon's *Unit 101*. This embittered many Border Guard policemen, especially when their fallen comrades only received the briefest of mentions while an IDF casualty warranted large headlines and a day of national mourning. Their lack of acclaim stemmed from numerous reasons, among others the fact that they enjoyed a close, though introverted *esprit de corps*. Service in their ranks was by choice, rather than by the universal 'nation-building' experience of conscription, and many of Israel's fresh immigrants avoided what they saw as a 'native' (Arab-like) unit, thus leaving the Guards to further reinforce their élitism and separatism. Tragically, when publicity did befall the Border Guards, it would be highly negative; it emerged out of one of the most murderous incidents in Israeli history.

October 1956 witnessed some of the greatest tension in the history of the Arab-Israeli conflict. War was literally in the air, as Palestinian *fedayeen* guerrilla cross-border attacks into Israel prompted the IDF to respond in kind, with equally devastating paratroop retaliatory raids. Anti-Israeli propaganda from Egypt, and Israel's military mobilization, only escalated the Middle East's tense atmosphere one notch closer to the brink. Most of the Palestinian raids originated from the Egyptian-controlled Gaza Strip, which became one of the decisive factors in Israel's decision to participate in the joint Anglo-French plan in the hope of ousting Egyptian President Gamel Nasser in the Suez fiasco. Exacerbating the situation, Egyptian military intelligence coerced Jordan's King Hussein into opening a second *fedayeen* front against Israel along the very long Jordanian border on the West Bank of the River Jordan. Israel countered this move with dramatic military action. In a move to disguise its forthcoming invasion of Sinai, the IDF positioned large forces directly opposite strategic routes into Jordan. Hours before war was to begin, IDF OC Central Command, Major-General Tzvi Tzur (an eventual Chief of Staff), ordered the front to be 'kept absolutely quiet', and placed many Arab towns near the border with Jordan under curfew.

One such village was Kfar Kasem, situated in what was known during the British Mandate as the 'Triangle' – an area outlined by the towns of Jenin in the north, Qilqilya in the west, and Nablus in the south-east. On 29 October, as Israeli paratroopers were boarding their C-47 Dakotas for the trip to the Mitla Pass and the opening salvo of Israeli's invasion of Sinai, a company of Border Guards *under IDF command* moved into Kfar Kasem to enforce the curfew. The Border

Guards, equipped for full-scale combat, were given very specific orders regarding the curfew: 'No inhabitants were to leave their homes during the curfew; anyone leaving their homes would be shot. There would be no arrests.'[1]

With a few IDF officers supervising, the Border Guards moved into the village square. The village *muchtar* or chief was informed of the impending curfew at 1600 hours, only half an hour before it was to commence and in insufficient time to warn the townspeople. Unaware of any such order restricting their movement, the Kfar Kasem residents returned home from their fields between 1700 and 1800 hours only to find dozens of Border Guards policemen with their Czech K98 Mauser rifles cocked and aimed. The subsequent mêlée saw dozens of villagers shot and fatally wounded in cold blood. Many women and children, also unaware of the curfew order, tragically left their homes to see what the shooting and cries for help were all about – only to find themselves the target of Border Guard volleys too. As a Border Guard radioman relayed the unfolding events in a chilling and methodical fashion, senior commanders ordered the shooting stopped. But this was too late: 49 Kfar Kasem residents lay dead, and thirteen were seriously wounded. Israeli Arabs compared the events at Kfar Kasem to the infamous 1948 massacre at Dir Yassin by 'soldiers' from Menachem Begin's *Irgun* underground.

The Israeli Government could not cover up the brutal killings of Kfar Kasem, and, subsequently, eleven of the officers involved were put on trial. Eight of them received prison sentences ranging from eight to seventeen years, although many were later reduced upon appeal and review. Colonel Isachar Shadmi, commander of the IDF's 17th District Brigade and the officer who had ordered the Border Guard battalion commander, Major Shmuel Melinki, to enforce the curfew so rigorously, received the outrageous fine of 'one piaster' (the smallest demonination of Israel's then monetary system). 'Shadmi's piaster' became a battle cry for Arab rage. The incident, and Israel's indifferent reaction to it, caused lasting resentment among the Arab population and the Border Guards' reputation was marred forever. They were considered brutally insensitive policemen, their green berets and shiny silver badges symbols for harshness and cruelty.[2]

In the years to follow, the Border Guards profited in their task from the terror which the Kfar Kasem incident instilled into the subject population. In 1964, mainly as a result of the formation of the Palestine Liberation Organization, Defence/Prime Minister Levi Eshkol decided to expand them, sending one hundred IDF conscripts into their ranks. Eshkol and many of his senior defence commanders never expected much of Border Guard policemen, and so they filled their ranks with 'sub-standard' material the IDF rejected, men of poor intellectual and social backgrounds usually from the Arab diaspora, *Sephardim* who were considered 'not much better than Arabs' themselves. Despite the contempt in which they were held by many racist *Ashkenazim* (European Jews) in the ruling élite, the Egyptian- and Syrian-sponsored Palestinian guerrilla attacks in 1965 meant that the Border Guard's responsibilities were increased to include the protection of the ultra-sensitive National Water Carrier, which ferried the sweet water of northern Israel and the Sea of Galilee to the remainder of the desert nation.

When the 1967 Six Day War erupted, Border Guard units were immediately rushed into the ex-Jordanian West Bank and entrusted with the herculean task of keeping the peace in the large towns of Bethlehem, Jenin, Tulkarem, Nablus, and Hebron. The ability of most Border Guard policemen to speak Arabic, as well as their understanding of the cultural behaviour of the local inhabitants, was a decisive plus in keeping the peace during the initial days of occupation. As the dark-green personnel carriers sporting their emblem rolled through the streets of the major West Bank towns, frightened residents were heard to say 'The men of Kfar Kasem have arrived'.[3]

The abilities and reputation of the Border Guards were apparent even to PLO Chairman Yasir Arafat. After the initial IDF capture of Nablus, Arafat and several of his most senior lieutenants remained behind to assess the situation. Upon seeing the Green Berets begin to patrol the city's winding ancient alleyways, Arafat fled in a panic, leaving his men to do battle with the policemen. In the ensuing firefight with the Arafat entourage the Border Guards gave little quarter.

Following the 1967 War, the IDF fought a vicious three-year conflict known as the '1,000 Days War of Attrition'. Along the frontiers, Israeli forces fought Palestinian terrorists attempting to infiltrate into the Galilee and Jordan Valley from their bases in Lebanon, Syria, and Jordan, while at the same time countering Arab conventional forces in fierce aerial and artillery barrages compounded by spectacular commando strikes. Inside the occupied territories, however, it was the Border Guard that served as the vanguard of Israeli attempts to quell determined attempts by Palestinian groups to establish operational terrorist cells. While the IDF was well suited for military operations, its forces, even the much vaunted Military Police, had little if any actual policing experience. IDF infantry forces, for example, were not trained in proper arrest procedure, nor were they familiar with the sensitivities of the locals, such as never entering a house where only a female was present and never verbally insulting the male head of the household in front of his children. The Border Guards were also the lone Israeli force trained in crowd control, and internal-security arrangements. Although they understood the mentality of the 'locals', the Border Guards' reputation for brutality preceded them, and the local inhabitants of the West Bank went out of their way to feign respect and courtesy to the much-feared *tarbush al-ahdar* (Arabic for green berets).

Distinctive in their tan khaki fatigues, dark-green berets, British-style rank insignia and well-polished FN FAL assault rifles, Border Guard units patrolled the *casbahs* of Hebron and Nablus with great effectiveness. They became expert in identifying suspicious individuals, their fluency in Arabic allowing them to overhear sometimes invaluable chitter-chatter in the streets and market place. The fact that many of the policemen were Druze, Circassian and Bedouins facilitated the transition from Jordanian to Israeli occupation into an easy, even indistinguishable one. The presence of the 'minorities' reminded many of the West Bank old-timers of the days of the Turks and British; their penchant for enlisting the Druze and Circassians for police duty, as well as their habit of raising fists and clubs at the smallest infractions, only reinforced this traditional image. Many of the locals – used to the 'iron fist' brutality of the controlling Jordanian and Egyptian regimes – were apathetic to the Border Guards' presence, sentiments which contrasted starkly with the hostility vented against the 'conquering Jewish IDF'.

The Border Guards' police training was an invaluable asset in the West Bank as much of the home-grown hostile terrorist activity was financed through organized criminal activity such as robbery, extortion, prostitution, and narcotics. The Green Berets' ability to be both soldier and patrolman served its dual purpose brilliantly, but unfortunately it passed without due merit. Even though every Border Guard policeman underwent an all-inclusive IDF-style infantry basic training, their IDF 'brothers in arms' never considered them equal entities. The racial gulf referred to earlier remained, indeed it was inforced as the years passed; the IDF paratroop and infantry units serving garrison duty inside the West Bank came to be seen as the reserve of the clean-cut, 'respectable' Jews from the élite *kibbutz* and affluent Tel Aviv suburbs. Such racial tension was heavily ironic in a nation which owed its existence to the concept of tolerance in such matters. The IDF, however, always suppressed their prejudices when they needed help, and this they needed in abundance during the chaotic situation which had developed in the Gaza Strip during 1970–1. The Border Guard came to their rescue; their efforts were forceful and highly successful.

With the conclusion of the War of Attrition and the dire need of a Border Guard presence in the Gaza Strip, life returned to its somewhat traditional routine for the Green Berets. Israel's newly expanded frontiers made the Border Guards' historic role of frontier duty almost obsolete. With borders five times their original size, the then less than four thousand Border Guards could never hope to secure such a vast area and, as a result, their presence along the frontiers was dwarfed by the IDF. They would, however, become a staple in the daily lives of the residents of the numerous refugee camps around Bethlehem, Nablus, and Hebron, imposing curfews, searching for terrorists, and trying as best as possible to keep the peace. They also manned constant road-blocks, checking all West Bank vehicles entering and exiting Israel proper. As opposed to the standard yellow Israeli vehicle licence plates with black numerals, West Bank and Gaza vehicles were forced to put on distinctive blue plates, with the first letter of the owner's home city prominently represented as well.

The Green Berets also became a fixture of the Jerusalem land-scape, with Border Guard policemen keeping the now unified City of David at peace. Along the rooftops of the two-storey Jerusalem stone buildings overlooking the narrow alleyways of the *suq* or marketplace of the Old City, Border Guard policemen, assault rifles at the ready and eyes fixed on potential problems, kept a constant vigil, protecting the thousands who soon flocked to the Holy City.

The removal of the minefield and barbed wire barriers after the unification of Jerusalem not only allowed greater freedom of travel for Israelis, but also greater access for Arab terrorists into Israel proper. As a result, Jerusalem became a city on the edge. Arab east Jerusalem merged with the Jewish western half, with only the tenacious efforts of the Border Guard averting a bloodbath. In the Israeli capital, the Border Guards' service earned them the much honoured nickname of 'the infantry of the police'.

The Border Guards were very soon considered the élite of the National Police. Just as the paratroops had set the standards for the entire IDF to emulate, so too did the Border Guards fulfil this role for the National Police. Junior police officers began to volunteer in con-siderable numbers.

Internal security was not the original mandate of the Border Guards, but it soon became their principal responsibility. Following two murderous Palestinian terrorist attacks at Lod Airport (renamed Ben-Gurion International Airport in 1973) in 1972 – Black September's 8 May hijacking of a Sabena airliner to Lod, and the Japanese Red Army's bloody 30 May 1972 grenade and automatic weapon attack at the arrival hall – the Border Guards became synonymous with safeguarding Israel's ports of entry. The city of Lod was in fact home base for the Border Guards, and their dark-green ex-Egyptian Army BTR-152 APCs became a familiar sight along the tarmac at the airport. Every visitor to Israel soon found a heavily armed Border Guard policeman supervising each take-off and landing, as well as examining *every* vehicle entering the airport. A car with Israeli yellow plates was generally whisked through, while cars with suspicious passengers or originating from the 'territories' were subjected to thorough searches.

In August 1972, a Border Guard company was brought from the rough and tumble of urban warfare in Gaza for a new kind of urban mission: Tel Aviv. Israel's largest city had witnessed a rash of brazen bank robberies and assaults by organized criminals, with the 'blue' civilian police (a reference to the colour of their officers' peaked caps) at a loss for a solution. It would be the first time heavily armed Border Guard units had operated on the fashionable boulevards of Tel Aviv and the Green Berets treated their mission with the dire seriousness characteristic of frontier duty. They secured vital intersections of the city and patrolled poor neighbourhoods once controlled by organized crime gangs. Within a few weeks, they had not only helped the police to capture the wanted perpetrators, but had also helped reduce crime in

Tel Aviv to an all-time low. The company commander for this mission was Second Superintendent Pinchas Shachar (a rank equivalent to the IDF's lieutenant-colonel), a future commander of the Border Guards.

The *official* entry of the Border Guard into an internal security role came in the aftermath of disaster. On 15 May 1974, a three-man terrorist squad from Nayif Hawatmeh's Democratic Front for the Liberation of Palestine (DFLP) crossed the heavily fortified Israel-Lebanon border and attacked a schoolhouse in the frontier town of Ma'alot, seizing almost a hundred teenage students on a nature bivouac. The terrorists demanded the release of 26 Palestinian terrorists (one for each year of Israeli independence) from Israeli prisons in exchange for the lives of the students – otherwise *everyone* would die. Israel's top military and political leaders soon gathered round the beseiged school-house and entered into tense negotiations, while at the same time finalizing details for the inevitable rescue assault.

Although terrorist attacks were commonplace in Israel, they usually involved planting bombs on buses and firing Katyusha rockets from the safety of bases in southern Lebanon and north-west Jordan. The first true terrorist hostage-taking drama to occur on Israeli soil was the hijacking of the Sabena flight on 8 May 1972. Israeli police units had little experience in hostage rescue operations an the IDF's various élite units had specialized their efforts in lightning strikes against *conventional* targets, not in storming an airliner or a schoolhouse full of youngsters held by suicidal fanatics.

The hijacked airliner was subsequently stormed, the terrorists killed and captured, and all but one of the 99 hostages rescued by commandos from the IDF's élite and highly secret General Headquarters Reconnaissance Unit (*Sayeret Mat'kal*). They masqueraded as air mechanics and succeeded in neutralizing the potentially disastrous situation within a matter of seconds. Once news of the Ma'alot incident broke it was again this unit that was called up, but this time the ending was a disaster. When the green light was finally issued for the commandos to storm the schoolhouse, the assault techniques had yet to be perfected, and the force's co-ordination, deployment, and effectiveness was severely hampered. Exacerbating the situation was the *kamikaze* mentality of the terrorists, who first fired their weapons at the doomed hostages before engaging the assaulting soldiers. The final death toll of the massacre was 22 students killed and more than seventy seriously wounded.

The failed rescue attempt at Ma'alot is still considered one of the most controversial episodes in Israel's war against terrorism, and precious little information regarding the incident has emerged in the years to follow. There were many operational reasons as to 'why' the rescue attempt failed and in order to reduce or, it was hoped, eliminate the chances of a repetition it was felt necessary to co-ordinate responsibility for internal national security among the Israeli defence community. In late 1974, a government memorandum handed responsibility for

Israel's internal anti-terrorist duty, as well as an expanded policing role, to the Border Guards. Their once unique task of safeguarding the most desolate and precarious frontiers, in jeeps, with rifle in hand, had been changed for ever. The Border Guard would become a combat unit like any infantry force the IDF could field, only their area of battle would include the entire State of Israel, ranging from the desolate fields of northern Galilee to the slums of southern Tel Aviv.

Safeguarding northern Israel from terrorist attack was a sacred undertaking for the Green Berets. Since their inception in 1950, the Border Guards have done some of their finest work in northern Galilee, protecting the spartan agricultural settlements along the Lebanese and Syrian borders from infiltrators, smugglers, and thieves. Most of the Border Guard officers and NCOs lived in the area which they policed and entered each operational foray with the thought of protecting their own wives and children. This analogy became much more than a cliché, especially in the wake of the Ma'alot tragedy.

Among the 22 students killed at Ma'alot, a brother and sister became an emotional rallying cry for the Border Guards in their war against Palestinian terrorism. Yehudit Mader, a 17-year-old student in a Safed religious high school, and her 15-year-old brother, David, had fatefully taken part in a Youth Battalion [or *'Gad'na'*] nature trip which brought them to the Ma'alot schoolhouse. After the first news of the terrorist take-over was broadcast on the radio, Yehudit and David's elder brother Haim, then 28 and an NCO in a Border Guard Northern Company, commandeered a unit jeep and raced to the scene, his mind consumed with anger and anguish. During the tense negotiations with the terrorists outside the schoolhouse, the stone-faced Haim tried to gather whatever bits of information he could find. When he learned that a rescue assault was about to take place, he unofficially attached himself to the attack force, dodging bullets and shrapnel while searching for his brother and sister. Haim failed to find them either inside the building or at the emergency aid station set up outside the school grounds. He learned of their deaths the next day, feeling painfully impotent for not having been able to save them.

The Border Guard comrades of Haim Mader viewed the deaths of Yehudit and David as a tragedy they swore would never be repeated. The Border Guards look upon themselves as a large family, where the loss of 'one of their own' is mourned collectively, and the family of the fallen is 'looked after' in the same manner. A Senior Master Sergeant loved by officer and NCO alike, Haim Mader became a stoic symbol fo the Border Guards' resolve against terrorism. Tragically, however, he would also become one of their martyrs, falling in the line of duty in Lebanon eight years later.

Another outcome of Ma'alot and the decision to allocate internal security duties to the Border Guards was the formation of a counter-terrorist hostage rescue force. Much like the West German *Grenzschützgruppe*-9 (GSG-9) anti-terrorist strike force attached to the Federal Border Guard, which had been created in the aftermath of the September 1972 Munich Massacre, the new Israeli force was intended to fulfil the operational needs of the National Police for a force of professional commandos whose sole mandate would be hostage-rescues and delicate arrest operations. Unlike the various *conscript* élite units of the Israel Defence Forces that undergo periodical changes of manpower, and must master commando-tactics against both conventional as well as irregular forces, the Border Guard anti-terrorist team would have the single mandate of anti-terrorist operations inside the confines of Israel, and would be on call 24 hours a day and 365 days a year to execute that mandate.

Organized along the lines of GSG-9, the Border Guard anti-terrorist force adopted the mysterious name *Ya'ma'm* (Hebrew acronym for *Hayechida Hameyuchedet Lelochamah Beteror* or Special Unit for Combating Terrorism). It was a volunteer force of active duty Border Guard policemen searching for a greater challenge; also prominent were recently discharged commandos from various IDF *Sayerot*, especially from the disbanded Northern and Central Command reconnaissance forces who found the unique Border Guard *esprit de corps* a pleasant alternative to the rigidity of IDF service, and a modest civil servant's salary preferable to the bleak economic prospects Israeli civilian life promised. Although identifiable by their tank khaki canvas *patauga* boots, and commando physiques squeezed into Border Guard uniforms, most Israelis did not even know the *Ya'ma'm* existed. They are thought to have played a role in two incidents during the 1970s. The first of these happened on 5 March 1975 when a seaborne *Force 17* group landed at Tel Aviv's beachfront and proceeded to take hostages at the Savoy Hotel nearby (*see* page 157). The second came on 11 March 1978 when eleven *el-Fatah Force 17* terrorists landed on the shores of *Kibbutz* Ma'agan Michael, situated halfway between Haifa and Tel Aviv on the Mediterranean coast (*see* page 159). Following their less than perfect début, techniques were refined to the point where the Ya'ma'm are today possibly Israel's most expert hostage rescue unit.

During the last half of the 1970s, the Border Guards once again expanded, with brigades assigned to Jerusalem, The West Bank (Judea and Samaria), central Israel, and northern Israel. They were also ordered to co-ordinate their efforts with the regular police in Israeli cities and rural areas, helping to protect the *Kibbutzim* and *Moshavim* against agricultural thefts. The Green Berets also performed their duties in such diverse locations as government buildings in Jerusalem and Tel Aviv's often tumultuous Central Bus Station – acting as both a deterrent and a reactionary force against terrorist attack.

In the occupied territories, and the West Bank in particular, the Border Guards succeeded where the IDF and the civilian police had failed. As opposed to an IDF unit which is often rotated, a Border Guard company remained in a single location for a number of years, allowing the policemen to acquaint themselves with the intricacies of a particular neighbourhood and allowing the locals to get to know the Border Guards. In addition, an IDF reservist, for example, will not enter a tour of garrison duty with the same determination as a professional Border Guard policeman, whose pride in his task and uniform is total. The distinction became particularly evident when anti-Camp David demonstrations developed into PLO-led riots, and the IDF's desperate lack of training in riot control would become all too apparent. When their dark-green jeeps reached a riot, the Border Guard's proficiency in tear-gassing and swinging batons was enough to quell any disturbance. They managed to enforce curfews and undertake terrorist pursuits with fewer casualties than those conducted by the IDF.

Oddly enough, for a force once considered vehemently 'anti-Arab' because of its large representation of *Sephardic* Jews and Druze, some of the Border Guards' principal adversaries in the early 1980s were Jewish. In Jerusalem, Border Guard units, some on horseback, sometimes savagely beat off fanatic Orthodox Jewish riots opposed to archaeological digs in the Old City. When the last phase of the Israeli withdrawal from Sinai took place in the spring of 1982, in accordance with the Camp David peace accords, Border Guard units were called into the fray which developed between fanatic Jewish settlers refusing to leave the Sinai town of Yamit and the IDF forces ordered to remove them. The fighting was cruel and often hand-to-hand, but on the whole it was routine police duty.

On 3 June 1982, Shlomoh Argov, Israel's Ambassador to Great Britain, was critically wounded by Palestinian gunmen from the notorious Abu Nidal Faction after a diplomatic reception in London. Immediately, and inevitably, a fierce border war developed between the IDF and Palestinian forces in southern Lebanon. Israeli aircraft bombed Beirut, IDF artillery batteries pounded Palestinian refugee camps, and Palestinian Katyusha rockets rained down upon the Galilee settlements.

For Border Guard Northern Brigade commander Chief Inspector Gabi Last, a hard-spoken man with an iron will, the news of the Argov shooting and the ensuing artillery war ignited ominous thoughts in his mind as well as those of the men in his brigade's Safed HQ. To Gabi Last, the Border Guards were much more than a corps, they were a way of life – and their lives were soon to be drastically changed. Something big was brewing, and the Border Guards were to be an integral part of it.[4]

From Invasion to Destruction
The Saga of the 20th Company in Lebanon, June to November 1982

On 6 June 1982, a formidable IDF invasion force consisting of tens of thousands of soldiers burst across the northern frontier into Lebanon.

The IDF's mission was clear and apparently unilateral: remove the PLO presence from southern Lebanon and bring 'peace to Galilee'. For the IDF, the Middle East's most powerful military force, the objective of removing a few thousand irregular Palestinian fighters from southern Lebanon appeared to be a modest undertaking. Many IDF commanders likened the invasion to the virtually uncontested March 1978 Operation 'Litani', a mini-invasion of southern Lebanon in response to the Country Club Junction massacre. Lebanon, however, would prove to be a battlefield unlike any other in Israeli history, and Operation 'Peace for Galilee' would prove different from any war Israel had yet fought.

The Israeli invasion force consisted of armoured divisions sporting the awesome *Merkava* main battle tank (MBT), mechanized elements ferrying paratroops and *Golani* infantrymen, and second-to-none aerial capabilities including the F-15 and F-16 fighter-bombers. But the IDF unexpectedly found itself facing a stubborn and unrelenting enemy, and fierce fighting ensued. Even though IDF spearheads made it to the outskirts of Beirut by the end of the first week of fighting, and the Palestinian refugee camps around the urban centres of Tyre and Sidon had been 'neutralized', the IDF found itself involved in a counter-insurgency/police action it was ill-prepared to carry out. Its battle-tested armoured forces were trained in conventional combat, to defend ground and advance through hails of anti-tank projectiles on bat-tlefields such as the Golan Heights. They were *not* trained in identifying and pursuing fleeing terrorists amid a large and hostile population. Not a single IDF unit, including the paratroops and the constabulary Military Police, was sufficiently well trained or informed for such scenarios. The IDF had entered Lebanon to protect the citizens of northern Israel but who would now protect the IDF?

As experienced IDF generals such as Avigdor Kahalani and Yitzhak Mordechai looked over the landscape towards Beirut they knew that only one force existed whose experience, function and human character was tailor-made for the maelstrom they had entered. After a flurry of telephone calls between Tel Aviv, Jerusalem, Lod and Safed, the call-up was ordered, the equipment gathered and the Green Berets crossed the border they had so long protected and headed north.

In 1982 the Border Guards were commanded by one of the most controversial, feared and effective men in their history: Chief Superin-tendent Tzvi Bar. A man known more for his combat prowess than judicial experience, Tzvi Bar had reached the Border Guards following 22 years of service in the IDF as a highly acclaimed paratroop officer. During his rise up the IDF ladder of command, he participated in the 1966 Samua operation, the 1967 War battles for Gaza, the spectacular 1968 raid against Karameh and the epic fighting on the Golan Heights in 1973. He had commanded a Paratroop Brigade and *Ba'had 1* – the IDF's Officer Academy – before joining the ranks of the Green Berets in 1975 as its deputy commander. He would become a Border Guard commander whom policemen and Arab alike would respect and fear.

The transition from a military to a police framework was an easy one for Bar, who found the Border Guards a police force living and operating under military conditions. He brought to the Border Guards a unique brand of innovative thinking, typical among IDF paratroop officers, which he translated into an 'élite' brand of military training among operational Border Guard units. The Border Guards proudly and consecutively won numerous IDF physical and marksmanship competitions, beating the likes of the Golani Brigade and several paratroop reconnaissance units. By 1982, Tzvi Bar's Border Guards were prepared physically and mentally for any mission they would be summoned to carry out.

At the time of the invasion of Lebanon, the Border Guards consisted of 4,300 policemen, the vast majority of them being 'lifers' or professional NCOs and officers serving until retirement. Seventy-two per cent of the Border Guards' make-up was Jewish, sixteen per cent Druze and the remainder Circassian, Bedouin, Christian or Muslim.

After careful negotiations between the Ministry of Interior, the Ministry of Defence and the IDF, the decision to 'advance' Border Guard units into the Lebanon fray was finalized on 15 June 1982 – nine days after the first IDF units crossed the heavily fortified frontier. Although most of the responsibility for a Border Guard presence in Lebanon would fall on the shoulders of Northern Brigade commander Gabi Last, Tzvi Bar had the utmost confidence in his men. While Border Guard units enjoy the luxury of being stationed in permanent locations, they are by nature and design a rapid deployment force. A company which is stationed one evening in an anti-terrorist ambush in Hebron, might find itself in an anti-drug patrol in a Tel Aviv slum the next. As many Border Guard policemen would wryly joke later, 'The trip from our base in northern Israel to southern Lebanon is the same distance as a ride to Tel Aviv.' Lebanon, however, would prove to be a world away from Tel Aviv.

Under the brief orders bringing the Border Guards into Lebanon, their principal objective was joint-security operations in the IDF rear, concentrating on the south Lebanon cities of Tyre and Sidon. Both Tyre and Sidon were ancient Phoenician port cities and had witnessed nearly a decade of incessant fighting and destruction even before the Israeli invasion. Both cities are surrounded by dozens of Palestinian refugee camps – the largest around Tyre being Rachadiye and El Ba'as, and the notorious and overcrowded Ein el-Hilweh dwarfing much of Sidon. Tragically, the presence of the Palestinian camps made their host cities natural targets of Christian, Syrian and Israeli attacks. During the Lebanese Civil War, the Christian and Palestinian bloodletting destroyed much of the ancient port cities, as did the Syrian use of ZSU-34 self-propelled anti-aircraft guns to root out Palestinian snipers! Since 1968 the Israelis had also contributed their share of the destruction, as the IAF mounted frequent retaliatory bombing raids against 'terrorist bases' in the Palestinian camps of southern Lebanon in response to acts of terrorism – which inevitably scarred many of the nearby Lebanese towns and villages.

Although the awe-inspiring mountainous landscape of southern Lebanon resembled northern Israel, the likeness stopped there. Law and order had been absent from Lebanese society since 1975 and the local inhabitants had been brutalized for years by war and occupation at the hands of renegade Palestinian terrorists. Shoppers carried AK-47s to market, business disputes were settled with Semtex and 10-year-old children toting Walther PPKs drove Mercedes sports cars. The shell-shocked streets were filled with countless pregnant 13- and 14-year-old Christian and Shi'ite girls who had been raped by Palestinian guerrillas and then abandoned by their families who couldn't bear the shame. Lebanon was a deranged land and once the IDF entered into it the hatred of the inhabitants was focused on the new occupier: the Israelis.

Oddly enough, in a land where the Druze, Christians and Muslims were deadly and violent rivals, the integrated Border Guards did not fall victim to internecine temptations. Joint-security duty amid the shell destroyed ruins of the camps and two-storey buildings of the Tyre and Sidon *casbahs* was similar to a stint in the territories. Keeping peace amid a hostile population was after all a Border Guard trademark, but in Lebanon the probability of violence was far higher; this likelihood weighed on the minds of every heavily armed and flak-vested Green Beret policeman walking his beat in Lebanon. Every window might hide a sniper and every suspicious object could be a booby-trapped explosive device. To counter this threat, the Border Guards would soon enlist the services of National Police bomb disposal experts. The *Ya'ma'm* also travelled north, on call for the most challenging of situations.

The Border Guards' primary role during the early days of Israel's presence in southern Lebanon was the capture of known and active Palestinian terrorists whose names, addresses and photographs were on captured PLO rosters. The initial IDF onslaught had killed more than a thousand PLO regulars, but IDF Military Intelligence estimated that there were still thousands of heavily armed, well-trained and determined Palestinian terrorists in the area from Beirut to the Israeli border. These men, many of whom swapped camouflage fatigues for the blue jeaned uniform of a refugee, had to be identified and caught, and their substantial arms caches seized. In the summer of 1982, as the IDF fought the Syrians in the Beka'a Valley and near Beirut and while the Lebanese capital was subjected to an incessant siege, Israel's Green Berets initiated a precarious game of cat and mouse, hunting a very cunning and elusive enemy. The hunter would also inevitably become the hunted; unfortunately for the Border Guards, their Kfar Kasem reputation of intimidation and brutality would have little if any deterrent value on the hardened Lebanese and Palestinians.

The Border Guards' purification of southern Lebanon was not to be conducted in a brutal, Kfar Kasem-like fashion, however. The Green

Berets were policemen under a mandate to keep the peace, not a stormtrooper force ordered to destroy a fortification. As a result, they received *strict* guidelines dictating their use of fire-power and deadly force. When entering a suspect house, they were not permitted to fire bursts of automatic fire nor were they allowed to use hand-grenades. They could only fire when directly threatened and only when civilian casualties could be avoided. This practice hindered many military operations and led to the injury of many Border Guard policemen.

Unlike the vast majority of IDF units in Lebanon, Border Guard units had regularly undergone extensive house-to-house assault training prior to their transfer north of the border. Special techniques were developed which trained policemen in proper and safe procedures for forcibly entering dangerous confines during a search operation. The tactic consisted of the following: two policemen would enter a house, their M-16s and *Galil* poised for action, and concentrate on one room and its inhabitants, while a second two-man team would burst in, followed by another team. The division and quick deployment of force allowed a potentially confusing situation, which could result in civilian casualties, to become an orderly procedure. These methods would prove invaluable in southern Lebanon as Border Guard units entered *thousands* of homes in search of terrorists, weapons and information.

Although much of the Israeli attention in the summer of 1982 centred around the siege of Beirut, the force of Border Guards in Tyre and Sidon – which never numbered more than a few hundred – were concentrating on Palestinian bases. Relying on their fluency in Arabic, experience in pursuing terrorists and ability to cow the locals, the Green Berets soon proved their worth out of all proportion to their numbers. The IDF *Ansar* detention facility for terrorists and suspects soon swelled with angry young men who could not evade the Border Guard dragnets. Senior IDF officers were surprisingly impressed by the Border Guards' performance and efficiency and there wasn't a single brigade commander in southern Lebanon willing to relinquish the services of the Green Berets.[5]

The IDF's presence in Lebanon was so overwhelming that many of the soldiers viewed their tour duty as a foreign adventure. For an army not known for visiting exotic locales, Lebanon soon became a very short-lived colonial bonanza. El Al opened a regional sales office in Sidon, offering one-way escape packages to anyone with enough cash to leave the nightmare. IDF soldiers soon learned the Byzantine mystique of Lebanese economics and became joyful shoppers purchasing smuggled videos, watches and cigarettes. Paratroopers and Phalangists exchanged blouses and berets and even a few romances developed between conquering Israeli soldiers and Christian Lebanese women. As many IDF veterans would comment, 'Were it not for the fighting, Lebanon could even be considered a vacation on the IDF's tab!' For the Border Guards, however, the trip north was not an amusing journey. Their operations were incessant and tiring. They mounted day-long patrols of the refugee camps and the Tyre and Sidon *casbah*s, only to return in the dead of night for an ambush or curfew enforcement. Their home became the heavily armed dark-green Command Car they patrolled in, its canvas roof providing protection from the brutal heat, its vehicle-mounted FN MAG machine-guns providing protection against the well-armed and numerous enemies waiting for their moment to attack. Rest time was scarce and leave home to loved ones was few and far between.

The first and one of the most effective Border Guard forces to operate in southern Lebanon was *Plugat Chaf* or 20th Company. Commanded by Chief Inspector Shraga Levi, a warm man with a fatalist's approach to his work, 20th Company was largely made up of northern Israeli natives, policemen whose vigilance in Lebanon literally kept terrorists away from their wives and children. Many of the 20th Company's seasoned veterans, who until Lebanon had never seen combat, found southern Lebanon a maddening, though fascinating experience. Besides searching for terrorists, the Green Berets had to enforce a delicate balance of law, order and security operations in one of the most dangerous hot spots in the world. Some of the 'incidents', as they are known in Border Guard jargon, were comical while others only reinforced the need for a Border Guard presence in southern Lebanon.

Nowhere was the show of the Border Guards' flag more important than in the refugee camps. Ein el-Hilweh was the largest of these and certainly *the* hotbed of Palestinian nationalism in Lebanon. It was home base to many of the PLO's smaller and more revolutionary factions and the breeding ground for future generations of suicidal *fedayeen* who would continue the eternal struggle against Zionism. During the Israeli invasion, Ein el-Hilweh was the scene of some of the most intense fighting. It was finally captured after an IDF task force of paratroops, infantrymen and armour units waged a *jihad* against hundreds of entrenched, heavily armed Palestinian fighters who fought to the death. The camp's inhabitants, aware of their precarious situation as Palestinians in Lebanon, cherished their weapons with religious devotion as a guarantee for their integrity. For weeks after the camp's capture, the Border Guards uncovered thousands of tons of weaponry hidden in the labyrinth of caves, hutches and tunnels. They included everything from brand-new Czech Vz-52 assault rifles to US-made recoilless rifles. The vast amount of military hardware uncovered served notice to many of the Border Guard policemen that there were still hundreds of weapons out there and this presented numerous operational dangers. One incident, however, underscored both the fragility of the situation and the 'diplomacy' needed to defuse it.

On one July night, a Border Guard patrol was 'awakened' from the end of an average fourteen-hour day by the crackling of an automatic-fire burst through the air of the Ein el-Hilweh camp. Racing to the scene in full battle gear, the squad of Green Berets were both amused and shocked to learn that the source of the gunfire was a Palestinian wedding. The volley of AK-47 fire was providing a ceremonious send-off to the bride and groom. Flabbergasted and adamant (and covered by a force of heavily armed policemen), the Border Guards' officer demanded that the guests relinquish custody of their weapons to the assembled policemen. They refused. Without wasting a second in negotiations, the Border Guard Inspector supervising the incident took custody of the groom, refusing to return him until all the assault rifles were surrendered. Realizing that the paid-for wedding reception could not continue without the hapless groom and that they were hopelessly over-powered for a fire-fight, the guests acquiesced, respectfully realizing that the Green Berets were not to be crossed.

Border Guard patrols also mounted a constant vigil along the Mediterranean waterfront, preventing terrorist reinforcements from entering the south by sea and stopping escaping terrorists from fleeing to Cyprus or Tripoli in the north. Historically the Lebanese are seafarers, and the possibility of one of the Border Guards' 'most wanted' slipping away warranted a clampdown on all fishermen and ferry services. Border Guard policemen were able to utilize their Arabic skills by examining pre-civil war Lebanese Government fishing licences and searched almost each fishing vessel returning to its home port of Tyre or Sidon. Sometimes the 'catch' was highly profitable, as RPGs, recoilless rifles and mortars were confiscated, prompting the vulnerable IDF/Navy patrol vessels stationed off-shore to offer their Green Beret comrades a hearty 'Job well done!'

The Border Guards capitalized on many of their inherent skills to maintain law and order in Tyre and Sidon. They seized control of key intersections, their most notable position being at the entrance to Tyre, where their heavily armed Command Cars surveyed each indigenous vehicle entering and exiting the city. The Green Berets also co-operated to an extent with the local Lebanese gendarmerie who for years had been a nonentity in local affairs, using them for their information, experience and informants. For their trouble, the Lebanese were given the power of arrest and the right to carry nothing larger than a sidearm.[6]

The proliferation of all types of weapons in southern Lebanon provided the Border Guard policemen with dangerous operational difficulties. Almost every home had at least one weapon, and many served as arms caches for the PLO, or rented warehouse for more obscure, though equally dangerous, factional militias. The threat of a fatal fire-fight weighed heavy on the minds of every 20th Company policeman as he engaged in an anti-terrorist search or pursuit. When intelligence provided the name and address of a known terrorist, an intricate and detailed planning of the snare would be undertaken. Heavily armed Border Guard officers conducted pre-raid reconnaissance of the targeted location, as well as closing off much of the area surrounding the target to limit any chance of escape. Nothing was taken for granted.

The Border Guards' reputation for meticulous methods was reinforced in Lebanon by their considerable success. From 17 June to 9 September 1982, the few hundred Border Guard policemen serving in Lebanon captured 1,500 *known* and *documented* Palestinian, Lebanese and foreign terrorists and 471 *suspected* terrorists. From mid-September to mid-October 1982, they captured an additional 178 terrorists and 132 suspects. Many of the suspects were later released when evidence of terrorist involvement was lacking, only to reappear on the streets and alleyways of southern Lebanon openly confronting the same Border Guard policemen who had arrested them. Many no doubt turned to armed resistance following their experiences at the Green Berets' hands but others had always been active and their promises while in captivity not to 'get involved in trouble' were hollow, and the more experienced Border Guards knew it.

During this period the Border Guards seized more than 1,000 assault rifles, more than 100 RPGs and recoilless rifles, more than 200 hand guns, dozens of silencers and a remarkable *seven* tons of high-explosives. Much of this material was sent to Israel for public display, and thousands came to view this frightening find, which by itself justified Operation 'Peace for Galilee'.

The sheer volume of 'incidents' made the 20th Company's southern Lebanon home base a concentration of tension and raw nerves. The hissing chatter of the incessant radio communications filled the air, as did never-ending clouds of cigarette smoke which more often than not covered a huge map of Tyre and Sidon. Nicotine and caffeine in fact became a staple of the Border Guard diet, Bedouin coffee laced with cardamom helped maintain morale, as well as keep sleepy eyes open. Unlike most of the IDF reservists who milled back and forth through Border Guard controlled areas, the Green Berets were not on a one-month call-up, counting the days before their return to normal life in Israel. They were professionals, serving in order to provide for their families. While an IDF officer who for political or moral reasons refused to serve in Lebanon received an obligatory prison sentence, a Border Guard policeman refusing service in Lebanon was dismissed immediately with no chance of appeal.

There were other reasons for high Border Guard morale and the unique Lebanon *esprit de corps* especially among the Druze NCOs and officers. For many of Israel's Druze, service in Lebanon was considered a litmus test of their long-questioned divided loyalty. Israel's propping up of the Christian Maronite Phalangists, the historic enemy of the Lebanese Druze, created a situation which could have led to brother firing on brother in the Shouf Mountains.* Instead, many of the Druze Border Guards viewed their Lebanon service as proof of their worth as soldiers, policemen and as a family of fighters. The Druze also took

---

* During Israel's involvement in Lebanon, four Druze IDF soldiers defected to the ranks of their Lebanese brethren fighting in the Shouf, while no Border Guard defections were reported.

great pride in their uniforms and rank; in many of their villages around Mount Carmel in northern Israel, a policeman with a high rank or a medal of valour was placed first in line when the local council allotted land or building permits. Many Druze women also chose a husband according to his rank and status in the Border Guards.

In addition to the thousands of terrorists captured, the Green Berets also caught several of the PLO's top officers in Lebanon, including one of the most wanted of them all: Colonel Azmi Zerayer, the PLO's *el-Fatah* commander of Tyre. During the civil war and after, he oversaw the deaths of hundreds of innocents; his renegade bands of guerrillas brutalized the local Shi'ite and Christian women, raping and murdering many of them. Oddly enough, many in the Arafat hierarchy considered Zerayer an Israeli agent, since Israeli Defence Minister Moshe Dayan had personally released him from prison in 1970. Whether or not Zerayer was a murderer or a double-agent, the Border Guards had long held his name on their 'most wanted' list. Yet they had little luck in locating the elusive colonel until one of his lieutenants was captured and made to talk during a 20th Company raid in Tyre.

In a deserted villa due east of Tyre, surrounded by a citrus grove, Zerayer had set up a temporary home base. His barbaric reputation and huge sums of dollars secured him a fair degree of anonymity from the nearby villagers. Zerayer was not the average PLO officer and the Border Guards did not expect to be able to tackle him in a routine manner. They therefore summoned the commandos of their élite hostage-rescue unit who established a vigilant stake-out, stalking Zerayer until they felt him to be vulnerable and accessible. According to foreign reports, the *Ya'ma'm* operates in 24-man platoons, divided into two 12-man squads. As a unit, they are highly agile and tactically innovative, stemming from the fact that many were ex-Naval Commando and *Sayeret* veterans.

For several days, the commandos watched the villa while 20th Company reinforcements secured the surrounding villages. All the Border Guard units were heavily armed and wore flak vests, expecting Zerayer to put up a determined resistance. On 26 August 1982 they struck, bursting into the villa and surprising Zerayer as he lay in bed. He tried to get his assault rifle to defend himself, but never had a chance to pull the trigger, and was killed by a burst of automatic fire. The killing was one of the most notable Border Guard victories in Lebanon, although Border Guard OC Chief Superintendent Tzvi Bar was outraged that the newspaper credited Zerayer's death to security forces and not specifically the *Ya'ma'm*.[7]

By late 1982 the war in Lebanon had 'stabilized' into a political tug-of-war and the Border Guards settled in for a long stay and a dreaded Lebanese winter. The 20th Company continued its brilliant work, capturing dozens of terror suspects and bringing a modicum of law and order to the country. The 20th Company now began a series of impressive and selective ambushes in and around the refugee camps of

Tyre, making sure that terrorists who had evaded the initial IDF *Blitzkrieg* in June did not return to re-establish their pre-war terrorist cells. During quiet periods, when they weren't participating in anti-terrorist patrols, supervising curfews and working with the IDF, the 20th Company trained hard to increase their marksmanship scores and refine assault techniques.

Several outstanding soldier-policemen emerged from the 20th Company's first few months in Lebanon; these included platoon commander and company master tactician, Senior Inspector Stephen Daniel, a man noted for his ability in assessing situations and locations, and Senior Master Sergeant Yoel Baranas, the 20th's jovial guardian angel, who at home base cared for his men's needs and in the field took charge of their safety.

On the morning of Friday, 11 November the IDF's Military Administration Headquarters in Tyre collapsed in a gas related implosion of disintegrating concrete and twisted steel. The eight-storey building, approximately one kilometre due north of the city, was also home to the regional Military Police command, a Shin Bet desk, an IDF liaison office for Major Haddad's South Lebanese Militia and home base to the Border Guards' 20th Company. The building was completely destroyed; it had folded like a house of cards and was the worst single disaster in Israeli military history. Attempts to rescue those trapped inside the rubble went on for days, but the end result was devastating: 75 Israelis had died in the disaster, including 34 20th Company policemen. Among the dead were dozens of family men; a sense of shock, grief and mourning pervaded many of the towns and villages of northern Israel.

Also among the dead was 20th Company's Senior Master Sergeant Haim Mader. As a result of the deaths of his sister and brother in the Ma'alot massacre, he was not required to serve in Lebanon, but he felt that the safeguarding of the remnant of his family from the Palestinians' terrorist infra-structure in Lebanon was paramount. Tragically, and typically for some Israeli families, his family would be burying its third child in eight years.

The destruction of the Tyre HQ became known as the 'Tyre Disaster'. For Shraga Levi's 20th Company the loss of 34 of their own was catastrophic. The survivors found themselves in a state of shock and anger. Men who had served together for dozens of years and considered themselves closer than brothers had to gaze at the empty cots of their fallen comrades, realizing that they would never be coming back. Collective mourning transcended cultural barriers. Jewish policemen participated in Druze mourning ceremonies as if they were Muslims, and Druze, Bedouin, Circassian and Christian policemen rose and recited *Kadesh*, the Jewish prayer for the dead, as well as sitting the traditional *Shiva*, a Jewish seven-day period of mourning, at the homes of fallen comrades. Most of the men grew beards as a symbol of their sorrow, eulogized the dead and vowed to return to Lebanon.

After a year of rehabilitation and rebuilding, 20th Company would return to Lebanon, ironically enough replacing their own replacements following the second Border Guards' 'Tyre Disaster'.

Duty with Honour
The Border Guards in Lebanon, November 1982 to June 1985

The mysterious destruction of the Israeli Military Administration building in Tyre on 11 November 1982 was the first link in a chain of disasters Israel had begun to suffer in Lebanon. Until then the IDF had fought an efficient military campaign which had seen the destruction of Syrian SAM bases in Lebanon, the downing of 92 Syrian fighters for no IAF losses, and the ending of the PLO threat to Israel's northern frontier. But the decision was taken to enter Beirut and the IDF's legions of armour and men quickly became bogged down in the outskirts of the city and a bitter siege commenced. Palestinian tenacity increased as the promised Christian Phalangist military participation on Israel's behalf evaporated and a political nightmare ensued. Home-grown misdeeds were also hampering Israel's war against the PLO, as the renegade attempts of Defence Minister Ariel Sharon to create a new political order in Lebanon became painfully apparent and irreversible. It was the first political war the IDF had ever fought and it would also be the nation's most lingering conflict.

The adversity of Lebanon and the international criticism levelled at Israel for its invasion and its incessant siege of Beirut seemed inconsequential when on 1 September 1982 the first of more than 14,000 Palestinian and Syrian fighters were evacuated from the Lebanese capital. The exodus was supervised by a multi-national force (MNF) of peace-keepers consisting of US Marines, Italian infantry and military police units, and French paratroops. They were originally meant to protect the Palestinians of West Beirut from the Israelis and Christians, but would later, and inadvertently, contribute to Lebanon's new pro-Western order. For Israel, a national-security victory comparable to the Six Day War seemed imminent. The terrorists responsible for countless outrages and massacres were to be expelled once and for all from Israel's northern frontier and dispersed throughout the Arab states, all enforced conveniently and peacefully by foreign soldiers.

But the Israeli fantasy ended abruptly and in explosive fashion. Lebanese president-elect and Phalangist warlord Bashir Gemayel was assassinated on 14 September 1982 by a powerful bomb planted by an agent from the obscure, though fanatical, Syrian Socialist Nationalist Party (SSNP) commanded by I'zam al-Mahairi. The IDF responded by entering West Beirut in direct violation of the agreement under which the PLO had orginally been evacuated, claiming it was protecting the Palestinians from the wrath of Gemayel's grief-crazed militiamen. It was five days later, while engaged in this role, that the IDF allowed the Phalangists to enter the Sabra and Shatilla refugee camps, ostensibly to search for the source of muted gunfire heard hours before. Less than 24 hours later, more than 700 unarmed Palestinian men, women and children lay slaughtered. Lebanon was a land with a history of massacres; during the civil war Palestinian guerrillas had butchered thousands of Christians in Damour, and the Christians had responded in kind by slaughtering thousands of Palestinians during the siege of Tel Za'atar. But these murders of Palestinians in the camps carried intense ramifications for the Lebanon of the future, as well as for all the foreign powers attempting to alter its precarious make-up. The MNF was forced to return to Lebanon to keep the peace and keep the fledgling government of Bashir's brother Amin alive. Finding itself entangled, the IDF was unwilling to leave until the Palestinian threat had been removed, and their occupation of a good portion of Lebanon began to look permanent. This military occupation soon stirred up a new enemy, Lebanon's Shi'ite Muslims, who were to become a new and mystical force the world has yet to comprehend. In trying to rid itself of one enemy Israel created another. In southern Lebanon the IDF dug in.

For the men of the 21st Company of the Border Guards, Lebanon would become a treacherous tour of duty. Unlike 20th Company, they would not enjoy the magic and mystery of Israel's initial presence in the Lebanon. The Palestinian and Lebanese terrorists still at large were not the part-time warriors who had been snared before they could set fire to their lizard-pattern camouflage fatigues, but hard-core cell organizers determined to harass the IDF rear with decisive guerrilla attacks. By late 1982, hit-and-run attacks against fixed IDF positions and troop movements had become commonplace. Grenades were hurled at patrols, RPGs fired at buses ferrying troops home and occasional machine-gun fire trailed helicopter flight patterns. The most damaging attack was a Palestinian ambush of an IDF transit point near the Shouf Mountain town of Aley on 3 October, when six Israeli soldiers were killed and 22 seriously wounded.

Oddly enough, as the number of terrorists captured by Green Beret dragnets increased, the attacks grew bolder and deadlier. Tactics also changed. Instead of the traditional Palestinian method of attack – a sniper, camouflaged by strolling women and children, opening fire against an IDF or Border Guard patrol – more sophisticated and destructive means were found. Prior to the 1982 War, hundreds of Palestinian guerrillas were sent to distant outreaches of the Soviet bloc to take courses in everything from operating a T-34 tank in Hungary to learning the intricacies of booby-trapped *punji* stakes from the battle-expert Vietnamese. They were taught the most effective means to conquer conventional military might by the best in the business and soon learned to cherish the value of the hit-and-run attack and the indiscriminate use of hidden explosives. As a result, the new nemesis of the Israeli soldier became the roadside booby-trapped device. The mountainous and spartan underbrush terrain of Lebanon afforded great camouflage for the home-made bombs which often consisted of kilograms of high-explosive wrapped in a tin drum packed with shrapnel. Activated by a trip wire or by a brave trigger-man, the devices began to take their toll on Israeli personnel on 23 December 1982 when two Israeli soldiers were killed by a booby-trapped device conveniently planted near a roadside pile of rubbish. A week later on 31 December, a Border Guard patrol seized five Grad missile-launchers hidden in a villa in the village of Majdel es-Slim. The stakes of the Lebanon occupation had been dramatically raised.

The snowy winter of 1982/3 did not bring a withdrawal for the thousands of Israeli personnel serving in Lebanon, nor did it end the killing. The outnumbered men of 21st Company found themselves in the thick of a labyrinth of police activity they were ill-equipped to handle. The PLO Command had returned to Tripoli in Lebanon and was issuing orders to its 'freedom fighters' to make the IDF occupation as costly as possible and at the same time attempt to bring *terror back to Galillee*. This compounded tensions in the Border Guard camp. They were not only safeguarding the IDF rear and policing the chaos of southern Lebanon, but they had now returned to their sacred task of protecting northern Israel with one small exception, they were on the wrong side of the fence!

The 21st Company was almost identical in make-up and character with 20th Company. Both were under the command infra-structure of Deputy Superintendent Gabi Last's Northern Brigade and both were made up of professionals who had spent most of their career safeguarding either the northern frontiers as policemen or the northern settlements as part of *Mishmar Hayeshuvim*, a para-military component of the Border Guards which provided internal security to the very exposed *Kibbutzim*, *Moshavim* and small Druze, Circassian and Bedouin villages of Galilee.

Formed in 1974, 21st Company was created as a special strike force to help the 'Blue' civilian police combat difficult criminal situations in many of the poorly developed towns of northern Israel, mainly populated by new immigrants. Originally organized around a cadre of toughened veteran policemen, they proved to be an élite Border Guard force serving an area from the Lebanese border to the smart Tel Aviv suburb of Kfar Saba. Around their home base of Netufa near Shfaram in the Galilee, their dark-green jeeps and Kelly-green berets became as much a part of the natural landscape as the plush eucalyptus trees and the rolling hills.

During the war in Lebanon, 21st Company was commanded by Chief Inspector Nachum Mordechai, an amiable and jovial officer whose endearing personality was combined with his love for his command, his men and their mandated task of counter-terrorism. A northern Israeli Sabra or native, the chain-smoking Mordechai understood the mentality of the terrorist and, as a result, feared him greatly. Then 38 years old, though looking older than his years, Mordechai was an ex-paratroop officer with many years of experience as a military commander and as a policeman in the territories. Service along the northern frontier had taught him that a terrorist exploits the weaknesses and mistakes of security forces and he was determined to close all windows of opportunity to his PLO enemies. Anxious to prevent his men from becoming casualties, the tireless Mordechai went to great lengths to brief his men prior to every patrol and engagement. From their entry into Lebanon until 31 January 1983, 21st Company captured 74 Palestinian terrorists (including three much feared females) and arrested 192 terrorist suspects.[8] Countless Border Guard convoys also ferried truckloads of captured assault rifles, heavy machine-guns, RPGs and recoilless rifles back to IDF arsenals throughout Israel.

Mordechai's company was assisted in their task by dozens of survivors from 20th Company, whose volunteered return to Lebanon duty shocked many hardened IDF officers, but surprised few in the Border Guard camp. Their anti-terrorist experience in Tyre, Sidon, Aley and Beirut was an invaluable asset to Mordechai, much as it was also an invaluable boost to the company's morale. Even though Border Guard living conditions were spartan at best, with no canteen and the telephone service to 'the real world' an enigma, dozens of 20th Company survivors opted to leave their beloved rugged landscape of northern Israel to return to Lebanon and ensure terrorism was kept north of the border. As will be seen later, however, many would not be able to cheat death a second time.

At 1100 hours on 11 January 1983 a new type of weapon was brought into the fray. While a 21st Company foot patrol slugged its way through the winter's mud around the central square of Tyre – nick-named 'Shmuck's Square' for the endearing qualities of the city it represented – a vehicle parked in too legal a fashion for the Lebanese aroused the suspicions of the patrol commander. Fearing the worst, he positioned his squad in a defensive perimeter, ordering his machine-gunner to cover the open thoroughfare – to counter the escape of any terrorist vehicle – and ordering his riflemen to aim their M-16s at open windows to deter snipers. As the heavily armed officer approached the sparkling clean grey Peugeot 504 his caution was justified when he noticed electrical wires leading from the steering compartment to the driver's window. Within minutes hastily summoned Border Guard units had imposed a midday curfew in Tyre, while a National Police bomb disposal expert received the dreaded call.

The service of the National Police bomb disposal experts, or *Hablanim*, alongside the Border Guards in Lebanon is worthy of mention. While the legal mandate of the National Police did not permit a bomb disposal expert north of the border, many veterans volunteered, realizing that service in Lebanon was but an extension of their busy workload in keeping the streets of Jerusalem, Haifa and Tel Aviv safe from disaster. One such veteran expert was Dani Peretz, who was given the task of neutralizing the car bomb in Tyre.

Car bombs were not new to Israelis and most policemen remembered the destructive effects of the PFLP's car bomb in Jerusalem's Machane Yehuda market in 1968. As a result, the appearance of a vehicle loaded with explosives warranted great fear and apprehension. With a devastating blast a likelihood, dozens of nervous Border Guards established a security zone around the car, while civilians and soldiers alike were evacuated to a safe distance. Unlike a bomb call in Israel, however, Peretz could not work at a leisurely pace. He was still in Lebanon and the threat of the booby-trapped vehicle being a diversion from a greater plan of destruction was a firm possibility. With his Kevlar protective gear making his movements cumbersome, Peretz gingerly approached the vehicle, wiping the sweat from his helmet's plexi-glass visor and watching out for the barrel of a Dragunov sniper rifle pointing out of a neighbouring window. After a few hours of gentle labour and luck, Peretz succeeded in disarming the vehicle-bomb, eventually removing 120 sticks and thirty fingers of TNT – each stick weighing 200 grams – as well as 30 pieces of RDX, two gas cylinders and an additional 70 kilograms of Semtex hidden under the passenger seats. The device was designed to be triggered by a radio signal, but was dismantled before it took its murderous toll of Israeli soldiers and local civilians alike.

Other Border Guard patrols would not be so lucky. On 18 October 1983 a terrorist held in Border Guard custody complained of severe abdominal pains following a Green Beret interrogation in the Sidon HQ. He was taken to a field hospital a few kilometres south of the city in an ambulance escorted by two heavily armed Border Guard jeeps. After the medical examination and a clean bill of health, the terrorist was returned to Sidon. As the convoy neared the city centre, it was pounded by heavy machine-gun bursts and intense bazooka and grenade fire from terrorists waiting in ambush. The fire-fight was fierce, brief and deadly. Two Border Guard policemen in conscript service, Shalom Shvili and Meir Cohen, were killed. Shvili had been a policeman in the 20th Company and had been on the seventh floor of the Military Administration building in Tyre when it collapsed. At the time of the disaster, Shvili was guarding PLO prisoners, a task he amazingly continued to execute even after the destruction of the building. After digging himself out of the rubble, a badly shaken and bleeding Shvili dug out his surviving prisoners and held them at gunpoint until he was relieved. Meir Cohen was also a 20th Company survivor and had devoted all his free time to helping the widows and families of his fallen comrades. Only weeks before his death, Cohen was involved in another fire-fight, in which one high-ranking terrorist was killed and another captured.

The Border Guards' avenged their dead comrades a week later, when a patrol killed two heavily armed terrorists and captured seven others near the town of Al-Asu'a. The group had participated in an attack against IDF forces along the Tyre–Sidon road and had been on the wanted list for a long time.

The loss of policemen Shvili and Cohen was a blow to the morale of the Green Berets in Lebanon; they likened their task in Tyre and Sidon to 'a surgeon treating a case of cancer with an aspirin'. Sniping attacks gave way to booby-trapped devices, which were replaced by car bombs. A little over a year after the conventional combat of Operation 'Peace for Galilee' had ended, Israeli casualties were mounting and reaching unacceptable levels. Lebanon continued to come apart at the seams: Christian fought Druze, Palestinian fought Palestinian and Muslim fought Muslim, while Syria manipulated them all for her own political ends. What this fratricidal bunch had in common was a hatred for Israel. Israeli forces garrisoned knee deep in the mess had to absorb it and hope for a political solution; unknown to them a new force was about to strike them, one more fanatical than they had faced before.

One fact of Israel's first year in Lebanon was the co-operation and friendship of the Shi'ite Muslims of southern Lebanon. The Shi'ites had always been the poorest of all the religious factions in Lebanon and subsequently received little political representation or much-needed protection. In the south, the Palestinian guerrillas operating against Israel had long victimized the local Shi'ites, stealing their homes, abusing their women and randomly murdering family heads, villages elders and religious leaders. The presence of a PLO mini-state and base of operations against Israel amid the Shi'ite villages also attracted the attention of the Israeli Air Force who frequently flew raids against them, inevitably killing innocent Shi'ites in the process. By the time the IDF invaded Lebanon in June 1982, the frustrated and hapless Shi'ites viewed the Israelis as liberators and cheered the arrival of their *Merkava* tanks with bouquets of roses, showers of rice and victorious cheers. The *mullahs* preached that the Shi'ites' time of liberation was at hand; the invasion from the south was to be their true salvation amidst the anarchy of Lebanese politics.

The delicate alliance between the IDF and the Shi'ites of the south could not evade the realities of Lebanon's new political order and it would soon become eroded in bloody fashion. The accession to the Presidency of the Maronite Christian Amin Gemayel together with the apparently permanent Israeli occupation polarized the Shi'ites into military action. The Shi'ite-led Islamic revolution in Iran and Ayatollah Khomeini's call for a *jihad* against the Zionist and Western enemies of Islam found a receptive ear among the poor, illiterate and futureless young Shi'ites in Lebanon.

The militant Shi'ite fundamentalist movement in Lebanon can be traced to the world-wide expansionist aims of the Iranian revolution. In

1980, Iran's Ayatollah Khomeini made several failed attempts to bring his zeal and heavily armed Revolutionary Guards into the Beka'a Valley, but secular Syrian President Hafez el-Assad thwarted these efforts, not at all happy with the prospect of a religious earthquake on his doorstep. When Israel invaded Lebanon, Assad finally permitted the Revolutionary Guards to enter the Levant and help in the fighting; he was relying on their zeal, and many of the Iranians thought it was but a stepping-stone in the Islamic liberation of *el-Quds* (Jerusalem).

During the war, a few hundred Revolutionary guards took part in the fighting around Beirut and, most notably, in their suicidal attempts to defend the Shouf Mountain resort town of Aley against IDF para-troop and infantry forces.[9] The Iranians, though, had other objectives than the ousting of the Israelis and they concentrated their religious fervour into setting up a base of operations in the ancient town of Ba'albek, previously noted more for its awe-inspiring Roman ruins than terrorist training camps. Posters of the Ayatollah began to appear throughout the city streets, as did graffiti calling for 'Death to America' and 'Death to Israel'. Ba'albek was a means of bringing the Islamic revolution to the one million Lebanese Shi'ites. Their first goal was to oust the enemies of Islam from Lebanon. With complete backing, for different reasons, from Iran and Syria, shock troops of the revolution prepared to confront the 'American and Zionist devils'. According to one Shi'ite militiaman, 'Revenge would be taken against the Israeli invaders and their American backers.'

There were several Shi'ite militias and terror groups in Lebanon which soon targeted Israel and America. *Amal* (an Arabic acronym for 'Movement of the Disinherited', a political organization formed by the doomed Musa Sadr in Ba'albek in 1974) was the oldest and most moderate, commanded by the lawyer Nabih Berri. He was considered more anti-Palestinian than revolutionary and after the Israelis seized Beirut they even allowed his militia to keep their weapons. After 1982, the fundamentalist *Amal Islami* was formed by Hussein Musawi, a schoolteacher and military commander in *Amal* who accused Berri of abandoning 'Islamic principles' for the political spotlight. Almost simul-taneously, the radical cleric Sheikh Hussein Fadlallah gathered a hard-core cell of the 'waiting to be martyred faithful' into a shadowy terror group known as *Hizbollah* or 'Party of God'. Another even more secretive terror group, *Jihad al-Islami* (Islamic Holy War) would also feature prominently in the events to follow.

The first engagement between Israeli and Shi'ite forces occurred on 22 June 1983 when a Green Beret patrol outside the Shi'ite village of Arab as-Salim was pounded by murderous gunfire which resulted in the death of a Border Guard NCO. Arab as-Salim had been a 'troublesome' village for some time; posters of Khomeini had been followed by anti-Israeli graffiti and then culminated with sniper attacks against Border Guard patrols. The attacks from Arab as-Salim caused most IDF and Border Guard commanders to realize that they were about to face a host of security problems from Shi'ites; the suicide truck bombing of the US embassy in Beirut on 18 April 1983 (in which 63 were killed) was viewed as 'blood-soaked writing on the wall' – the act was repeated with the 23 October suicide bombing of the US Marine and French paratroops compounds in Beirut (in which 241 Marines and 59 paratroopers were killed, respectively). The poor defensive arrangements around the destroyed US Marine base were studied, and security around *all* IDF facilities considerably tightened. Yet as one IDF officer who examined the disaster at the Marine base later commented on Israeli TV, 'No existing security arrangement will stop an individual willing to martyr himself.'

Israeli Military Administration and Border Guard Headquarters Tyre – Friday, 4 November 1983. As the first rays of sunlight burst across the windswept Lebanese coastal landscape, many 21st Company policemen began their day in typical fashion by smoking the morning's first cigarette and preparing their gear for 0800 hours inspection. The barracks were more or less empty that Friday morning as many had headed home the night before to wives and children, for three days of food, sleep and attempts to forget about their Sunday return trip to Lebanon. Their headquarters was a comfortable complex of three multi-storey buildings which housed a makeshift prison, the local Shin Bet office and the Border Guard HQ. The compound was silent, the only noise being the muted shouts of Palestinian and Lebanese terrorists held in custody and the muffled sound of an approaching car motor. It was too early for vehicles to be milling about so close to the HQ, but the tell-tale noise aroused little suspicion.

For the unidentified Shi'ite driver of a green Chevrolet pick-up truck heading slowly towards the Tyre compound, Friday was his day to meet Allah; the religious culmination of his short life. A member of *Jihad al-Islami*, he had been dispatched to meet the enemies of Islam in a vehicle laden with half a ton of high-explosives. His adrenaline and confidence grew as he passed three unmanned IDF check-points along the Rosh Hanikra–Tyre Highway, even smiling and waving at the nearby UNIFIL (United Nations Interim Force in Lebanon) check-post before making the fateful turn and heading towards the Border Guard HQ complex.

In the light of the Shi'ite attacks against the American and French bases, IDF commanders were cognizant of a possible suicide attack against their positions in Lebanon and had ordered security arrangements to be increased to a heightened state of alert. Stone-filled barrels and cement 'tiger teeth' obstacles had been sited to slow down all approaching vehicles, while a heavily fortified machine-gun post had been set up at the base perimeter gate to stop any unwelcome visitors. The man entrusted with keeping 'unfriendlies' away that Friday morning was Nakad Sarbuq, a Druze policemen from the village of Beit J'an. When he first saw the green pick-up truck, Sarbuq followed routine procedure by shouting warnings in Arabic and then cocking his .30 calibre machine-gun and aiming the sights straight at the driver's head. As the Chevrolet passed the first concrete barricade, Sarbuq held his breath and squeezed off a burst of fire, but a second and finally a third barricade were all overcome. The sounds of gunfire shook the still sleepy-eyed policemen who were busy grabbing a quick shower, shaving or cleaning their weapons. Within seconds dozens of anxious policemen covered with towels, soap and shaving cream had grabbed their weapons and headed outside.

As the vehicle approached the main gate, Sarbuq's incessant .30 calibre volleys were hastily joined by a second Border Guard gunner, David Illouz. After frantic seconds of point-blank shooting, their combined efforts resulted in a flurry of lead ripping through the body of the Shi'ite *kamikaze* bomber. They fired without ceasing but the vehicle kept on moving. Its bumpers gently ripped off the hinges of the main gate and slowly rolled into the main perimeter, absorbing hundreds of bullets as it reached the centre of the compound where its half-a-ton of

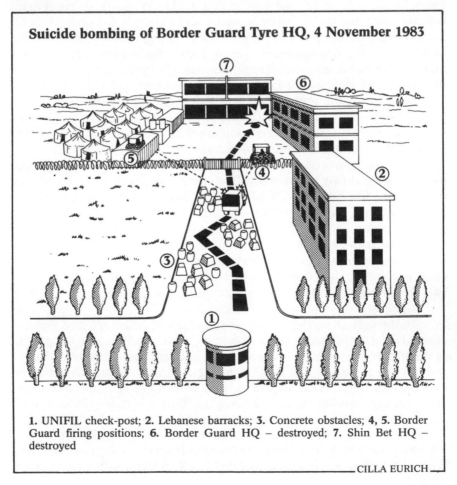

Suicide bombing of Border Guard Tyre HQ, 4 November 1983

1. UNIFIL check-post; 2. Lebanese barracks; 3. Concrete obstacles; 4, 5. Border Guard firing positions; 6. Border Guard HQ – destroyed; 7. Shin Bet HQ – destroyed

CILLA EURICH

high-explosives detonated with a thunderous blast. The alertness of the Border Guard sentries had prevented the Chevrolet from slamming into the main building, but devastation had been complete. The entire area was shaken, and many people as far away as Sidon thought that a major earthquake had occurred. For the second time in two years, a cloud of dust and smoke shrouded a scene of death and horror around a Border Guards Headquarters.

As the buildings burned and the wounded cried for help, the badly shaken policemen of 21st Company began to tear at the debris with their bare hands, looking for survivors and tending the numerous wounded. IDF units stationed nearby were rushed to the chaotic scene, as were rescue dogs and medevac helicopters. A dead body was recovered almost every five minutes and the badly mangled corpses covered with IDF-issue grey blankets soon filled a parking lot for identification and return to Israel for burial.

The next day, IAF aircraft struck at any Druze, Palestinian or Shi'ite positions in Lebanon conveniently within range.

Just as 20th Company had been devastated by the first 'Tyre Disaster', so too was Mordechai's 21st Company ravaged by the 'Second Tyre Disaster'. The final death toll was 28 Israelis killed, including nineteen policemen from the 21st Company. Dozens of others were severely injured.* Most of the dead were Druze and the rural village of Beit J'an found itself immersed in a state of grief and despair. Tragically, one of the dead, a 43-year-old Bedouin Senior First Sergeant and seventeen-year veteran named U'gla Hamadi, left behind twelve children.

For the survivors, the first week after the explosion was marked by funerals, visits to the bereaved families, trips to wounded comrades in hospital and countless hours of discussions with Border Guard psychiatrists. They had been severely traumatized and their healing as individuals and as a fighting unit was of paramount importance. The doctors and company commander Mordechai both agreed that the best therapy for the hard-hit 21st was to remain in Lebanon, in Tyre and in the area of their destroyed HQ. The IDF hierarchy, however, had other plans and dispatched the remnant of Nachum Mordechai's proud fighting force back to their home base of Netufa.

Although disappointed with the decision to pull back, Mordechai was a soldier and had to follow orders. He realized that the true rehabilitation of his men would only be when they resumed training, regained the feel of their weapons and returned to Tyre. Only nine days after the blast, Mordechai was quoted as saying proudly: 'Its only a matter of time before we return to Tyre. In the one year that we've been there, our forces captured more than 3,000 terrorists and retrieved tons of weapons and ammunition. Whenever there would be an "incident",

---

* Also killed in the blast were 32 Palestinian and Shi'ite terrorists captured in recent 21st Company operations. *Hizbollah* and *Jihad al-Islami* knew of their presence in the Tyre compound, but decided to martyr them nevertheless.

the Border Guards would respond in less than *five* minutes and always before the IDF. Ninety per cent of those responsible for terrorist activity in *my* sector were captured. Because of this unique work which only the Border Guards – 21st Company – can accomplish, I'm sure that all the survivors, as well as the new recruits will want to return to Lebanon.'[10] These views were shared with equal passion by Shmuel Levi, a hardened platoon commander in the 21st and brother of 20th Company commander Shraga Levi who fervently felt that, 'No IDF unit is capable of doing our work with the same effectiveness, success and zeal.'

The sincere and sometimes obsessive desire of men like Mordechai, the father of four children, to return to Lebanon voluntarily personified more than anything, the Border Guards' unique and altruistic *esprit de corps*. Following the 1983 destruction of the Tyre HQ, dozens of Border Guard veterans from companies throughout Israel submitted their requests to transfer into the 21st Company, with availability not always matching the great demand. Sons, brothers and fathers of the 21st Company men who had fallen literally begged Mordechai and his commander Gabi Last for permission to enlist into the Border Guards and assume the places of their dead kin. Many of the severely wounded left the secure comfort of their hospital beds in Haifa and Safed to hitch-hike rides up north to visit their buddies and talk about the incident. Most important for many was a discussion with the company commander to secure a position in their unit upon release from medical treatment.

For the survivors of 21st Company, rehabilitation was a slow and painful process. These were simple men who had assumed an enormous task, but had been overwhelmed by circumstance. In a forum meant to sooth raw nerves and, it was hoped, preserve the cohesion of the force, Northern Brigade commander Gabi Last visited the 21st Company home base at Netufa. With the chain-smoking company commander Mordechai by his side, Last reiterated the possibility of a return to Lebanon to dozens of men, some with blood-stained bandages, who viewed such a prospect with intense fear and anxiety. Many career NCOs who had spent what appeared to be a lifetime in anti-terrorist operations pleaded not to be returned to Lebanon. Some said that 21st Company had already spilled more than its share of blood, while others promised that a return to Lebanon would cause the majority of them to go crazy. The Northern Brigade commander responded in true Gabi Last fashion, promising to attach additional psychiatrists to the company and vowing that should the order to return to Tyre arrive on his desk, then Tyre it would be!

Tyre and much of southern Lebanon was instead returned to Shraga Levi's 20th Company, which at the time of the second Tyre disaster was garrisoning Sidon. The routine of incidents, arrests and 'keeping the peace' in a war-torn land remained a Border Guard exclusivity. It would also have its heavy price.

On 27 December 1983, one of 20th Company's most beloved and effective officers, Senior Inspector Stephen Daniel, led a routine patrol into the Palestinian shanty town of Kiya, due east of Sidon. He was the 20th Company's operations officer and had always briefed his men extensively as to the dangers of the patrol, hoping to return to base with all his policemen 'in one piece'. He religiously examined the latest intelligence reports prior to each outing, as well as tapping the usual source of informants to ensure that he would not be taking his squad into an ambush. A Sidon patrol was something he had led hundreds of times; it consisted of glancing at open windows, looking over one's shoulder and suspecting every crate of oranges of hiding a powerful booby-trapped explosive device. The worst part of the patrol was entering the city's claustrophobic *casbah*. The ancient alleyways and bustling mercantile activity made vehicle passage impossible and patrols had to make do on foot. With the Command Cars, their radios and their FN MAGs left out of any possible fire-fight, all Green Beret patrols in Sidon left incredibly vulnerable. The smiling fruit vendor could easily hurl a grenade, any rooftop might be hiding an RPG gunner.

As part of that day's patrol, Daniel called at a house which intelligence sources listed as a possible bomb factory. He had it surrounded in the routine manner – policemen securing a perimeter while the vanguard of the patrol raced up a flight of stairs and secured all exits. In characteristic Israeli fashion, Stephen Daniel led the patrol from the front and was the first one up the stairs.† After pounding on the iron door and identifying his force as Border Guard policemen, he burst through for the search operation. Intelligence was correct, Daniel's squad had surprised three heavily armed terrorists, catching them red-handed while busy assembling high-explosive booby traps. In the close quarters of a primitively furnished room a fierce fire-fight ensued. Although he was wearing his cherished protective flak vest, Daniel was struck by a 9mm pistol round at point-blank range and fatally wounded. In the exchange of gunfire, two other Border Guard policemen, squad leader Nazam A'jmayah and 20th Company Sergeant Yoel Baranas, were also wounded. A profusely bleeding Baranas emptied two full Colt AR-15 thirty-round magazines into the terrorists. The Border Guard policemen uncovered dozens of assault rifles, RPGs, explosives and Soviet-made silencers. Subsequent reports suggested that the terrorists killed in the Kiya house had been responsible for most of the thirty attacks against Israeli forces during December 1983.

Thirty-year-old Stephen Daniel was the fifty-fifth Border Guard policeman to fall in Lebanon. He had realized that as a survivor of the 'first Tyre disaster', he was living on borrowed time, but was adamant about remaining in Lebanon with his men. The death of the brilliant young officer was a bitter blow to 20th Company which had already had

† Although a component of the Israeli Police, Border Guard officers undergo all command courses within an IDF framework. As a result, they perform in the field in the same effective way as IDF officers.

its fair share of dead and wounded. To many, his death signalled that the time had come to order the Green Berets home from Lebanon. In an interview given to Israeli Television just days after Daniel's death, the new Border Guard commander, Chief Superintendent Pinchas Shachar, dourly remarked, 'We've been called upon to perform a most difficult task; one which we've tirelessly achieved in Lebanon since the beginning of Operation "Peace for Galilee". The burden which has fallen upon our shoulders has been enormous, with 10 per cent of all Israeli casualties in Lebanon being Border Guard policemen. What are we when compared to the *giant* IDF, but a force minuscule in proportions. Accordingly, we've *donated* our fair share in the security operations in Lebanon – Tyre and Sidon particularly – in a most positive and effective manner and the time has come for us to *leave* Lebanon. However, should the decision stand that the Border Guards remain in Lebanon, we will continue to perform our duties in the same, *positive* and effective manner.'

Even though the death of Stephen Daniel and the heavy Border Guard casualty toll made a Green Beret withdrawal from Lebanon only a matter of time, the IDF was not willing to relinquish the services of the Border Guards just yet, and with good reason. In late March 1984, three Arab terrorists succeeded in slipping through an IDF-controlled sector of southern Lebanon and crossed the frontier into Israel. The tenacious group made their way to Jerusalem where they struck on 2 April amid a midday crowd of shoppers in Jewish West Jerusalem. They indiscriminately fired automatic weapons and hurled fragmentation grenades at anyone in sight, killing one man and severely wounding 59. One terrorist was killed by an armed off-duty policeman, the other two were captured by a Border Guard patrol hours later.

The Jerusalem attack served as justification for the IDF/Border Guard presence in southern Lebanon to continue, but terrorist attacks and their ensuing casualties increased. Dozens of Israeli soldiers were killed and wounded in deliberate attacks against IDF positions, while mortar rounds and Katyusha rockets were fired against Border Guard bases in Sidon and Tyre. On 7 November 1984, two Border Guard policemen, Avraham Zohar and Eli Mizrahi, were awarded the Israeli National Police's highest decoration for valour for their role in killing a three-man terrorist squad in Sidon. The terrorists, armed with a variety of Soviet bloc weaponry, had opened fire on an IDF convoy escorted by Border Guard vehicles. Zohar and Mizrahi instinctively jumped off their Command Car and opened up accurate bursts of 5.56mm fire. That same day diplomatic negotiations began between Israel and Lebanon to co-ordinate the long-awaited and inevitable IDF pullout.

Israel's three-stage withdrawal from Lebanon was announced on 14 January 1985 and was intended to bring quiet to the north; it only proved to exacerbate the Shi'ite and Palestinian wrath against IDF personnel and installations. An IDF pullback from Lebanon was an outspoken statement of defeat for Israel, whose enemies were now racing to fire their parting shots against the 'hated Zionist occupier'. Palestinian groups returned to eastern Lebanon and Shi'ite suicide bombers, both male and female, killed almost as many Israeli soldiers as had fallen during the conventional fighting during Operation 'Peace for Galilee' three years before. On 5 February 1985, a Shi'ite car-bomb was used against IDF forces at Burj Shemali, killing one and wounding nine others. The most costly attack, however, occurred on 10 March 1985 when a suicide car bomber detonated his explosive-laden automobile alongside an IDF convoy near the Israeli town of Metulla. The blast killed twelve soldiers and wounded fifteen. It illustrated painfully not only how the war in Lebanon had failed to remove completely a Palestinian terrorist presence from the northern border – the PLO had returned to Tyre and Sidon – but that the fanatical spark of Shi'ite fundamentalism was now situated uncomfortably along the northern border as well.

In less than three years in Lebanon, the Green Berets had captured 1,958 male terrorists and six female terrorists and arrested 1,909 suspects.‡ They seized 1,169 AK-47s and 5.56mm assault rifles, 200 bolt-action rifles, 162 RPGs, 187 pistols and revolvers and fourteen silenced automatics. Much of this weaponry was American and West German, from arms shipments to conventional Arab armies that had conveniently been diverted to terrorist stockpiles in Lebanon. The Border Guards also captured dozens of recoilless rifles, hand-grenades and communication devices, but probably their most important haul was the astounding seven tons of explosives. Two companies of Border Guard policemen accomplished more than full brigades of élite IDF troopers. But they paid the price for their impressive numbers: the Border Guards had lost 55 dead, 36 seriously wounded and nine men who had to be discharged from active duty. Many Border Guard policemen felt bitter about the lack of recognition they received back home for the tremendous work they had accomplished.

As the convoys of IDF armoured personnel carriers and Border Guard Command Cars departed Lebanon for the short, though precarious ride home, a Border Guard policeman was quoted as saying, 'The day that we can return to guarding the borders of this country, is the day we'll know that peace has finally arrived.' His optimistic hopes would not be realized.

In the years since Israel's withdrawal from Lebanon and the establishment of a 12-kilometre-wide 'security zone' in southern Lebanon, terrorist attempts to infiltrate into northern Israel have been many and varied; they have included attempts by Palestinians, Shi'ites and Syrian-sponsored suicidal fanatics. The IDF and the Border Guards tried to reinforce their northern barrier with the help of the joint Christian Shi'ite SLA (South Lebanese Army) working with 'unofficial occupiers' in the form of heavily armed IDF units. But dozens of

† The total number of terrorists captured by the IDF in Lebanon was approximately 7,500.

attackers have succeeded in reaching the security fence of barbed wire, electronic sensors and a sandy road which allows the Bedouin and Druze tracker to see any footprints made by infiltrators. In 1987 alone, the IDF and the Border Guards protecting northern Israel killed 230 Palestinian and Lebanese Shi'ite terrorists. Among the more important incidents were:

19 April. Eighteen *Hizbollah* terrorists killed in a mass, suicidal charge against SLA and IDF positions just north of the Israeli border.

6 September. A Border Guard patrol picked up A'li al-Rahman, an Egyptian recruited by Syrian intelligence to carry out a suicide attack against an IDF patrol.

4 October. A force of Golani Brigade infantrymen intercepted a five-man *el-Fatah* force along the security fence, who were heading towards Nahariya to take hostages and, according to their written orders from PLO Command, 'commit widespread murder.'§

Although the IDF retaliated with force against every terrorist attempt to infiltrate into Israeli territory, one unique terrorist attack that year was to have unforeseen political repercussions, as well as once again bringing the Border Guards to the forefront of the war against terrorism.

Sticks against Stones
Legacy of Lebanon:
the Border Guards v. the Intifadah

At the time when remnants of the Border Guard's 20th Company shared a joint security role with IDF units along the Lebanese frontier and 21st Company resumed its routine internal security duty in Galilee, a unique and historically significant terrorist attack took place near a northern Israeli city long synonymous with terrorism, murder and massacres.

The IDF were vigilant patrollers of both the Security Zone they had created in Lebanon and the northern frontier security fence. The soldiers manning the border in Command Cars and APCs realized that their gunsights aimed across the concertina wire and minefields was *the* decisive factor in preventing bands of marauding Palestinians from entering Israel and committing a massacre such as the ones perpetrated in Ma'alot, Misgav Am and Kiryat Shmoneh years earlier. They had attempted to infiltrate into Israel through a variety of cunning means,

§ In 1988 the number of incidents increased three-fold, amounting to 26 attempts – twelve made inside the security zone and fourteen along the northern fence. Twenty Israeli soldiers and policemen were killed in the fire-fights, which also killed dozens of Palestinian terrorists.
   The greatest number of infiltration attempts were made in April, the start of Israel's 40th anniversary celebration, resulting in several Israeli casualties, especially among *Giva'ati* Brigade forces stationed along the precarious Mount Dov sector. Most of the attackers were terrorists under the command of Doctor George Habash's PFLP, and Nayif Hawatmeh's DFLP.

ranging from cutting their way through the wire obstacles with clippers, to crude and unsuccessful attempts to tunnel under. To avoid detection by Israel's Bedouin trackers, the terrorists went so far as to coat their fatigues in the excrement and blood of sheep and wrap their rubber-soled shoes in goat skins. In 1980–1 ingenious attempts were made by terrorists from the Palestine Liberation Front commanded by Muhammad Zain Abu Abbas of *Achille Lauro* fame to cross into Israel by hot air balloon and hang-glider. Both attacks ended in embarrassing failure.

At 2130 hours on 25 November 1987, Maludin A-naja, a terrorist from Ahmed Jibril's Damascus-based Popular Front for the Liberation of Palestine General Command (PFLP-GC), allowed the Lebanese mountain winds to carry his motorized red-and-white hang-glider high across Israel's security fence into a field of thorny mountain flowers. He was armed with an AKMS, a silenced Tokarev pistol and dozens of grenades. He was to have been joined by a second airborne comrade to attack a block of flats in Kiryat Shmoneh and take hostages, but the second terrorist's hang-glider suffered engine failure and crashed inside the IDF security zone. Alone, armed to the teeth and suicidal, A-naja took it upon himself to change the objective of his mission and proceeded towards the IDF base at Beit Hillel – only 200 metres down the road. His foray would be the first Palestinian terrorist attack against an IDF installation in Israel proper since the 1960s and would contribute towards one of the more bloody and controversial periods in Israeli history. As fate would have it, the high-flying terrorist chose his target well.

The base at Beit Hillel was home to a Fighting Pioneer Youth (*Na'ha'l*) infantry battalion, a force of farmer-soldiers who split their three-year national service between military training and agricultural toil on frontier settlements. Their ranks were once filled with the most dedicated, able-minded and able-bodied of Israel's conscriptable men, and they were considered the IDF's *premier* strike force. During the war in Lebanon, however, their units suffered very badly, absorbing a disproportionate number of dead and wounded which many attributed to poor leadership and a lack of combat proficiency. Some half-a-dozen such infantrymen were taken prisoner in Lebanon by guerrillas from the PFLP-GC. They were seized as a result of their own negligence and, much to the outrage of the Israeli public, later exchanged for *1,150* convicted Palestinian terrorists in Israeli gaols – many of whom jubilantly returned to their homes in the West Bank and Gaza.

This particular night, intelligence reports had warned of a possible terrorist attack in the Kiryat Shmoneh area and a state of high alert was ordered, but precautions were ignored at the *Na'ha'l* encampment. After Israeli ground radar had observed A-naja's hang-glider in flight, urgent orders were issued to *all* IDF northern bases to gear up for battle, but the farmer soldiers at Beit Hillel continued their off-duty activities of reading, sleeping and playing backgammon. In fact, only one inexperienced soldier, Private Roni Almog, manned the perimeter gate.

A-naja's first target as he raced towards Beit Hillel was an IDF Peugeot tender. He placed his AKMS on full-auto and raked the vehicle with incessant bursts of 7.62mm fire, killing the officer driving it and critically wounding a female soldier passenger. The muffled crackle of automatic gunfire should have stirred the base into a decisive response, but it did not. By the time A-naja reached it, firing wildly and throwing grenades, Private Almog was overcome by fear and left his post without even firing a warning shot. Once inside the camp, A-naja was in a perfect position to fulfil the murderous deed for which his mentors in eastern Lebanon had so calculatingly trained him. Squeezing off bursts of fire indiscriminately and throwing grenades, A-naja managed to kill five infantrymen and wound dozens of others before a wounded sergeant managed to hit the young terrorist with fire from his *Galil* assault rifle. That dark and ominous night in northern Israel would become known as the 'Night of the Hang-Glider'.

Days later, a cycle of irreversible bloodshed between Arab and Jew commenced in what became known as the *Intifadah* or uprising. In early December 1987, a semi-trailer truck driven by an Israeli worker in Gaza accidentally ran over a group of four Palestinian workers waiting at a bus stop – killing them all. Their tragic deaths proved to be the spark which lit the discontent felt by the inhabitants of the Israeli-occupied West Bank and Gaza; they expressed their hatred for the occupying force with violent outbursts of rioting and nationalistic yearning. For the first time stones and deadly Molotov cocktails were directed against the Israeli soldiers policing the area. The killing of the six *Na'ha'l* infantrymen in the north revealed the once much feared Israeli soldier to be a real and tangible target. With their shield of invincibility no longer a factor, the Palestinians were able to express their rage, frustration and bitterness in explosive fashion.

Gaza was the principal centre of the riots and incidents of stone-throwing, but the popular uprising soon spread to the West Bank towns of Hebron, Nablus, Ramallah and, at Christmas time, even to Bethlehem. Outlawed Palestinian flags soon appeared throughout the occupied territories, as did posters of Arafat, Habash and Jibril. The breakdown of law and order was obsolute. General strikes were ordered by secret PLO directives pulblished by covert printing-presses, and mobs of fearless youngsters known as the *shabab* kept perplexed and overwhelmed IDF units at bay.

The *Intifadah* was soon much more than a spontaneous public uprising. The United Palestinian Leadership emerged to try and direct it and exert some form of PLO control over events; the 'outsiders', those in exile in Syria, Jordan and elsewhere, were surprised to find the 'insiders', those living under Israeli rule, expressing themselves in this way and attempted to lend assistance via coded radio broadcasts from 'Radio Monte Carlo' – the PLO's powerful radio station. On the ground, various PLO elements were soon represented who began to organize resistance committees much more efficiently and to try to co-ordinate disturbances in the streets. The particular factional allegiance of the *shabab* was represented by the colour of the traditional *kefiyeh* or headscarf worn. A stone-thrower allied to Yasir Arafat's *el-Fatah* factions would wear a *kefiyeh* adorned with a black design, while one adhering to a more radical group such as the PFLP or PFLP-GC would wear a red *kefiyeh*. The most feared 'colour', in what amounted to gang warfare, was the green *kefiyeh* of the Islamic fundamentalists.[11]

The IDF initially responded to the challenge of the *Intifadah* with traditional performances of blinding tear-gas and mass arrests – but the uprising was larger than any Israeli Defence Ministry strategist could ever have foreseen. When the riots increased in ferocity and Israeli casualties began, the use of live ammunition was ordered and Palestinians were killed. The rapid death toll of protesting teenagers inevitably resulted in negative publicity for Israel: images of heavily armed Israeli soldiers firing tear-gas canisters and bullets at point-blank range into crowds of teenagers led to an outcry from many of Israel's Western allies.

In fact, one of the factors exacerbating the spreading fires of the *Intifadah* was the absence of a decisive Israeli solution. For an army known for establishing innovative solutions to impossible situations, the absence of a distinctive IDF policy was embarrassing to the Israeli hierarchy, especially to Defence Minister Yitzhak Rabin and Chief of Staff Lieutenant-General Dan Shomron – a man known as a master of problem-solving, since his command of the 1976 Entebbe rescue operation. Yet both men knew that they faced a political struggle which could not be resolved by military means. As they waited for the politicians, or a miracle, to quell the rage of the *Intifadah* and its attendant growing international support for the Palestinian cause, the death toll mounted. The political drawbacks of shooting protestors led to the issuing of wooden batons to soldiers and a policy of 'break their bones' was ordered. While the scenes of Israeli infantrymen shooting indiscriminately into crowds and beating Palestinian teenagers to death with firmly held clubs still enraged world opinion, the use of supposedly less-fatal rubber and plastic bullets was ordered. For Israel, suppressing these uncontrollable demonstrations of frustration was a public relations nightmare. The once admired IDF was now likened to the brutal SS and South Africa's repressive security forces. PLO Chairman Yasir Arafat seized the political initiative in countries where his gunmen once wreaked havoc, and his decision to accept the right of an Israeli State to co-exist with any Palestinian nation brought international credit and gentle nods of approval from Washington.

The end of 1988 brought the *Intifadah*'s first deadly year to a close. Throughout the West Bank and Gaza, more than 400 Palestinian men, women and children had been killed and countless others wounded. The Israelis erected a detention facility in the Negev Desert called 'Ansar 3' (a reference to the makeshift prison of the same name near Tyre during the war in Lebanon). 'Ansar 3' housed thousands of arrested young men whose 'crimes' ranged from merely showing the Palestinian flag to throwing Molotov cocktails at crowded passenger buses. Dozens of *Intifadah* ringleaders were captured and exiled to Lebanon, while the homes of convicted stone- and petrol-bomb throwers were demolished by Combat Engineer sapper units.

Other counter-*Intifadah* tactics were also tried. In October 1988 it was revealed that Israel had set up two specially trained, clandestine military units. These were code-named 'Cherry' or *Duvdevan* (the West Bank unit) and 'Samson' or *Shimshon* (the Gaza Strip unit). They were developed to smash the leadership and *esprit de corps* of the uprising head-on, and had *carte blanche* to use whatever means necessary to perform their duties. The soldiers were armed with light, concealed weapons and posed as Palestinians as they toured the territories in confiscated vehicles with Arab licence plates. Their tactics were effective and their results were immediate but controversial. In Gaza, soldiers from a Samson unit were reported to have posed as a group of Arab workers and savagely beaten and then arrested a PLO enforcer squad threatening to kill shopkeepers unwilling to comply with a PLO-ordered strike. They also posed as PLO agents from rival factions in attempts to spark internal dissensions and violence. In the West Bank, Cherry units had equal success; it was as a result of their activities here that journalists unearthed their existence when investigating Palestinian claims of 'Death Squads'. It was said that they had machine-gunned to death two Palestinian strike leaders in the town of Yatta near Hebron on 9 October; two men in plain clothes driving a blue van had been seen killing the men.[12] Such exposure soon had Shin Bet agents masquerading as journalists and cameramen to gain intelligence and increase the risks for and limit the proliferation of bona fide reporters. Another killing, this time by a sniper, was claimed in the village of Yabat and periodic 'claims' have been made constantly ever since, including agents dressing as tourists and then opening fire. These more organized and covert actions, targeted directly at grassroots organizers of the uprising, were an ominous development and signalled a trend towards 'discreet' forms of warfare.

The IDF also attempted to defeat the rebellious Palestinians with technology, including a monstrous vehicle fitted with a specially designed cannon to fire marbles or gravel at demonstrators. This was known as the *Hatzazit* or 'Demon of Unrest' and, needless to say, its successes were limited. Now, it is reported that hot air balloons are going to be deployed over camps to observe trouble spots and direct troops on the ground via live relay pictures.

As the number of Palestinian dead grew and the *Intifadah*'s objective of bringing about a Palestinian State remained unrealized so, in the face of increased Israeli tenacity, bolder and more violent means of resistance were found, and several Israeli soldiers patrolling the *casbah*s of Hebron and Nablus were killed when heavy blocks of concrete were dropped on them. It also came to light that Palestinian terrorists, sometimes disguised as Orthodox Jews, had begun to abduct hitch-hiking Israeli soldiers and brutally murder them. These trends, indicating a more deadly Palestinian campaign – signs supported by several rare firearm incidents – led to a meeting of minds between OC Central Command Major-General Amnon Mitzna and OC Southern Command Major-General Yitzhak Mordechai, the two men entrusted with neutralizing the uprising. Both generals were highly experienced combat leaders and Mordechai in particular was quite familiar with terrorist tactics and the iron hand needed to suppress them. The one thing upon which both men agreed was the failure of attempts by the IDF to douse the uprising. Conscript combat units were losing invaluable training time fighting teenagers, while the reservists, brought into the fray for 62 *days a year* for their patient and moral leanings, were equally ineffective. An unflinching police force was needed and the call once again went to the Border Guards.

The decision to bring the Green Berets into the fight took almost a year in coming, but should have been Israel's obvious response from the start. The Border Guards had extensive experience in security duties inside the territories and had long ago mastered the most effective means of quelling violent disturbances. They were the only combat-type unit trained in riot-dispersal, the only force with tear-gas canisters as a staple weapon and the only force at Israel's disposal able to understand the mentality and cultural expressions and aspirations of the local inhabitants caught in the crossfire of rebellion.

Experience and age were also factors in the decision to send in the Border Guards. Men aged 40–50, who had survived security operations such as Gaza in 1970 and Lebanon in the 1980s, were not as likely as the young IDF conscripts to respond to mere stones and taunts with bursts of automatic gunfire. One of the first Border Guard units sent into the *Intifadah*-affected areas was the re-built 20th Company, who patrolled East Jerusalem amid hails of stones, petrol bombs and hand grenades – one of which claimed more than a dozen 20th Company wounded in the Old City. Statistically, Border Guard units showed the greatest patience before opening fire; they also reported the fewest percentage of casualties when neutralizing a riot, or demonstration.

In the past, Border Guard units stationed in the West Bank and Gaza Strip had managed to keep the peace – often, admittedly, by way of harsh methods. When a terrorist incident occurred in Hebron or Nablus, for example, the Border Guards would enforce a curfew then bring all the males of the district between the ages of 10–60 into the local mosque – and keep them there until, a name, witness, or confession was obtained. Their unconventional service in the territories was reflected in their often distant relationship with the local populace. It was a well-documented fact that Druze Border Guards frequently brought their wives to the Nablus *suq* or marketplace for Saturday shopping (a practice stopped when a Border Guard policemen was fatally stabbed while haggling in 1985) and it was said that many Border

Guard NCOs were proud and overt clients of West Bank brothels, whose receipts, ironically, often financed a fair portion of Palestinian terrorist activity in the territories and inside Israel proper.[13]

The Border Guards' intimacy with the occupied areas and their inhabitants might have been one of the factors calling for their entry into the territories' crowds, but their violent history was certainly a substantial contributing factor in the initial decision to deploy the IDF instead of the Green Berets. With the world's media paying such close attention to the unfolding events in the territories, the IDF might have wanted to prevent the Border Guards' unpredictable behaviour from being transmitted on world-wide news broadcasts. The men of Kfar Kasem might have been summoned once again, but massacres were to be prevented at all costs; such a hope was soon shattered.

When the first Border Guard companies reached the Gaza Strip in March 1989, they were sent into the heavily populated city of Gaza as a vanguard force, the IDF playing only a support role. Their entry was impressive and their presence felt immediately. Along Nasser Street, Gaza's 'front line' of Palestinian nationalism, women who once hurled petrol bombs at the mere sight of an IDF patrol now ran in fear at the sight of a Green Beret. According to a resident of Gaza's notorious Jebalya refugee camp, 'When the *shabab* saw the red berets they threw rocks and stones and petrol bombs. When they saw the purple and brown berets of the *Giva'ati* and Golani Brigades, they threw from far away. When they now see the dark green beret of the Border police, they get the hell away and fast!'

In the proud words of Riyad, a Druze company commander in northern Gaza, 'Two jeeploads of Border Guards can hold the Shatta refugee camp with less incident than a full battalion of reservists.' Reputation alone would not spare the Border Guards from the violence, however. On 23 March 1989 three Border Guard policemen were critically stabbed in Gaza by three wanted PLO terrorists during a routine patrol of the city.

The distinctions between the IDF and the Border Guards in dealing with the *Intifadah* were striking. The sight of middle-aged reservist soldiers in bulky combat gear awkwardly chasing lightfooted Arab youths was an embarrassing cause of concern among senior IDF officers trying to quell the attacks. Although they were excellent warriors in past conventional combat, the IDF's conscripts and reservists proved to be lousy policemen! The young, inexperienced conscripts often lost their tempers when youngsters spat at them and insulted their mothers and sisters. Reservists on the other hand, spent as much time cooling the conscripts down as they did worrying how to return safely to wives, children and unattended business. It also took the IDF units weeks of painful and eventful foot patrols to familiarize themselves with the local alleys, hiding-places and caves, as well as when to recognize the tell-tale signs of trouble. By the time they had mastered their area of operations, they were rotated by another force of 'green' soldiers.

The Border Guards on the other hand were able to use age to their advantage because it meant experience; they were used to being stationed in one specific area for lengthy periods of time. Operationally, the policemen were divided into small teams, usually driving fast jeeps, boasting effective radio communications with superior officers stationed at conveniently located central command posts. The Border Guard officers tended to be older and more experienced than IDF officers and, as a result, a 40-year-old Border Guard company commander would judge a dangerous and developing situation far more calmly than an IDF lieutenant straight out of officers' course.

Another contrast between the IDF and Border Guards existed in the bureaucracy of size. While IDF combat units are built around an enormous, almost overwhelming command and control apparatus, the Border Guards function in a thrifty manner, affording quicker decision-making in unconventional crises. The integrated configuration of the Border Guards' Jewish, Druze, Circassian, Bedouin and Christian policemen also prevented volatile situations from exploding into bloodshed. A Druze policeman, for example, would settle a potentially dangerous confrontation with a local leader over a cup of Turkish coffee, where an IDF officer might have used tear-gas and rubber bullets. The intrepid Gaza youngsters also knew that escaping deep into the labyrinth of the camps would not deter a pursuing force of Green Berets, who were quite happy to chase them anywhere.

Most importantly, perhaps, was the Border Guards' standard riot training received at their basic training base at Beit Horon. IDF soldiers would use their issue truncheons in attacking youths and for random beatings, while the well-trained Green Beret policemen used these same tools to push crowds back. The lack of IDF police training led to the all too many instances of soldiers shooting their way out of mob scenes, causing injury and death. Although the Border Guards were heavily armed, they were seldom *forced* to use their weapons.

The Green Berets' entry into the *Intifadah* seemed to have meant an end to the massive casualties, public relations setbacks and violence, but controversy could not escape the Border Guards.

On 13 April 1989, a Border Guard unit responding to the display of the outlawed Palestinian flag in the town of Nahlin, in the hills just south of Jerusalem, encountered crowds of youngsters hurling stones and burning tyres. The Green Berets responded against existing orders by placing their automatic weapons on full automatic and firing indiscriminate volleys of 5.56mm bullets into the crowds. Some have suggested that dum-dum bullets were used. In a matter of minutes eight Nahlin residents were killed and dozens of others seriously wounded before intervening IDF units managed to force their way into the chaos and rescue the town. Tragically, it was not the first time violence had come to Nahlin for in Operation 'Lion' on the night of 28/29 March 1954, a task force of paratroopers and *Unit 101* commandos attacked the Jordanian village, in response to the murder of a Jewish policeman in Jerusalem, and killed ten. The incident was one of the *Intifadah*'s most murderous days.

An IDF internal investigatory commission released its findings in May 1989 and found that Border Guard policemen had carried out an 'uncontrolled shooting' in an operation which was poorly planned and executed. The commission condemned two senior Border Guard officers for their role in the incident and ordered that the three officers commanding the operation be removed from their posts, and their senior officer reprimanded.

The killings at Nahlin was yet another stigma, in the vein of Kfar Kasem and the two Lebanon disasters, which had befallen the Green Berets. They seemed doomed to calamity, even though their vigilance, courage and experience has saved countless innocent Israeli lives. Unheralded and unnoticed in Israel due to their lack of flamboyance, the Border Guards continue their task of keeping Israeli citizens out of harm's way. Security operations along the Lebanese and Jordanian frontiers continue; as does the vigil at Israel's ports and points of entry, inside the major cities and throughout the isolated and rustic agricultural settlements. Through action, sacrifice and diverse areas of operation, the Border Guards are Israel's true guards without frontiers. Their work continues, and their full and eventful history cannot yet be written.

Caretakers of a most unpleasant Task

The Israeli National Police Sappers

'... *internal terrorism is after all a particularly barbaric form of unconventional war, and political leaders and decision-makers need to make* tough *and unpleasant decisions to safeguard the security of State and citizens.*'

Professor Paul Wilkinson[14]

Among the thousands of souvenirs that the IDF and the Border Guards seized in the Palestinian refugee camps near Beirut in the summer of 1982, were what appeared to be hundreds of plastic toys wrapped in cellophane. Found in cartons marked 'Made in Pakistan', the small toys, with dimensions of $11 \times 14 \times 17$ centimetres, were shaped in the likeness of cute dolls and cuddly kittens. Upon further examination, however, the Israelis were able to determine that these 'cute and cuddly' playthings were anything but playful: they were deadly. They were formed from 600 grams of cast TNT and, according to PLO documents seized in Operation 'Peace for Galilee', were to be smuggled into Israel and distributed to terrorist cells operating in the Occupied Territories. With only the slightest of modifications, a trigger or timing mechanism, the TNT toys were to be planted throughout Israel to explode as booby traps in the hands of the unfortunate souls who picked them up. The capture of these seemingly innocent items shocked many experienced IDF officers, but caused sighs of relief among a very select and enigmatic group of Israeli policemen who make their living beating terror head-on.

Terrorism in its truest form is pure, unadulterated theatre dominated by spectacular acts of destruction. By perpetrating hijackings, taking hostages and murdering protected diplomats, small obscure terror groups obtain international notoriety through their gestures. Yet grand acts are not the terrorists' sole domain. Their principal objective is, after all, to terrorize, to strike fear and to destroy all semblances of a society's normal existence. The terror groups comprising the PLO have run the entire gamut of means and methods for striking against Israel, from attacking her aircraft in Europe to massacring school children in her frontier towns. But on the whole they have met with bloody and disappointing failure. To keep the plight of the Palestinians burning in the hearts of every Israeli citizen, the Palestinians have traditionally resorted to the most effective, bloody and cowardly means of terror: the planting of bombs in public places – on buses, in schools and in crowded marketplaces. The task of combating this prolific threat has fallen upon the shoulders of the Israeli National Police and in particular their bomb disposal experts known as the *Hablanim* or sappers. If the Border Guards are Israel's unheralded combatants against terrorism, the sappers are surely the nation's busiest. They are a small but crucial element in Israel's struggle against terrorism.

In Israel *today*, the sappers are constantly being summoned by sightings of suspicious cardboard boxes and abandoned automobiles; any of which may conceal a sophisticated explosive device. In 1988 alone, the sappers responded to an astounding 49,378 calls from citizens regarding suspicious objects, 16,601 calls on potential car bombs and conducted 385,102 reconnaissance forays and deterrent patrols. Their courageous day-to-day operations have saved countless innocent lives.

For Israelis, both Arab and Jew alike, the sight of a 'suspicious object' is a cause of great fear and anxiety. The uttering of the phrase, 'Whose is this?' sounds a warning note and starkly reveals Israel's security predicament. During the years since the 1967 War when the physical barriers separating Palestinian and Israeli were removed, hundreds of Israeli citizens have been killed and maimed by exploding devices. Innocent objects turned into bombs have sadly become as natural a fact to the average citizen as the Mediterranean sunset and the rolling green hills of Galilee. In Jerusalem alone, more than 75 people have died from bombs camouflaged in anything from bundles of clothing to an open Norman Mailer novel. Travellers' alarm clocks packed with explosives have been planted in hotel rooms, saccharin bottles loaded with *plastique* and a timing device have been discovered in popular restaurants, and winter parkas abandoned on bustling city streets have been packed with enough explosive material to kill dozens and produce a five-metre deep crater in a concrete pavement. The planting of a booby-trapped explosive device inside the binding of a book can kill one unlucky individual and wound dozens, while a Volkswagen crammed with Semtex in a crowded Jerusalem thoroughfare might kill hundreds. These tactics are meant to bring terror at every turn and remind every Israeli of his precarious existence so long as the Palestinian problem remains unsolved.

The bomb was the Palestinians' chosen weapon during the years following the 'disaster of 1967'. They are relatively cheap to produce, easy to plant and destructive. The disguises are cunning – from abandoned suitcases to a loaf of bread with a grenade and trigger mechanism. In the mid-1970s, a powerful explosive device was attached to a crate of eggs and placed in a crowed market. An abandoned refrigerator full of explosives killed fifteen when it exploded in downtown Jerusalem and, in 1979, a potent amount of *plastique* was placed in an expensive racing bicycle chained to a lamp post in Jerusalem's busy pedestrian area of Ben Yehuda Street. It exploded before even raising an eyebrow among the already suspicious Jerusalemites, leaving two persons dead and wounding 38.

By turning the most innocent of objects into deadly weapons, the terrorists have attempted to disrupt the daily pattern of life and sense of security for Israelis. Their objectives have largely failed as a result of the Police sappers. This force of highly trained volunteers works tirelessly and skilfully to keep the towns of Israel from turning into a Beirut or a Belfast.

Prior to the Six Day War, the National Police boasted fewer than a dozen bomb disposal experts. Although bombs were a natural element, given the tumultuous history of the Arab-Israeli conflict and their earlier use by the Israeli underground, they were rarely used by Palestinian terrorists against Israeli civilian targets. The first police bomb disposal experts were mainly police pensioners who had been rogue sappers serving the British Army during the Second World War and who now received their training from the IDF. They were once kept very busy by responding to calls from irate farmers complaining of misguided military ordnance landing on their fields following IDF manoeuvres gone wrong, or from builders uncovering unexploded mortar shells during ground-breaking work. Their tools, training and operational methods were all obsolete, but sufficient to meet the then meek challenge mounted by Palestinian terrorists operating from across the frontiers.

The occupation of the West Bank and Gaza Strip after 1967 heralded a new era; when a powerful PFLP car bomb exploded in the midst of shoppers in Jerusalem's bustling Machane Yehuda Market on

22 November 1968, killing twelve and wounding 68, the potential for mass carnage was signalled for all to see. Although the police sappers were not yet properly mobilized to meet a massive terrorist bombing offensive, the Machane Yehuda blast was the last successful car bomb to bring double figure death tolls to Israel's streets. A significant contributory factor toward Israeli success was the fact that the Palestinian bombings were not co-ordinated into an effective operational strategy. Isolated murders were the norm.

In 1972, for example, the high point of Palestinian terrorism, both world-wide and inside Israel, Tel Aviv (Israel's largest city) employed a single police bomb disposal expert: Nissim Sasson. An ex-*Haganah* and British Army veteran, Sasson was the Israeli National Police's first sapper and served in its ranks for 22 years, responding to calls during the day and lecturing at universities, schools and symposia at night. On 1 February 1972, he was summoned from an evening meal to examine a booby-trapped package addressed to a senior police official from a Yugoslav return address. Unable to gain access to the Tel Aviv police's lone suit of protective gear, Sasson examined the package alone and unprotected. The booby-trapped device exploded and Sasson was critically wounded, severely disfigured and retired from active service. At that time, remarkably, only an inexperienced trainee was available to take Sasson's place and protect Tel Aviv from terrorist bombs.[15]

The true turning-point in the National Police's initiative in the war against bombings was 1974, when the police were given their internal security mandate. This was a year of terror on all Israel's fronts. A demoralized nation attempting a painful comeback from the shock and losses of the 1973 Yom Kippur War faced a mass of successful Palestinian attacks against her national aircraft abroad, against her northern frontier settlements and on her streets. In early 1975, in response to growing incidents of random and deadly bombings, senior police officers conscripted the services of an ex-IDF Combat Engineer lieutenant-colonel and created what is known today as the national sapper formation. They searched for volunteers, mainly IDF Combat Engineer officers and NCOs, who were keen for a challenge and looking for a unique and extremely pressurized working environment. Gathering such volunteers was initially a difficult undertaking for the National Police, a body which had a reputation for negativity, laziness, and incompetence. The police had a mandate to fill and they needed an élite group of well co-ordinated professionals.

For this group of newly gathered ex-military sappers, the transition to being policemen was not easy. They had been trained in the art of planting explosive devices, not neutralizing them. In addition, men who were schooled on conventionally produced hardware now had to master the intricate, diabolical and sometimes ingenious explosive devices employed by the various Palestinian terrorist groups. Their endeavours and capabilities were greatly enhanced by the work of the Israeli National Police Criminal Indentification Unit (CIU), whose work ranged from determining burglary fingerprints to corroborating terrorist devices with their parent organizations. They also painstakingly reconstructed exploded devices to provide the sappers with working models for the future, and a somewhat *ad hoc* but technically sound operational doctrine. Today, the CIU has mastered its craft to such an extent that it is the *sole* Israeli police body that investigates hostile terrorist activity (HTA).

Before engaging in a massive, unco-ordinated and ineffective campaign to rid Israel's streets of explosive devices, police planners realized public education was of paramount importance. The training, tools, technique and courage of a police sapper was useless if a woman walking her dog would not know enough to telephone the police emergency number when she sighted an abandoned suitcase. Not only did the police want the Israeli public to be their 'eyes and ears' they planned for them to be the front line of a deterrence force. Faced with an alert public, a terrorist attempting to plant a bomb in a marketplace or bus would have to try doubly hard and possibly make twice as many mistakes in order to achieve his task.

The enlistment of the public has also helped keep a human face on Israeli society. Were it not for the responsible reaction of the average Israeli in the war against terrorism, their streets would look like an armed camp with bags checked on every bus and the fragile liberties of democracy would be severely curtailed.

According to Deputy Superintendent Shlomoh Aharonishky, who at the time of this book's writing is the commander of the National Police sapper formation, 'Every Israeli citizen was transformed into a front-line soldier in the war against terrorism for a simple and pragmatic reason: Israel is too poor a nation to field hundreds of thousands of policemen and public participation is our only realistic resort!'[16]

As a result of this inherent lack of manpower, the sappers have been forced to instruct as well as serve. Realizing that its ranks were too thinly spread to protect airports, schools and large recreational areas, the sappers instructed workers on the intricacies of securing an area and preventively searching for explosives, as well as crowd control and evacuation techniques. Workers in Ben-Gurion International Airport frequently mount their own search operations (even though the Border Guards and Shin Bet both maintain a constant vigil of their own), schoolteachers regularly search classrooms for suspicious objects and not a single movie-goer in Israel can ever enjoy a film before having his or her bags thoroughly searched.

The police succeeded in educating a stubborn and fiercely independent-minded public through barages of mass media public service advertisements. TV commercials depicted seemingly peaceful locations, such as restaurants, playgrounds and beachfronts, where civilians milling about are suddenly decimated by powerful blasts originating from such docile objects as books, Coca-Cola bottles and wallets filled with cash. The commercials educated an already war-knowledgeable public on the wide variety of means employed by terrorists and of the advantages of an alert society. Daily ads were placed in newspapers and magazines reminding the public to 'stay alert'. In addition, stickers and large signs were positioned in every bus and post office giving the ominous warning: 'Beware of suspicious objects'. As a result, impatient 'strap-hangers' began to take notice of unclaimed kitbags and postmen began noticing bulky packages from exotic locations which appeared to be somewhat suspicious. Complementing this effort were large, red-coloured stickers placed on every parcel, warning citizens in Hebrew, Arabic and English 'not to open the package before checking the return address'. It is important to emphasize that funding for these commercials, posters and signs comes directly from the police's anti-terrorist budget.

No precautionary system, no matter how far-reaching, can be 100 per cent successful. Bombs got through and severe casualties were inflicted. Homes, offices and crowded commuter buses (particularly in Jerusalem) were destroyed by deadly blasts. Since 1974, the most notable incidents have been:

11 December 1974. A grenade attack in Tel Aviv's *Chen* cinema results in two dead and 66 injured.

20 December 1974. Twenty civilians critically injured by a bomb planted in Jerusalem's Zion Square.

28 March 1975. Eleven seriously injured by an explosive device planted on a No. 12 bus in Jerusalem.

4 May 1975. One woman killed and twenty critically injured by a bomb planted in a block of flats in Jerusalem.

4 July 1975. Fifteen killed and 62 seriously injured by a powerful bomb planted in an abandoned refrigerator on Jerusalem's Yaffo Street, adjacent to a crowded cafe.

27 October 1975. Eight seriously injured by a car bomb placed outside Jerusalem's Eyal Hotel.

13 November 1975. Six killed and 46 injured when a bomb planted in Jerusalem's Zion Square.

28 April 1976. Two police officers killed and four seriously injured by a booby-trapped box in Jerusalem's Shtrauss Street.

3 May 1976. One woman killed and 32 seriously wounded by a booby-trapped device on Jerusalem's Ben Yehuda Street. A female security officer was killed and eight critically injured when a booby-trapped suitcase exploded upon inspection at Ben Gurion International Airport. The West German terrorist carrying the suitcase was also killed in the blast.

18 August 1976. Eleven seriously injured when a bomb hidden in a bag detonated on a commuter bus between Kfar Saba and Tel Aviv.

11 November 1976. Four injured when a bomb blew up in a Petach Tikva supermarket.

24 April 1977. 31 critically injured when a bomb exploded on an Israeli commuter bus in the West Bank.

6 July 1977. A woman shopper killed and twenty injured by a bomb hidden in fruit bundles in the Petach Tikva central market.

27 July 1977. Eleven critically injured by an explosive device in Tel Aviv's bustling and chaotic Carmel market.

28 July 1977. 28 seriously injured by a bomb planted in Be'er Sheba's market.

13 November 1977. Two dead and four seriously injured by two explosive devices which detonated simultaneously in Jerusalem.

29 December 1977. Two dead and dozens injured by an explosive device planted near a sea-side cafe in Nahariya.

14 February 1978. Two dead and 41 injured by a bomb planted on a bus in Jerusalem's Geulah neighbourhood.

1 March 1978. Two senior citizens killed when a bomb hidden in a grove detonated in Tel Aviv's affluent Hadar Yosef suburb.

26 April 1978. Two West German tourists killed and six injured when a bomb planted on a tourist bus exploded in Nablus.

2 June 1978. Six killed and nineteen injured when a bomb blew up a bus in Jerusalem.

23 June 1978. Two dead and 43 injured when a bomb hidden in produce blew up in Jerusalem's Machane Yehuda market.

3 August 1978. One killed and 51 wounded when a bomb hidden in produce blew up in Tel Aviv's Carmel market.

19 November 1978. Four killed and 49 injured when a bus was blown up in Jericho.

28 January 1979. Two killed and 32 seriously injured by a powerful bomb planted on a Netanya street.

7 March 1979. Twelve seriously injured when a bomb blew up on a tourist bus crossing the Allenby Bridge between Jordan and Israel.

10 April 1979. One killed and 34 injured when a booby-trapped device blew up in Tel Aviv's Carmel market.

23 May 1979. Three women killed and fourteen seriously injured when a bomb blew up in Petach Tikva's Central Bus Station.

19 September 1979. Two killed and 38 injured when a bomb exploded on Jerusalem's bustling Ben Yehuda Street.

24 August 1980. One killed and eleven injured when a powerful bomb hidden in a rubbish bin exploded at a garage in Abu Gosh.

4 December 1980. Twelve critically injured when a bomb detonated in Jerusalem's King George Street.

25 February 1983. Five Bedouin killed and three wounded when their vehicle detonated a sophisticated mine device in the Negev Desert, planted by terrorists who had crossed the 'peaceful' Egyptian frontier.

6 December 1983. Five killed and 50 seriously injured when a bomb hidden under a seat destroyed a bus in Jerusalem.

7 July 1985. Five seriously injured when a powerful explosive device hidden near a bus shelter exploded at Holon Junction just outside Tel Aviv.

14 February 1986. Four critically injured when a bomb exploded on a bus in the Orthodox neighbourhood of Bnei Brak.

4 February 1987. Nine passengers seriously injured when a booby-trapped device exploded on an inter-city bus travelling between Haifa and Jerusalem.

Although the above-mentioned attacks are but a small fraction of those perpetrated during the years 1968–88, bombings have accounted for 22 per cent of the 8,000 terrorist attacks committed *inside* the boundaries of Israel by Palestinian terrorists. Although the attacks have been murderous, the overall Israeli murder rate remains well below those of many Western nations. In addition, each attack gave the sappers and their support personnel in headquarters, invaluable intelligence as to the terrorist's capabilities and what to expect the next time out.

Another source of invaluable intelligence for the sappers came from Lebanon. When the Border Guards were sent into Lebanon, the top brass at National Police Headquarters also saw fit for teams of sappers to assist the beleaguered IDF legions. The sapper *esprit de corps* was so great in fact that few teams had to be mobilized as many experienced officers rushed to volunteer.* In Lebanon, the sappers had a golden opportunity to view the enemy's capabilities first hand. By touring terrorist training centres set up in the ex-UNRWA schools of the refugee camps surrounding Tyre, Sidon and Beirut, the sappers were able to examine and understand how the PLO taught its disciples to produce explosive devices. Captured terrorists interrogated by IDF, Border Guard and police CIU officers provided additional data, including booby-trap techniques and where such devices were likely to be encountered next. The information was processed at the Israel Bomb Data Centre (known as the IBDC and one of six such departments world-wide) and dispatched to several 'friendly' European police forces who also have had their share of trouble with terrorist bomb-makers.† It is important to add that the Israeli sappers also received valuable intelligence from other police bomb disposal units, especially from the British and Spanish who encounter what are considered by InterPol to be the élite in the bomb-making field; the IRA and the Basque ETA terrorists.

What many sappers witnessed in Lebanon frightened them. In a country just a few hundred kilometres from the centre of Israel, tons of high-explosive were waiting to be used against Israeli targets. Although one police sapper was killed in Lebanon during the Border Guards' first

---

* Under Israeli military service laws, policemen are *not* required to serve in the reserves. Nevertheless, many sappers even put in written requests demanding an opportunity to return to their conscript IDF units and serve in Lebanon.

† On 8 March 1989, Israeli Police Minister Lieutenant-General (Res.) Haim Bar-Lev signed an agreement with his Italian counterpart ensuring an exchange of intelligence regarding counter-terrorism and criminal/hostile terrorist activity identification.

Tyre disaster, they left the country virtually unscathed but more experienced. As one sapper with dozens of Lebanon incidents behind him would wryly comment, 'For a sapper, Lebanon was the Oxford of universities.' Like a 'university student', a sapper is only as good as his internal discipline, his tools and his techniques.

A sapper 'attacking' a suspious object on Tel Aviv's Dizengoff Street is undertaking a dramatic act of life and death which requires an 'actor' of amazing qualities ranging from daredevil courage to even-tempered common sense. The requirements for being a sapper are simple: twelve years of schooling, a satisfactory military record (combat units only) and the yearning for a challenge. Naturally, not every applicant is accepted for the $600 a month employment. He must pass a stringent set of psychological examinations, followed by an intensive four-month training course and it is believed that less than half of those wishing to become sappers make it to the field.

Many find it difficult to understand the mental state of a person who volunteers to tinker with explosive devices. They are, on the whole, a quiet, highly superstitious (no photographs or mentioning of rank are ever allowed) family of fighters who fool about, play the lottery and gamble daily on their own very precarious existence. The certainties of their work are pressure and non-stop chaos. They do not don their Kevlar protective vest for fanatically induced bursts of patriotic fervour, nor are they cowboys eager for dangerous thrills. In fact, the sappers are on the whole as apolitical a bunch as one could find in Israel. They care very little about the politics of terrorism or about the motivations of the groups which plant the bombs. Their sole concern is how the device is put together and how it can be safely destroyed. The abstract world of the Middle East is of little importance to a sapper, who must worry about why one wire leads to another and the stability of the explosive agent he is handling.

Although many sappers will candidly admit that 'a sapper unit is only as good as the citizens who alert them to potential danger', their equipment is certainly one of their most important assets. Their tools range from the high-tech to the primitive. Obviously, the most important article of a sapper's equipment is the protective clothing. Specially designed Kevlar flak vest, Kevlar leggings and Kevlar helmets fitted with plexi-glass visors provide a semblance of physical protection from explosive devices. Although very heavy and cumbersome to wear in the average 30°C temperatures of Jerusalem and Tel Aviv, they are a necessity and are constantly modified for the sapper's specific requirements. Unlike a sapper in London, for example, who might respond to one call a day, an Israeli sapper will respond to dozens. While he will not gear up for each alarm, he *must* be able to get suited-up in a matter of seconds. The protective apparatus, which weighs more than 15 kilograms, is light compared to similar equipment used world-wide, but is highly effective. The Kevlar vest and leggings offer substantial protection from fragmentation, and the helmet, while hot and uncomfortable, is shrapnel-proof. It sometimes amazes the onlooker observing a sapper in action just how delicately he functions with his bulky layers of clothing, but the gentle movements of a sapper are what keep him alive. In addition, the sappers also wear khaki rubber-soled canvas *Patauga* boots which increase their agility and comfort. Completing their gear is a 9mm Beretta automatic tucked unobtrusively inside a back holster. They are, after all, policemen!

The Israeli sapper's second most important piece of equipment is his vehicle. The importance of mobility is crucial, as reaching a scene in seconds can be the deciding factor between an averted disaster or an explosion. The principal vehicle is the jeep. Fitted with a small illuminated sign identifying it as a sapper's vehicle, the jeep affords a team speed, all-terrain mobility and enough cargo space for two sets of Kevlar protective gear and other, smaller tools of the trade. The sappers also deploy from larger police vans, which house their third most important piece of equipment: the robot. Mechanized mini-tanks designed to handle delicate explosive devices, all bomb-disposal robots operate on the same principle. The robots move on six to eight wheels, or on tracks, and are sufficiently manoeuvrable to climb stairs and go around corners. They are fitted with video cameras to facilitate remote control operations via a monitor in the van and have high-powered lamps for night-time operations.

The *Hablanim* primarily employ three types of robots: the British produced Kentree 'Hobo' Remote EOD Robotic Vehicle, the British Morfax Wheelbarrow Remotely Controlled EOD Vehicle and the Israeli-produced 'Bambi'. The Hobo is a large, six-wheeled vehicular robot controlled by cable or by radio via a console in a strengthened transit case. It carries all standard explosive disposal tools, including a shotgun, disrupters, an X-ray, sniffer, microphone, acoustic detector and telescopic boom. Because of its large size – 1.47 metres long and weighing 228 kilograms – it is primarily used for large suspicious devices such as car bombs. The Wheelbarrow is lighter (195 kilograms) than the Hobo, is controlled by a detachable 100-metre-long cable and uses a TV monitor to guide its tank-like treads.[17] The Bambi is the lightest of the three and has been designed to suit specific Israeli sapper needs.‡ Weighing less than 50 kilograms, the Bambi is meant for small explosive devices (2–10 kilograms), deals with approximately 75–80 per cent of all suspicious objects reported in Israel, and can be deployed from every police vehicle.

The robot is in fact the sapper's shield, allowing him to operate from safe distances while examining a suspicious object. Through their mechanical arms, robots can transport potential bombs to convenient locations while a shotgun fixed just below the video camera can fire a cartridge of tiny pellets into the explosive material and detonating device. The projectile pellets disperse the explosive material faster than

‡ The British-produced robots have also undergone classified Israeli modifications which make them more effective in Israel's unique environment.

it can ignite and, as a result, destroy the device before it can go off – contrary to the popular belief that it is simply blown up. The Israeli sappers rarely disassemble an explosive device in the costly fashion of the British experts who neutralized unexploded bombs dropped by the Germans during the Second World War. Such a practice is too costly in human terms; the national cemetery at Mount Herzl in Jerusalem is already home to too many sappers. Nevertheless, the sapper will eventually have to face the object alone and hope that luck, his training and his cool will enable him to write the obligatory report hours later.

The robot is not usually used initially, but comes into play if a suspicious object is deemed too risky to handle manually. Usually, a sapper will approach an abandoned attaché case or kitbag and make an immediate field decision. If a risk factor is possible, the sapper will disperse the crowd, gear up and generally hook a long cord to the object – giving it a sharp yank in the hope of spilling the contents open or disconnecting the detonation device. Its a tricky and volatile tactic and one meant to save time, as another 'emergency' call is always just minutes away.[18] Unfortunately, such a practice might result in an explosion, injury and property damage. Every victim of a terrorist incident is eligible for financial compensation from the Israeli Government and the sappers realize only too well that the money saved in legal payments means added equipment for their own use. In addition, the sappers have recently been supplied with portable X-ray machines, which can examine the contents of packages without the risk of haphazardly testing them with the unofficial 'yank technique'.

Actual explosive devices, once dealt with, are all stored in a macabre museum of destruction. In a cold storage room deep beneath the National Police headquarters in Jerusalem, hundreds of once potent bombs sit in a now peaceful display. The objects range in diversity from a piece of pipe, to a high school year-book, an old black-and-white television set to knitting needles jabbed in a ball of wool. All these objects are identical, however, in that they are entangled with wires, primitive timing devices and explosive matter. There are also hundreds of grenades in storage, ranging from volatile Ottoman-era grenades uncovered in excavations, to modern day Czech RG-4 anti-personnel devices captured in terrorist arms caches in the Judean hills. Also evident in the vast collection are some sophisticated devices produced by ex-IDF personnel who were part of an ultra-right wing terror group of Jewish West Bank settlers which was compromised by the Shin Bet in 1984. According to a senior sapper officer named Aharon, 'These devices showed some of the finest handiwork ever seen by the Israeli police.'[19]

The primary target of terrorist bomb attacks in Israel is, of course, Jerusalem, the centre of the Israeli national government infrastructure. Its historic and religious legitimacy as the Jewish capital is contested, and the city's enormous numbers of foreign tourists are enticing to the terrorist. As a result, the Jerusalem sapper force is Israel's busiest, as well as its most famous. With targets such as the Wailing Wall, the Church of the Holy Sepulchre, the Yad Vashem Holocaust Museum and the Knesset (Israel's parliament), the Jerusalem sappers must secure vast and numerous sites, as well as answer hundreds of calls on a daily basis. Although their exact numbers remain classified, their beleaguered ranks are kept busy by the residents of Jewish West Jerusalem and even Arab East Jerusalem. Both Jewish and Palestinian terrorist groups have planted devices in the ex-Jordanian half of the city. The Arab residents realize that death does not distinguish between Arab and Jew and they dial the 100 Emergency police number just as frequently as their Jewish counterparts.

To prepare Jerusalemites for the threat of bomb attacks, the Jerusalem sapper force frequently conducts surprise drills. In one such recent incident in February 1988, a white Subaru with different front and rear licence plates was parked at a crucial intersection in the Machane Yehuda market awaiting a citizen's call to police. The sappers were immediately summoned and a Hobo robot deployed. It gingerly approached the suspicious vehicle and examined its contents, uncovering two large gasoline balloons hooked to a wire-controlled timing device. After the crowds were dispersed, traffic diverted and the area secured, the announcement that 'this is only a drill' relieved hundreds of very anxious individuals. Similar exercises are conducted throughout Israel, from Nahariya in the north, to Tel Aviv, from the resort town of Eilat and its tranquil waters to the Gulf of Aqaba. While Jerusalem might be the terrorist's primary target, numerous bombings have taken a heavy toll in lives and property throughout Israel. In May 1988 a large explosive device was planted by terrorists from Abu Mussa's *el-Fatah*'s renegade faction outside the Israeli Stock Exchange in Ramat Gan, but it detonated prematurely and missed killing crowds of employees.

The success enjoyed by the Israeli National Police sappers in safeguarding Israeli society from harm is continuous. As police capabilities increase, so do the means employed by the terrorists. The thousands of tons of high-explosives available through the arsenals of terrorist groups in Lebanon, coupled with their bomb-making skills, remain an ever-ominous threat the sappers will one day have to deal with. Because the Israeli borders, no matter how vigilantly patrolled, can never be completely sealed, the ingredients needed to manufacture a bomb will always be available. Stolen IDF ordnance and explosives obtained from the flourishing Israeli underworld, have also made their way into the hands of terrorist bomb-makers and on to the Israeli streets.

The potential also exists for terrorist bombs to employ chemical and even nuclear ingredients. In addition, powerful car bombs and letter bombs have once again appeared, prompting many to fear that with the *Intifadah* in its full fury, and growing Arab investment in chemical agents under way, the stakes in the sapper's war against terrorism have been raised. Shlomoh Aharonishky refers to the thousands of bomb sightings and alerts as 'nationalistically motivated'.

It seems that the phrase 'Whose is this?' will continue to be uttered in fear and the howling sirens of racing sapper jeeps will continue to be an integral element of life in Israel for years to come.

4. Israel's Naval and Air Campaign against Terrorism

'The carrying out of sea warfare by Palestinian fighters is an expression of the firm decision to continue and to escalate this armed struggle, whatever the difficulties may be ...'
Abu Jihad (*Al-Anba*, Kuwaiti daily newspaper, 24 February 1985)

On 21 October 1986, the scene in Athens' seedy Syngrou Avenue was typical as dozens of prostitutes, transvestites and heroin addicts cruised the filthy thoroughfare for a quick hustle. Yet the routine of drug abuse and rented sex was disrupted at 0200 when a car bearing rental licence plates erupted in a fiery explosion. The blast had been caused by a powerful, well-placed bomb which sent more than a hundred ball bearings through the driver's head, lungs and torso. The injuries inflicted were so horrendous the coroner had to submit what remained of the body to laboratory test to determine the gender. Although the murdered person's identity remained a mystery for some time to Athens Police officials, he was well known to senior members of the Palestine Liberation Organization for his name was Brigadier Monzer Abu Ghazala and he was the operations commander of Yasir Arafat's *el-Fatah* seaborne commando forces. The PLO quickly blamed Mossad for his death and claimed he was but another casualty in the 'naval war for Palestine'.[1]

Another casualty was the Haran family of the northern Israeli coastal city of Nahariya.

On the night of 22 April 1979, a heavily armed four-man terrorist squad from the Abu Abbas Faction of the Palestine Liberation Front (PLF) landed on Nahariya's picturesque sandy shore. After beaching their Zodiac rubber dinghy along a rocky breakwater, they gathered their AK-47 assault rifles and rucksacks loaded to capacity with banana-clip magazines and grenades and went looking for victims. Under the cover of darkness, the terrorists roamed stealthily through the empty streets of the sleepy town. They entered a block of flats and broke into numerous apartments in search of hostages. One flat they chose was that of Smadar and Danni Haran. They seized Danni and his four-year-old daughter and held them at gunpoint. Smadar had managed to take refuge inside a laundry cupboard together with her two-year-old infant daughter, whom she accidentally suffocated while trying to stifle the baby's screams.

The terrorists were preparing to make their stand in the block of flats when police units reached the scene. They panicked at the sight of an Israeli response force and, in a wild burst of gunfire, killed a Nahariya police officer. They then grabbed their two hostages and raced towards the beach for the final showdown. As hastily summoned IDF units began to arrive, one of the terrorists took a boulder and smashed the head of the four-year-old Haran girl, killing the child instantly before her anguished father's eyes. One terrorist then aimed the barrel of his AK-47 at Danni Haran's head and put the bereaved father out of his misery. Moments later, in a brief encounter with the vanguard of the IDF force, two of the terrorists were killed and the other two were captured.

The PLF attack on Nahariya and the massacre of the Haran family shocked and outraged most Israelis. The wanton savagery directed at innocent children brought a public outcry demanding the death penalty for such crimes, although the government resisted. The attack also underscored Israel's vulnerability to terrorist infiltration from a border not previously under serious consideration as a risk.

Israel's elongated border with Jordan, for example, is sealed with fortifications, barbed wire barricades, electronic sensory devices and heavily armed, mobile patrols who vigilantly safeguard the volatile frontier. This undertaking is complemented by Jordan's *own* curtailing of Palestinian terrorist activity on its soil. At the Adam and Allenby Bridges, the two River Jordan crossings which connect the two warring nations, all Arab visitors entering Israel are subjected to a lengthy body and property search procedure meant to prohibit the transfer of military equipment and terrorist paraphernalia into Israel. Vehicles carrying Arab goods into Israel are literally taken apart and then reassembled after they have been diligently searched by Israeli soldiers. A similar set-up attempts to protect the 'peaceful' Egyptian-Israeli frontier from terrorist infiltration, and the Lebanese border sees perhaps the greatest concentration of military force in the world.

As a result of the tight seal surrounding Israel's land frontiers, the Mediterranean has for years been the Achilles' heel of Israeli security. With approximately 180 miles of coastline, and most of the population centres concentrated along it, the coast appears indefensible and therefore an enormous segment of terrorist attention has been devoted to seaborne infiltration into Israel. Historically, such attacks have been the most murderous in Israeli history.

The Palestinians' naval war against the State of Israel began in 1967, when the creation of the 'Palestinian Arab Navy' was announced at a Pan-Arab meeting in Alexandria, just prior to the Six Day War. Initially, the Palestinians' seafaring capabilities were nil, consisting of little more than a few ex-guerrillas sporting naval uniforms, who envisaged large-scale attacks against Haifa and Tel Aviv. Following the 1967 War, the Palestinians saw fit to expand their naval efforts and enlisted fishermen, commercial divers and ship-owning smugglers. They managed to develop a small cadre of well-paid frogmen and naval commandos in a relatively short period of time and were able to enter proposed forays against Israel's coastline cities in their operating manuals. Oddly enough, the Palestinians' first waterborne point of access into Israel came from Jordan, across the waters of the Dead Sea. Using high-powered craft, Palestinian terrorists were able to penetrate Israeli territory and smuggle arms and explosives to cell commanders in the West Bank and, after a lengthy march, into the Gaza Strip as well. Their ability to cross the salt-water obstacle and then attack a significant Israeli civilian target was, however, minimal. Several Israeli air and paratroop raids in 1968 and 1969 succeeded in destroying these naval staging facilities altogether.*

In dozens of press conferences and political speeches following the 1967 defeat, various Palestinian resistance leaders vowed to open a new front against the 'Zionist entity'. After being defeated in the Gaza Strip and the Jordan Valley and after being expelled from the Hashemite Kingdom in 'Black September', the sea became their final option. Initially the concept of a Palestinian naval force was a communicational, rather than a military necessity. With Israeli forces sealing off most of the Jordan Valley to Palestinian guerrillas, the Sinai Peninsula entirely in IDF control and the Lebanese and Syrian frontiers extremely well protected, the sea was the only means to deliver important communications and instructions to agents in the Gaza Strip and the West Bank. In fact, a flourishing Palestinian guerrilla sea lane was established between Beirut–Gaza–Rafiah, with a well-run ferry service. Yet if agents and arms could be smuggled in from the Mediterranean, so too could heavily armed groups of attackers. Contingency plans were drawn up and men and women trained for battle. The Palestinians' first sea attack, however, would occur in entirely different waters.

On 11 June 1971, *el-Fatah* terrorists, operating from a speedboat, fired a volley of RPG grenades at the Israeli oil tanker SS *Coral Sea*, as she made her way around the Bab el-Mandeb towards Eilat. Although the attack publicized what were then rather covert oil shipments from Iran to Israel, it carried more anxious repercussions in IDF/Navy (*Heyl Hayam*) Headquarters in Tel Aviv. The use of speedboats, RPGs and mother ships represented new and fresh thought in Palestinian terrorist planning and signalled their intentions for a new front against Israel. Those fears materialized in March 1973, when PLO frogmen attached a mine to the hull of the Greek passenger liner SS *Soniyon* in Beirut harbour. *Soniyon*'s final destination was to have been the port of Haifa, but the mine detonated prematurely and the ship sank in Lebanese, not Israeli, waters.

---

* Today, the desolate waters of the Dead Sea are patrolled by the small, patrol craft called *Yatush* or 'Mosquito'. The ex-US PBR-type craft are armed with 2–3 light machine-guns (either .30 calibre or 7.62mm FN MAGs), a radar and have two geared diesel waterjets which make them capable of 25 knots. Although a little-known component of Israel's high-tech naval order of battle, they have denied Palestinian terrorists in Jordan access into Israel for almost twenty years.

On 25 June 1974 the *true* seaborne intentions and capabilities of the new terror front were displayed. Only a few kilometres off northern Israeli waters, three terrorists from *el-Fatah*'s *Force 17* lowered their motorized Zodiac rubber dinghy, from the deck of a Lebanese merchant vessel, acting as mother ship, into the murky Mediterranean. The Zodiac craft were loaded beyond capacity with thousands of rounds of ammunition, neatly packaged portions of high-explosives, dozens of grenades, combat rations, political propaganda and, most importantly, a map of the intended target: the town of Nahariya. Their plans for a massacre had to be drastically altered, however, when the heavily laden three-man team was discovered by a motley crew of part-time policemen from the Civilian Guard or *Mishmar Ha'ezrachi*. The guards, armed with antiquated M-1 carbines, were hopelessly ill-equipped to fight the terrorists, but their valiant attempts to do so alerted nearby police units and off-duty armed soldiers who raced to the area. The *Force 17* commandos were penned into a block of flats where they managed to kill a mother and two children before a unit from the Golani Brigade stormed the building and killed them. Although a greater massacre was averted, Israel's shores would never be the same.

At first, the IDF was baffled by the attack. Intelligence had indeed warned of intense Palestinian naval training, but terrorist attacks against vulnerable, heavily populated urban centres were hard to belive and, at the time, difficult to prevent. In 1974, the beleaguered IDF/Navy was hard put to defend the Israeli shoreline from terrorist infiltration. The small force had been built around a flotilla of extremely fast missile boats armed with Gabriel surface-to-surface missiles. In the Yom Kippur War, the IDF/Navy and its fleet of a dozen missile craft had been Israel's *sole* combat branch *not* caught by surprise by the Arab *Blitzkrieg*. The IDF/Navy was also the only combat arm that achieved an offensive military initiative during the early days of the war (during the eighteen days of combat, Israeli missile boats sank thirteen Egyptian and Syrian naval vessels without suffering a single loss). As a result of the sporadic 'war of attrition' still being fought against the Egyptians and Syrians along the front lines, the bulk of the missile and small patrol boat fleet were stationed on combat duty, safeguarding rear positions from attack by commando forces and intelligence-gathering units infiltrating behind secured lines. In 1974, the IDF/Navy encountered more threats than it was capable of handling.

The Israel Defence Forces have always adhered to an anti-terrorist doctrine of 'preventive retaliation'. On the night of 8 July 1974, this doctrine was transferred to the naval theatre as well. Under cover of darkness, an Israeli naval strike force systematically attacked *el-Fatah* naval training bases along the Lebanese coast, sinking more than twenty speedboats anchored in Tyre, Sidon and Ras as-Sheikh. The attack was meant to prevent a repeat of the landing at Nahariya, as well as push the amphibious raiders north, beyond the range of Israel. Israeli confidence in its Mediterranean shield was somewhat further restored on 10 August 1974, when an Israeli patrol craft intercepted a Zodiac craft attempting to ferry a heavily armed terrorist squad once again towards Nahariya. In a short burst of fire from the patrol craft's 20mm Oerlikon cannon, the infiltration squad were all killed. Three days later, IDF/Navy missile boats shelled the PLO's largest naval command base near Tyre with 40mm and 76mm cannon.

If the *el-Fatah* attack on Nahariya illustrated the vulnerability of Israel's Mediterranean frontier to the public, their bold and brazen seaborne attack on Tel Aviv in March 1975 pushed the naval theatre into Israel's front line against terrorism.

On the night of Wednesday 5 March 1975, eight *Force 17* terrorists, wearing camouflage fatigues and laden with ammunition, stood at attention on the deck of a freighter and saluted the Palestinian flag for the last time.† Then they threw their Zodiac craft into the choppy winter waters and commenced their short journey to the most significant of all terrorist targets in Israel: Tel Aviv. At 2315 hours, the eight gunmen landed undetected on a southern Tel Aviv beach. Jubilant at having reached the centre of modern Israel, they assembled their weapons and gear on the fashionable beach promenade and ran through the deserted streets firing and throwing grenades into the crowded 'Cinema 1' theatre. Nearby, two policemen on a stake-out expecting an underworld 'settling of scores' thought their shoot-out had arrived when they noticed the Palestinians' distinctive lizard pattern camouflage and returned immediate, though ineffective, gunfire. The terrorists ran into the small seafront Savoy Hotel and seized more than twenty hostages. As hundreds of Israeli policemen and soldiers surrounded the hotel for *yet* another terrorist siege, the failed rescue operation at the Ma'alot schoolhouse was at the forefront of everyone's mind and they vowed that it would not be repeated again.

The next morning, an impromptu rescue force of reconnaissance paratroopers, which, according to foreign reports, is thought to have been from the General Headquarters Reconnaissance Unit, and the Border Guards' *Ya'ma'm* commandos, broke through a hail of terrorist gunfire and burst into the hotel with guns blazing. Just as it appeared as if the attack would succeed, the terrorists detonated their dynamite charges as they had threatened to and the south-western corner of the hotel collapsed in a thunderous explosion. Eight hostages and three soldiers died in the débâcle, including assault force commander Colonel Uzi Yairi who carried an AK-47 captured during a February 1973 commando raid against Palestinian naval bases in Tripoli, Lebanon.[2] All but one of the terrorists was killed in the mêlée.

Israel Air Force aircraft and helicopters joined hastily summoned patrol and missile boats to search for the terrorists' mother ship, which

† Initial reports listed the terror squad as belonging to the notorious Black September Organization, mainly as a result of PLO offices in Beirut claiming that they belonged to the 'Abu Yusef Commando' named in honour of the Black September leader killed in Operation 'Spring of Youth' in April 1973.

they located hours later – a 150-ton ship without a name or national flag, heading fast towards sanctuary in Lebanon. Patrol boats escorted the vessel into Haifa harbour, where the crew was apprehended and interrogated. The ship had indeed ferried the terrorists towards Tel Aviv and it was learned that the operation had been the brainchild of *el-Fatah* military commander Khalil al-Wazir and enthusiastically approved by PLO Chairman Yasir Arafat. Khalil al-Wazir was better known by his *nom de-guerre* of Abu Jihad or 'Father Holy War' and had proven himself to be an effective terrorist planner. His name would feature prominently in spectacular events to come.

Following the successful Savoy operation, Palestinian naval training was accelerated in order to, according to captured PLO documents, bring death and destruction to the 'heart of Zion'. *Force 17*'s own naval efforts were complemented by expert training from Egyptian, Syrian and Soviet officers, as well as, it has been reported, ex-naval commandos and frogmen from Cuba and North Korea. It was in fact the Syrians who planted the seeds for the Palestinians' naval prowess by providing PLO officers with a two-year underwater combat and sabotage course. The small cadre of officers were then sent to various 'brother' states, such as Libya and Algeria, for further training and, finally, to advanced training facilities in friendly foreign countries such as Pakistan and East Germany. They trained in a meticulous fashion, concentrating on infiltration techniques, marksmanship and planting explosives (mainly to thwart any IDF-style rescue attempts once hostages had been seized). Most worrying to the Israelis was their penchant for suicide assaults and their readiness for martyrdom. As a result of the funding and unique attention the PLO High Command invested in them, *Force 17*'s naval warriors were considered an élite within an élite, prepared for dozens of spectacular operations, and only the very best candidates were chosen.

The objectives of the PLO's naval effort, as proudly proclaimed by Abu Jihad in numerous interviews, were:

■   To open a new front against Israel and to cause massive destruction, thereby necessitating the transfer of front-line forces from the Lebanese and Jordanian frontiers to the Mediterranean coastline.

■   To harass and depress the morale of the Israeli nation.

■   To infiltrate commanding officers, instructions and combat material into the Occupied Territories.[3]

The IDF was fully aware of the seafaring capabilities of the PLO and of *Force 17* in particular, and they attempted to destroy the Palestinians' naval threat by naval commando operations of their own. From July to October 1976, the IDF/Navy's Naval Commandos or *Kommando Yami* attacked the ports of Tyre and Sidon five times, destroying ships, ammunition dumps and facilities.

When Egyptian President Anwar es-Sadat began his historic *rapprochement* with Israel in 1977 and 1978, the Palestinians vowed to curtail the peace process through the bloodiest means possible. On 11 March 1978, they struck in another of Abu Jihad's well-organized operations – this time his signature of genius constituted the bloodiest seaborne terrorist attack in Israel's history. At approximately 0600 hours thirteen members of an *el-Fatah Force 17* commando unit, again code-named 'Kamal Adwan Commando', although on this occasion they were also said to be from the 'Dir Yassin Unit' (so named after the Palestinian village where Israeli forces from Menachem Begin's *Irgun* group massacred more than 200 Palestinian civilians during the 1948 War), boarded a small Lebanese fishing trawler off the tiny secluded port of Dabur, just due south of Tyre. They were all heavily armed and had enough ammunition for a protracted battle. The commander of this well-trained force was an 18-year-old female named Dalal Mughrabi, who had been expelled from Israel in 1969. She spoke fluent Hebrew.

After entering Israeli waters without being detected by ground or naval radar, the Kamal Adwan Commando force transferred into three Zodiac craft for the quick trip to shore. According to the plan conceived in Beirut, they were to seize a heavily booked hotel in the seaside Tel Aviv suburb of Bat Yam, take hundreds of hostages and demand the release of five Palestinian terrorist commanders held in Israeli gaols. Unfortunately for the terrorists, their navigating skill was inadequate and they landed approximately 50 kilometres due north of Tel Aviv, on the shores of *Kibbutz* Ma'agan Michael, halfway between Tel Aviv and Haifa. In addition to their navigating troubles, one of the Zodiac craft capsized at sea and the two terrorists it carried, laden with many kilograms of arms and ammunition, drowned immediately.

At 1600 hours the surviving members of the unit were ashore, had assembled their gear and prepared their propaganda leaflets written in Hebrew! But they could not understand where the hotels and crowds of tourists had vanished to. A few yards inland they encountered an American female photographer taking pictures of the wildlife; thinking the raiders were Israeli soldiers she was unperturbed and only realized her error when angrily asked, 'Where are we?' She was brutally killed. Hoping not to alert the heavily armed *Kibbutzniks* to their presence, the eleven raiders raced towards the bustling coastal highway connecting Haifa and Tel Aviv. After firing indiscriminately at the traffic, they commandeered two busloads of holiday travellers and headed south in a single vehicle, improvising their objectives as they neared Tel Aviv. Some of the terrorists thought their only chance of escape was to travel to Ben-Gurion International Airport and commandeer a plane to Lebanon. Operation commander Mughrabi, however, was determined to seize a hotel, not caring if it were in northern Tel Aviv or in Bat Yam.

The bus was stopped by a hastily assembled combined police-military force, including the *Ya'ma'm*, at Tel Aviv's Country Club Junction, just outside the middle-class suburb of Herziliya Pituach. A passenger took this opportunity to seize one of the terrorists' AK-47 and managed to kill three of the Palestinians. The sound of gunfire from inside the besieged bus was the green light for the Israeli assault since it was thought hostages were being systematically murdered. But a fire broke out on the bus and Israeli troops could not determine who was who! In the ensuing mêlée, more than 30 Israelis were killed (including a senior police officer) and more than 80 seriously wounded. Nine of the terrorists were killed in the battle, including Miss Mughrabi. Two terrorists escaped the night madness only to be captured hours later after almost 300,000 Israeli citizens were ordered into their homes while a massive search operation was conducted in Tel Aviv's northern suburbs.

The 'Country Club Massacre' demonstrated to every Israeli just how susceptible their coastline was to infiltration, even though the Savoy Hotel attack had led to increased vigilance with aerial and naval reconnaissance and shore-based radar defences. It should never have taken place for on 20 February 1978 an Israeli commando force had landed in the port of Tyre and sunk a number of *Force 17* speedboats, rubber dinghies and fishing trawlers in Operation 'Joy of Ages' ('*Hedvat Gil*'). Usually, IDF commando operations such as this discouraged terrorist operations for a time. The PLO's naval network, however, was so extensive and incorporated into the PLO's Order of Battle that a single Israeli raid, no matter how spectacular, could not thwart plans that were already afoot.

Prevention having failed, retaliation was taken when the IDF staged Operation 'Litani', a limited invasion into southern Lebanon during which 300 Palestinian guerrillas were killed and more than 5,000 sent north. Israeli missile boats blockaded Tyre and imposed a vehicular curfew along the once bustling Beirut coastal highway. The Israelis dedicated ten missile boats, at the time almost their entire flotilla, to the fray and fired more than 1,000 76mm and 600 40mm shells at Palestinian naval targets.

Following the bloody events of March 1978, the IDF/Navy increased its presence in the eastern Mediterranean. Missile and patrol craft attempted to secure vast pockets of open, supposedly international, waters while IAF reconnaissance flights beefed-up their operations, looking for any sign of a suspicious vessel approaching Israeli waters. On the ground, strategically established coastal radar stations were established to ensure that every kilometre of Israel's shore was covered in an electronic blanket of security. The *Force 17* response was to attempt a naval attack in an altogether different, and forgotten, theatre of operations.

On 30 September 1978, an IDF/Navy missile boat on a routine patrol of the Gulf of Aqaba, near the resort town of Eilat, intercepted the Greek freighter SS *Agaeus Dimitrius* as it headed towards Eilat from the Sinai coast at Dahab. The Israeli craft ordered the freighter to stop and identify herself, but the calls were ignored and a volley of .50 calibre warning shots were fired into the air. The *Agaeus Dimitrius* then made a desperate attempt to reach the Saudi shore, and the Israelis went to full battle stations. After the large and slow-moving target was acquired and the final warnings had been ignored, the missile boat's forward-mounted 40mm gun was unleashed. Its shells began ripping gaping holes in the freighter's hull, causing her to explode and sink. A total of seven terrorists were captured and interrogated. It seems they had planned to bring the freighter close to the crystal-clear waters off Eilat and then fire some 42 long-range 122mm Katyusha rockets at the seaside hotels crowded with Jewish New Year visitors. They were then going to run the freighter on to the crowded central beach and set off the three tons of high-explosives in the cargo hold. The terrorists hoped to leave the vessel at the last minute and escape to the Jordanian city of Aqaba in a Zodiac craft. If the attack had succeeded the carnage would have been horrific.

That same day, the IDF/Navy apprehended two terrorist mother ships, *Ginan* and *Stephanie*, in the Mediterranean *en route* to Israeli territorial waters. The *Stephanie* was to have sailed on a routine merchant route between Cyprus and Egypt past Israel and at a strategic point, close to its target, a small speedboat with a terrorist landing-party aboard was to have been lowered while still in international waters.

Although the last successful terrorist attack from the sea was the PLF's 22 April 1979 attack on Nahariya, Israel had paid a heavy price over the decade for her lack of prowess at sea. The IDF/Navy had always been the smallest and most neglected branch, but shore defence against lightly armed marauders rather than Egyptian, Syrian and Libyan missile-carrying cruisers was a national defence priority of the first degree.

From 1979 to 1984, an era which saw Operation 'Peace for Galilee' and the beginning of the IDF pullback from Lebanon, the IDF/Navy successfully thwarted thirty major terrorist attempts to infiltrate men and material into Israel. Many of the terrorist forays were deterred by patrol and missile-craft operations in Lebanese territorial waters, while a dozen terrorist craft were sunk *en route* to Israel's shores. Among the most notable incidents were: two failed attempts by the PLF to land at Nahariya and Rosh Hanikra in June and August 1979; the June 1980 destruction of a large terrorist craft heading towards *Kibbutz* Achziv; the June 1984 destruction of a *Force 17* craft six kilometres north-west of Tripoli in a fierce sea battle in which five Israeli sailors were seriously wounded; and the 20 October 1984 destruction off the coast of Lebanon of a mother ship *en route* to northern Israel. During this period, not a single terrorist infiltration into Israel through the Mediterranean was achieved.

Nevertheless, the PLO continued to invest heavily in *Force 17*'s capabilities and in its publicity value. In Beirut, their naval frogmen had regularly been paraded in full wet gear with their neoprene rubber suits and oxygen masks. Although many of these underwater terrorists would faint from dehydration in the hot Beirut sun during such military displays, they were touted as the 'vanguard force on their way to liberating Palestine'.

Perhaps the two most important and successful weapons in Israel's naval war against terrorism are the well-trained women radar operators and the agile and deadly *Dabur* patrol craft.

Although security considerations naturally prohibit the listing of the locations of IDF/Navy shore radar installations, they are numerous and cover the entire Israeli coastline. They are manned by female naval personnel, who all volunteer for the sometimes monotonous, though crucial task of tracking radar blips and forwarding the positions of all 'targets' to operation centres at naval headquarters. For the specific needs of the IDF/Navy, women radar operators are ideal. According to IDF studies, women soldiers are, on the whole, more intelligent, aware and meticulous in their duties than male soldiers. These radar 'eyes and ears' are considered the élite of all women soldiers.

Their skill and alertness would be pointless were it not for an advanced naval C^3 (Command, Communications and Control) infrastructure and the ability of the navy to co-ordinate and dispatch their second most important weapon into the fray: the fleet of 37 *Dabur* class craft. The *Dabur* or 'bumblebee' is an Israeli-produced small patrol boat armed with a wide variety of weaponry, including two 20mm Oerlikon guns, several .50 calibre and FN MAG machine-guns, 40mm grenade-launchers (not standard) as well as depth-charges and 324mm Mk 32 torpedo tubes for the American Mk 46 torpedo with ASW capabilities. *Dabur*s have a Decca Super 101 Mk 3 radar system and carry a complement of between six and nine, depending on the weaponry carried. With a speed of 22–25 knots, the vessel is fast and highly manoeuvrable and fully capable of meeting most of the craft employed by Palestinian terrorists.

To serve aboard a *Dabur* is at once the most relaxing and the most nerve-racking of military duties. Although such service is *not* voluntary, it is considered one of the élite combat forces within the branch. The crews are trained in a wide variety of heavy weaponry, such as the 20mm Oerlikon and the .50 calibre, as well as the lighter M-16/M203 grenade-launcher and *Galil* assault rifles in case a 'suspicious' ship has to be boarded and searched. Many *Dabur* commanders view their instinct as their most important piece of equipment. By knowing how to read a situation, such as boarding a suspicious ship, or dealing with a boatload of Lebanese fishermen who might be heavily armed *Force 17* terrorists, the commander's experience and intuition can be *the* deciding factor. The commanders are all young junior offices who must cut their teeth on the Bumblebee before getting the chance of a larger *Sa'ar* II, III or IV missile boat.

Safeguarding Israel's coastline is a task which often takes the Israelis to just off the Lebanese coast at Tyre where they search for the enemy and are often greeted by RPG, 14.7mm machine-gun and artillery fire. Although Palestinian shore fire has yet to claim its first *Dabur*, they are extremely vulnerable to the extensive modern terrorist's arsenal. Almost any Palestinian weapon can blow it out of the water, especially

RPGs and LAW rockets. As a result, IDF naval crews are trained to blast anything out of the water quickly and rely on the motto, 'Do unto others before they do unto you!'

The IDF/Navy's success could be attributed to numerous military, strategic and 'intangible' factors, but the Israeli experience in Lebanon is one which cannot be overlooked. When the IDF seized Tyre, Sidon and the dozens of sleepy seaside villages along the Mediterranean, they were quite impressed by the elaborate naval infrastructure the Palestinians had established. Bases, identifiable by small workshops had been set up for full-scale innovative production; these together with extensive arsenals were captured all along the Lebanese coast from the Israeli border to Beirut. Among the seafaring hardware the Israelis uncovered were:

■ Midget subs (bought in Western Europe from sporting goods store stocks) large enough to carry one determined 'suicide' terrorist.

■ Fast mini-reconnaissance ships obtained as a gift from Libya's Colonel Qaddafi.

■ Highly powerful fibreglass speedboats, some fitted with forward-firing 14.7mm machine-guns.

■ Dozens of rubber dinghies and Zodiac craft.

■ Tons of underwater and SCUBA gear and navigation devices.

Most ominous was the appearance of dozens of small, ingeniously designed rafts fitted with timing devices and multiple 122mm Katyusha rocket-launchers. Evidently based on the earlier SS *Agaeus Dimitrius*, the only possible use for such a ship would be delayed-action indiscriminate shelling of Israeli cities. With well over 50 per cent of the Israeli population living in Tel Aviv, Haifa and the other coastal cities, such attacks would cause enormous numbers of casualties. What surprised many IDF commanders was the innovation displayed by the Palestinians in their naval planning, especially its frightening resemblance to pre-independence Israel's fledgling naval efforts against the British *via* the *Haganah*'s sea commando force, the *Pal'yam*.

To protect their maritime investment, the Palestinians have attempted to obtain from the Soviets, the Western black market and from friendly Arab navies, small warships of their own and sophisticated coastal and naval radar stations. Seized documents also proved the suicidal nature of the planned PLO's naval attacks, as well as the logistical support such attacks were to have received from Abu Jihad's 'Western Sector' – the security command within *el-Fatah* which directs terrorist operations inside the occupied territories and Israel proper. In August 1982 and December 1983, after the expulsion of the PLO from Beirut and Tripoli respectively, *Force 17* was dispersed to the outer reaches of Tunisia, North and South Yemen and Algeria.

The loss of large segments of their Lebanon base might have severely hampered *el-Fatah*'s naval capabilities, but it did not destroy them. To keep the military and political pressure on Israel, as well as to underscore the futility of Israel's costly Operation 'Peace for Galilee',

Abu Jihad and *Force 17* commander Abu Tayeb (Colonel Mahmoud Ahmed Mahmoud an-Natour) decided to raise the ante of violence. This year 1985 was to be *their* year of decision, and the year the Palestinian naval offensive went international: from Israel to Italy; from Cyprus to Spain.

The Ein el-Hilweh refugee camp near Sidon is one of the most wretched places imaginable. Dirty, desolate, depressing and rat infested, it embodies everything that the Palestinians in the diaspora have endured since 1948. Its squalid homes and unpaved alleyways have become a tragic battlefield which, in the years since the Lebanese Civil War of 1975–6, has claimed thousands of Palestinian, Christian, Syrian and Israeli lives. Ein el-Hilweh is a frustrating place where hopes of a better life give way to fatal eruptions of rage. More than anything else it is a fertile breeding-ground for terrorists; here children learn the art of war at an early age; dying for one's national, or for that matter any, cause beats the hopeless misery of camp life.

It was for this reason, that Abu Jihad went to the camp to recruit a select group of young men who would be able to squeeze the trigger of an automatic weapon aimed point-blank at an innocent victim with zeal, and who would die willingly for a very special operation. It was to be a mission that would strike at the very heart of Zion and alter the rocky course of Middle Eastern history forever. When preparing the final details of the gambit in his Amman office, Abu Jihad chose a unit designation for his force which would embody the hate, fanaticism and desperation of the Palestinian revolution. The suicidal band of men chosen for this sacred sacrifice were to be called 'The Holy Martyrs of Ein el-Hilweh'.[4]

On the foggy night of 13 April 1985, Abu Jihad boarded the 1,000-ton, 60-metre-long SS *Attaviros* in an Algerian port for a ceremonious inspection. After supervising the planning, training and dress rehearsals for this historic undertaking, he was confident of his men's capabilities and of their chances for success. He joked with the captain, gave his men their final briefing, then saluted the assembled unit and the flag of Palestine for one last time. In all, twenty heavily armed *el-Fatah* terrorists clutched their AK-47s in salute; each had a specific task and each knew that in a matter of days he would be face to face with the IDF in an epic battle at the heart of Israel on the State's 37th birthday. The next night, they raised anchor and headed east.

A week later they were approximately 100 miles from the Israeli coastline when an IDF/Navy *Sa'ar* III missile boat located *Attaviros* heading suspiciously towards Israel. After several communication and identification attempts were ignored, the missile-boat commander realized he had not encountered an innocent merchant ship gone astray but a hostile vessel, whereupon he went to battle stations. At first Lieutenant-Colonel 'D', the missile-craft's commander, ordered flares fired followed by a volley of warning shots. These were answered by the tell-tale 'swoosh' of RPG-7 rocket-propelled grenades landing short of their mark, and incessant bursts of automatic fire from Soviet-made RPK light machine-guns. Cruising into a defensive position, the missile-boat retreated and prepared its radar-controlled 76mm gun for the inevitable battle. Minutes later, the *Attaviros* was pounded by well-aimed 76mm projectiles and sank shortly afterwards.

Although the Mediterranean waters were choppy and rough, Lieutenant-Colonel 'D' ordered a search for any possible survivors. Such a gesture was not simply a humanitarian one, the intelligence treasures an interrogated prisoner could provide were of enormous value. In all, eight Palestinians were plucked out of the sea while twenty of their comrades went down with the ship.

The objective of the *Attaviros* was simple: the 'Holy Martyrs of Ein el-Hilweh' suicide squad was to have landed on a secluded Bat Yam beach, seized several automobiles and headed for the *Kiryah* in Tel Aviv – a five-mile-square block compound which houses the Israeli Ministry of Defence and IDF General Staff Headquarters. It was Israeli Independence Day and the festivities of yet another year's survival were expected to have weakened the normally alert security apparatus around Israel's most sensitive base. After crashing through the *Kiryah*'s heavily fortified defences and overpowering the well-armed Military Police force guarding the installation, they were to have seized the General Staff HQ, taken dozens of hostages and demanded the release of 150 *el-Fatah* terrorists held in Israeli gaols. The terrorists fully realized that they were unlikely to be able successfully to negotiate their way *out* of the situation and had trained with diagrams and blueprints in planting explosives at strategic locations throughout the IDF General Staff HQ in order to kill as many of the enemy as possible before themselves being 'martyred'.

The attack would obviously attract international attention and highlight the PLO's claim to be the sole and legitimate representative of the Palestinian people, and its role in dictating the fate of the Palestinian revolution, in both its political and military forms. Abu Jihad gave an interview to the Saudi daily *Ash-Shark al-Awsat*, on 26 April 1985 in which he discussed the foiled raid:

> 'The action expresses the willpower and the strong determination of the Palestinian people to continue the armed struggle against the occupying enemy ... Our revolution will not forego the continuation of the struggle to hurt the enemy and to cause losses among his forces. The action is significant also as regards the masses of the Arab people, many of whom concluded, as they followed the PLO's political activity, that it was moving towards a political arrangement and political solutions, while in fact political does not preclude continuation of military actions.'[5]

Yet according to numerous reports, the operation's principal objective was the assassination of Israeli Defence Minister Yitzhak Rabin.[6] Even though the mission failed and Rabin's life was spared, the attempt represented a violation of an unwritten, secret 'gentlemen's agreement' against targeting the top leadership of either side. Abu Jihad, as PLO military commander, was therefore considered Rabin's Palestinian counterpart and now became 'fair game'. Yet before the Israelis would selectively deal with the elusive Khalil al-Wazir in their own way, further attempts to attack Israel by sea would be made, even as bodies from the *Attaviros* kept washing up on the Tel Aviv shore.

In the early hours of 8 May 1985, a *Dabur* patrol craft heading due east just south of Tyre spotted a small blip on its radar screen. The skipper followed routine engagement procedures by sounding battle stations and progressed towards the target. The ship turned out to be a small, motorized craft carrying five heavily armed *el-Fatah* terrorists *en route* to northern Israel. In a 30-second exchange the craft was blown out of the water by 20mm gunfire and all the terrorists were killed.

A few weeks later during a routine IDF/Navy patrol off the coast of Sidon, a 'suspect' merchant vessel poured heavy machine-gun fire at a *Dabur* craft, seriously wounding a sailor. Before the *Dabur* was able to achieve the offensive initiative, the merchant ship was heading back towards Sidon and the safety of Palestinian shore-based artillery batteries.

On the night of 24/25 August 1985, an IDF/Navy ship drew alongside the luxury yacht *Casselardit* as it sailed close to Israeli territorial waters. Israeli sailors boarded the boat and captured eight *el-Fatah* terrorists plus two foreign crewmen, an Australian and an American. After a lengthy, in-depth interrogation back in Israel, the terrorists admitted that their mission was to seize a commuter bus in Galilee and massacre its passengers. They had been trained in Tunis and Algeria then flown to Cyprus where they rented the yacht. The eight belonged to a new force within *Force 17* commanded by Abu Muatassem (a senior PLO military officer) which was to strike at Israel *via* the sea and also at Israeli 'diplomatic and intelligence' targets in Europe.

Six days later on 31 August 1985, the IDF/Navy seized yet another *Force 17* yacht attempting to infiltrate. The *Ganda* appeared more suited to the French Riviera than combat in the Middle East, but she was ferrying five veteran *Force 17* commandos towards another planned bus seizure in northern Israel.

Another major counter-terrorist *coup* pulled off by the IDF/Navy at this time was the seizure of the ferry boat SS *Opportunity* on 10 September 1985. She was on a routine midnight run between Beirut and Cyprus; the time and opportunity that this gave to travelling incognito made it a favourite among PLO personnel. That night, *Opportunity* carried one highly esteemed passenger, a man carrying tens of thousands of American dollars and Lebanese pounds and who held two passports. His name was Faisal Abu Sharah and he was a senior officer in *Force 17*. At this time, he was commanding the *Force 17* contingent in Beirut's infamous Shatilla and Bourj al-Barajneh refugee camps.

As Abu Sharah attempted a short night's sleep in his creaky cabin, dozing off with thoughts of his wife and children whom he would be meeting in Cyprus, he was woken by the blasting sounds of gunfire and blinding beams from searchlights. Seconds later, two fair-skinned soldiers in olive fatigues, carrying *Galil* and M-16 assault rifles, brusquely threw him out of his lumpy cot. They searched him for side arms and examined his personal effects, before blindfolding him and assisting him on to the swaying deck of an IDF/Navy vessel. He was taken to Israel and an IDF investigation centre for twenty days, then later moved to a Shin Bet facility 'somewhere' in central Israel. Twelve days after his capture, Defence Minister Yitzhak Rabin issued an administrative detention order holding Abu Sharah for six months.

The 21-year veteran of *el-Fatah* had 'escaped' Israel in 1964 for an active role in the Palestinian revolution. He volunteered for *Force 17* in December 1972 and served as a member of the Arafat entourage for almost a year. Although he had undergone a company commander's course in the Soviet Union, his specialty was logistics and the operational planning of terrorist attacks. Upon hearing of Abu Sharah's capture, *Force 17* offices in Amman, South Yemen, Algeria and Tunis were thoroughly searched for Israeli spies.

Although unable to uncover any Israeli intelligence agents in its ranks, senior *Force 17* commanders were convinced that Abu Sharah had been apprehended as a result of a security leak and not from the vigilance of the IDF/Navy. *Force 17* agents began intensive surveillance of all major Mediterranean ports used by their operatives, and of Larnaca (Abu Sharah's final destination) in particular.

On 25 September 1985, on Yom Kippur Day, *Force 17* terrorists, apparently targeting the first Israelis spotted as intelligence agents, stormed an Israeli yacht in the marina at Larnaca and murdered its three passengers – a middle-aged woman and two men. Although the PLO denied any involvement in the incident, the terrorists surrendered themselves to the Cypriot Police and confessed to everything. They admitted that they had been dispatched to Cyprus to kill Mossad agents; the three murdered on the yacht, though, were ordinary civilians on holiday – following an Israeli tradition of travelling to the closest and friendliest foreign neighbour for a quick escape from the frustrating routine of day-to-day life back home.

The three *Force 17* terrorists, believed to be members of Abu Muatassem's independent force, were identified as: Ali Nassif, a 24-year-old hired gunman who at one time guarded Yasir Arafat's office in Tunisia and had served the *Force 17* desk in Athens, where he would later take part in a failed attack against the Israeli mission; Mahmoud Khaled Abdallah, a 27-year-old *Force 17* veteran who had earned a fierce reputation as a soldier during the inter-PLO fighting in Tripoli in 1983. His commanding officer, a mysterious terrorist genius named Captain Turki, was captured by the IDF/Navy on the yacht *Ganda*; and Ryan Michael Edison, a 28-year-old British mercenary and neo-Nazi National Front faithful, who volunteered for *el-Fatah* in 1982 and served with *Force 17* in Tunisia and North Yemen.

On 1 October 1985, Israel took to the air in response to the *Force 17* naval offensive and the Larnaca murders in particular.

Israel has traditionally used its extensive military air power as a most potent weapon against terrorism. After its brilliant pre-emptive strike against Arab air forces on 6 June 1967, the Israel Air Force (IAF) has been justly considered one of the world's finest. Yet the IAF's ability to perform against conventional military targets in a SAM and MiG saturated battlefield environment has been overshadowed by its incessant campaign against terrorism. For every act of Palestinian terrorism committed both inside and outside the boundaries of the State of Israel, an IAF retaliatory air raid is an expected occurrence. Massive air raids against terrorist headquarters, training camps and installations have followed such terrorist incidents as the 1972 Munich Olympics massacre, the May 1974 Ma'alot massacre and the June 1982 attempted assassination of Ambassador Shlomoh Argov in London. Since September 1970, most of the attacks have been against terrorist targets on Lebanese soil.

The air raids have involved the IAF's principal combat aircraft, such as the A-4 Skyhawk, the F-4E Phantom, the F-15, F-16 and the *Kfir* series of attack aircraft. They have all been quick, surgical strokes meant to prevent large-scale civilian casualties, although these inevitably occur. While the raids are obviously destructive in nature, they also aim at keeping the terrorists occupied with their defensive precautions, rather than on proposed offensive strikes against Israeli targets. Most recently, the IAF has deployed low-flying helicopter gunships, such as the AH-1S Cobra and the Hughes 500 MD Defender, for selective, pinpoint attacks against terrorist positions. In Israel there are military observers who oppose the use of helicopters in such a role, due to their vulnerability to ground fire, but the whirling rotor blades and ability to appear from nowhere have had definite psychological advantages in the field.

To avenge the triple murders in Larnaca, however, the IAF could not deploy its fleet of attack helicopters nor could it settle for a mere retaliatory strike inside the Beka'a Valley, or along the Lebanese coast. The killings of the three Israelis and the prior attempts to infiltrate terrorists from the sea, amounted to a *Force 17* declaration of war and the Israeli military was determined to respond in kind.

Originally, a strike against *el-Fatah* naval installations and training bases along the Algerian coast was planned, but the positions were heavily defended by the effective Algerian Air Force and Soviet-designed SAM screens. Another possible target was Karaman Island, located just off the shores of North Yemen and home to '*Force 14*', the budding air component of *el-Fatah*. Although there is no Palestinian Air Force, *Force 14* is the nucleus for such and is made up of Palestinian pilots trained in Syria, Libya, Iraq and other friendly countries, on various combat aircraft such as the MiG-21 and MiG-23. In the mid-1980s, *Force 14* acquired several transport aircraft, helicopters and large shipments of SAM-7s. While an IAF attack on Karaman Island would not serve as just retribution for the Larnaca murders and the SS *Attaviros*, it would serve notice as to the 'long arm of Israel's aerial reach'. As OC IAF Major-General Amos Lapidot would warn the terrorists in a television interview, 'We can get you wherever you are hiding!'

Finally, the target chosen for Israel's retaliation was PLO headquarters at Hamam-Shat in Tunisia. A few kilometres from downtown Tunis, Hamam-Shat became Yasir Arafat's third home base following the PLO's forced evacuation from Beirut in August 1982. The seaside swimming-pools, shiny Mercedes limousines and neatly kept Mediterranean gardens around Hamam-Shat were a stark contrast to the shell-cratered labyrinth of death and destruction in Beirut. The 'Tunisian Riviera' afforded the PLO a sense of exiled class and legitimacy. The PLO's lair at Hamam-Shat, however, was anything but innocent. It consisted of a number of administrative buildings serving as Arafat's office, the world-wide communications and operations centre of *el-Fatah*, the PLO's central archives and office to the operations and command centre of Abu Muatassem. In addition, and most importantly, Hamam-Shat housed the largest *Force 17* HQ in the world (commanded by Abu Tayeb) together with a mysterious and much feared *Force 17* gaol and detention centre. There were some 1,300 heavily armed *el-Fatah* and Yasir Arafat loyalists stationed in Tunisia.

The attack squadrons of F-15s and F-16s had trained long and hard for such a deep penetration raid. At an air force base in southern Israel, the pilots had practised long-range surgical bombing runs and mid-air refuelling techniques for days. It was not the first time that the IAF had travelled far beyond the secure boundaries of home: On 3 July 1976, IAF C-130 Hercules transport aircraft travelled thousands of kilometres to Entebbe, Uganda, in Operation 'Thunderball', the spectacular rescue of 103 hostages held by the PFLP. On 7 June 1981, IAF F-15s and F-16s once again flew thousands of kilometres over Saudi Arabian and Jordanian airspace to destroy Iraq's Osirak nuclear reactor. In 1985, the IAF would emulate their previous successes.

On 1 October, at 1005 hours, the IAF struck. Flying in a steady formation above the Gulf of Tunis, two Israeli F-16s, identifiable by their Star of David markings, swooped like angry birds of prey and unleashed their loads of bombs and missiles at clusters of sand-coloured buildings surrounded by neatly groomed palm groves. The first two F-16s were followed by three other flights, also of two aircraft, and within minutes Yasir Arafat's command centre was reduced to a pile of twisted steel and crumpled concrete. Being far from home and in a hurry, the F-16s joined their covering flight of F-15 air superiority fighters and raced back towards Israel.

In the raid, 65 people were killed, including ten Tunisian security men. The IAF had taken great care in the attack, hoping at all costs to avoid inflicting innocent civilian casualties.

Among the 50 PLO officials who lost their lives in the operation were four very important men in the Palestinian's naval effort against Israel. They were:

■   Lieutenant-Colonel Abdallah Ghash, commonly known by his *nom de guerre* of Abu Shastri, a competent career officer in *el-Fatah*, and an officer in Abu Muatassem's unit. In Lebanon he had served as a battalion commander and in August 1985 he was responsible for planning the military and logistical details for the attack which was supposed to have transpired with the yacht *Casselardit*.

■   Shafiq Risa'a al-Ansar had belonged to *el-Fatah* since its inception and was a key Black September Organization officer in the early 1970s. He participated in the planning of several key Black September attacks in Holland, Italy and West Germany, including, it was believed, the 1972 Munich Olympics massacre. In October 1973, he was arrested in Vienna as a member of the group planning a hostage take-over of the Schoenau transit-camps for Soviet Jews, an attack many feel was part of the Arab intelligence screen prior to the surprise Egyptian and Syrian attack of 6 October. Shafiq Risa'a al-Ansar served as Yasir Arafat's personal bodyguard in 1978–9 and as a *Force 17* operations officer in Europe in the early 1980s.

■   Jlhad al-Ghol was the *Force 17* deputy commander in Tunisia at the time of the raid. His speciality was operations inside Israel and the training of special Palestinian murder squads in Europe.

■   Abu Ghosh was a senior operations officer within the *Force 17* bureaucracy, believed to have assisted Abu Jihad in planning the SS *Attaviros* attack on Tel Aviv in April 1985.

Yasir Arafat was conveniently out of the area at the time, demonstrating that he may indeed have nine lives. Other reports suggest that Arafat was even tipped off by a mysterious source, a source whose national interest demanded that Arafat remain alive and in charge of the PLO.

Like the Entebbe and Iraqi raids before it, the Tunis attack had been elaborately planned and meticulously executed. At dawn, eight F-15s took off from a base in northern Israel, followed 40 minutes later by a flight of eight F-16s. The F-16s were refuelled once, over the Mediterranean, during their 1,500-mile journey to Tunis by specially modified Boeing 707s. They flew only yards above the choppy sea to avoid radar detection, encroaching on Tunis from the south. While the F-16s bombed the PLO installations, the F-15s remained in reserve miles away as possible air cover. Off the coast of Malta, an IDF/Navy vessel stood by on alert, ready to launch helicopters to rescue any downed pilots. The whole operation took less than five hours to carry out. According to numerous foreign Press reports, the IAF had received in-depth intelligence data of the PLO's Hamam-Shat complex, including highly sensitive satellite information from Israel's spy in Washington, Jonathan Jay Pollard. Reports also indicate that Israel received detailed intelligence from American KH-11 satellites, an arrangement ostensibly secured in exchange for Israeli intelligence work following the US Beirut bombings, and Israel's role in the Iran-Contra Affair.* The raid was also meant to serve notice to King Hussein that opening a PLO office in Amman could result in the same devastation.

While the 1 October raid succeeded in curtailing *Force 17* naval activity for the time being, it could not arrest the cycle of killings. To prove its forces were still capable of striking at Israeli 'naval' interests, *Force 17* gunmen kidnapped two Israeli merchant sailors in Barcelona and brutally murdered them on the night on 5/6 October 1985.

Yet while Israel's attention was directed solely against the *Force 17* threat to her shores, a bizarre attempt to infiltrate Israel by sea was attempted by the other Palestinian terrorist group known for its seafaring adventures: the Abu Abbas faction of the Palestine Liberation Front (PLF).

On the night of 6/7 October 1985, the 23,629-ton Italian cruise liner *Achille Lauro* was mid-way through its eleven-day cruise from Genoa to Naples, Alexandria, Port Said, Ashdod, Limassol, Rhodes, Piraeus, Capri and back to Genoa. The passengers had table-tennis tournaments, shuffleboard games and lazy afternoons of sun and fun around the swimming-pool. The cruise ship had more than 750 passengers, mainly middle-aged Americans from New York City and New Jersey, and seemed a peaceful island of relaxation in the turbulent Mediterranean region. On the morning of 7 October, 666 passengers left *Achille Lauro* for a day of shopping and sightseeing in Cairo and would meet the ship at Ashdod in Israel, a day later. A total of 97 passengers and 315 crewmembers remained on board, including four young men who had boarded the ship in Genoa and rarely ventured outside their cabins since. The four, who mumbled to each other in Arabic and played loud cassettes with the sweet vocal tones of Fairuz (Lebanon's most famous female singer), claimed to be Norwegian students.

At dinner time, an *Achille Lauro* steward inadvertently entered the 'Norwegians' cabin, and discovered them cleaning dozens of AK-47 assault rifles, examining explosives and grenades and taking stock of their ammunition. After the almost comical moment of shocked silence, the terrorists realized that their cover had been blown and decided to take over the ship, and to play for time.

The ensuing developments are by now public knowledge. In cold blood, the terrorists murdered a 69-year-old wheelchair-bound Jewish American named Leon Klinghoffer and threw his body and the wheelchair overboard off the coast of Tartus. After Cyprus, Egypt and even Syria (mainly as a result of the PLF's pro-Arafat, anti-Syrian stance) refused docking privileges to the seajacked *Achille Lauro*, the terrorists were contacted by Abu Khalid (a *nom de guerre* of their leader, Abu Abbas) who searched for an 'honourable' way out. Having sworn that none of the hostages had been harmed, the terrorists' safe passage was

---

* Such satellite information was to be limited to purely defensive material following the 1981 Iraqi reactor bombing.

eventually secured by a frantic Egyptian Government, hoping to rid themselves of the incident, and by Yasir Arafat, who wanted to prevent a terrorist attack gone wrong from exploding into a politically damaging incident for his Movement. Throughout the episode, an IDF/Navy vessel shadowed the beleaguered passenger ship from a safe distance off the Lebanese coast.

The *Achille Lauro* returned to Egyptian waters and the terrorists were whisked away on a chartered Egyptian aircraft bound for Cairo Airport and a hero's reception by Abu Abbas. The US Ambassador to Egypt, Nicholas Veliotes, feared a PLF *fait accompli* and boarded the ship where he learned of Mr. Klinghoffer's tragic fate. Through a ship-to-shore radio link-up, he contacted his colleagues and said, 'I want you to contact the [Egyptian Foreign Minister], tell him what we've learned, tell him the circumstances, tell him that in view of this and the fact that we and presumably they, didn't have those facts, we insist that they prosecute those *sons of bitches*! The second thing: I want you to pick up the 'phone and call Washington and tell them what we've done. And if they want to follow it up, that's fine.'[7]

Washington did indeed follow up the incident. A flight of F-14 Tomcat fighters from the USS *Saratoga* and E-2C Hawkeye AWACS aircraft were ordered to intercept the Egyptair Boeing 737 jet ferrying Abu Abbas and his four 'heroes' in mid-air (also on board were several heavily armed Egyptian commandos meant to ensure the aircraft's safe return to Egypt!)† Foreign reports indicate that the US Navy F-14s were able to locate the Boeing 737 with the help of Israeli military intelligence communications specialists who monitored all 'pertinent' radio traffic in the region. The F-14s forced the aircraft to land at Sigonella Air Force base in Sicily where it was surrounded by commandos from the US Navy's élite counter-terrorist unit 'SEAL Team 6', as well as Italian carabinieri. Although the Italians pushed for the release of Abu Abbas, much to the anger of the US commandos (he was later rushed out of Italy to Yugoslavia and thence to the Middle East), the four seajackers were apprehended, prosecuted and, in due course, gaoled.

The 52-hour seajacking of the *Achille Lauro* and the murder of Leon Klinghoffer appeared to be a foolish act, but the terrorists had never meant to seize the ocean liner. Their objective was to land in Ashdod, a southern Israeli port where they had assumed Border Guard vigilance would be minimal. They would produce their weapons from large suitcases and kitbags, commit a massacre inside the passenger terminal and then seize the hundreds of *Achille Lauro* passengers embarking on a short tour of the Holy Land as hostages. The ultimate goal of the operation was to demand the release of 150 of their PLF

---

† A few weeks later, on 23 November 1985, that same Egyptair Boeing 737 (Flight 648) was hijacked by Palestinian terrorists from the Abu Nidal faction during a routine flight from Athens to Cairo. The aircraft was flown to Malta, where the terrorists killed eight people, including four Egyptian security agents and an Israeli woman. The next day, Egyptian commandos launched an unsuccessful rescue operation during which 58 were killed and 23 seriously wounded. The attack was in response to Egypt's 'misguided' handling of the *Achille Lauro* affair.

comrades rotting in Israeli gaols, *including* the two surviving killers of the Haran family in Nahariya, 1979.

It is impossible to ascertain whether the raid would have been a Palestinian 'victory', a bloody battle compounded by tragic casualties, or, as has been the case with most such hostage dramas in Israel, a pointless and violent débâcle. The *Achille Lauro* fiasco merely served to remind the world of the indiscriminate acts Palestinian groups remained capable of and it underlined to Israel that the Mediterranean Sea was one of the few operation venues that remained open to the Palestinians.

The Israelis continued in their attempts to frustrate the Palestinian's naval abilities in the waters off Lebanon and Israel and also farther afield with activities off the Italian shore. In early January 1986, two Palestinian-owned hydrofoils were blown up and sunk in a Messina shipyard. The hydrofoils were ordered by the PLO to facilitate the profitable Christian Phalangist-run ferry service between Larnaca, Cyprus and Junieh, near Christian East Beirut‡ Initially the blasts were blamed on rival Palestinian factions, but several published accounts implicate Israeli agents in the act of sabotage. It was believed to be a further preventive measure against Arafat's widening sealanes. According to Italian police, one of the explosive charges which failed to detonate was similar to that which claimed the life of PLO Information Minister Abu Shrar on 9 October 1981 (*see* page 58). They were also very similar to the bomb which killed Brigadier Abu Ghazala in Athens on 21 October; facts which pointed to the theory that Israel might be operating assassination and sabotage squads in countries bordering the Mediterranean.

The PLO would not allow the Israelis to seize the military and intelligence initiative, and further attempts to infiltrate by sea would continue in earnest and bloody fashion.

On 10 July 1986, an IDF/Navy patrol craft sailing in calm pre-dawn Mediterranean waters near the Lebanese frontier spotted a radar blip indicating that something was heading very rapidly towards the Israeli shore. It was a Zodiac craft and it carried four heavily armed terrorists *en route* to the unfortunate city of Nahariya for yet another early morning attack. Although the *Dabur* fired incessant bursts of 20mm cannon fire at the rubber dinghy, the four Palestinians proved to be elusive targets and succeeded in beaching their craft on the Lebanese shore, only yards from the heavily fortified Israeli frontier. As the early morning sunlight climbed over the Galilee hills in the east, the four terrorists assembled their mini-arsenal on the limestone cliffs and prepared a textbook ambush for the inevitable Israeli attack.

The IDF responded with helicopter gunships and Golani Brigade infantrymen. In a lengthy (three hours) and well-contested battle the

‡ Although the Phalangists had perpetrated the September 1982 Sabra and Shatilla massacres and were the historic rival of the Palestinians for military and political control of the Levant, they were blatant pragmatists in the Byzantine world of Middle Eastern politics.

Palestinians killed two Israeli soldiers, including a Bedouin tracker, and seriously wounded nine others before they themselves were overcome by superior Israeli firepower. The terrorist commander, wearing a Che Guevara T-Shirt and carrying more than a dozen AK-47 magazines, was clutching an elaborate map of the Nahariya seafront, which in the hot July sun would have been bustling with thousands of sunbathers. The attack was staged three days after Jordan's King Hussein abruptly shut down 25 *el-Fatah* offices in Amman, but it is doubtful if it was linked to that event because the dead attackers belonged to the Syrian-backed Popular Front for the Liberation of Palestine (PFLP). This had been the faction's first seaborne attempt. A day after the thwarted seaborne suicide operation, IAF aircraft punished *el-Fatah* 'anyway' by bombing their naval training facilities near Sidon.

Ten days later, on 20 July 1986, an IDF/Navy *Dabur* 'apprehended' the Cypriot merchant vessel SS *Anton*; its 'crime' was to look remarkably clean and seaworthy for the sort of ship normally ferrying cargo in the eastern Mediterranean. Upon further inspection, the *Dabur* crew captured several high-ranking *el-Fatah* officers. A month later, IDF/Navy vessels once again intercepted a PLO ship, this time ferrying arms and supplies, including high-speed racing boats, to bases near Sidon. Three months later, on 16 November, the IDF/Navy captured two Lebanese fishing boats carrying tons of ammunition and 50 heavy mortars, heading towards Israeli waters. And on 2 January 1987, the IDF/Navy apprehended two ferries, *Sunny Boat* and *Empress*, which were bringing PLO officers and their military hardware to bases along the Lebanese coast.

One of the largest and most important 'catches' the IDF/Navy have made in the Mediterranean occurred on 6 February 1987. At approximately 1200 hours, a missile-boat sailing in international waters between Cyprus and Lebanon discovered a small merchant vessel heading towards the Levantine coast. The 500-ton SS *Maria R*, was flying a Honduran flag and was manned by 'Egyptian' sailors. The missile-boat commander conducted a routine and distant inspection of the *Maria R* and learned that she was carrying more than 50 passengers. Other naval vessels were summoned and *Maria R* was taken to Israel for an elaborate search. Although not a single weapon was found, the fifty passengers were travelling on forged passports and were later discovered to be veteran officers of *el-Fatah*.

From the sinking of SS *Attaviros* to the seizure of the *Maria R*, the period from April 1985 to early 1987 was marked by crushing defeats for the Palestinian's naval offensive. During that 22-month period, the IDF/Navy killed more than 40 Palestinian terrorists, captured nearly a hundred more and prevented twenty *definite* planned terror attacks from reaching Israel. The military planners of *el-Fatah*, however, were far from raising the white flag and, in fact, escalated their offensive.

On 10 December 1987, the Israeli daily *Ma'ariv* reported that Palestinian terrorists were deploying suicide squads, four-man speedboats armed with RPG-7s, similar to the ones used in the Persian Gulf by the Iranian Revolutionary Guards. The objectives were not the facilitation of elaborate terrorist attacks against Israel's tranquil shore, but for *kamikaze* strikes against military targets, in this case the chief force restricting their ability to attack the Zionist heartland: the IDF/ Navy. Three days after that report was published a speedboat driven by such a squad, deployed in ambush from behind a fishing vessel and succeeded in drawing blood against a *Dabur* patrol craft off the River Litani tributary south-east of Sidon. At 2200 hours on 12 December, the *Dabur* was patrolling the busy waterways between Sidon and Tyre when it located a fast-moving target on a collision course. As battle stations were sounded and helmets and flak vests donned, the extremely agile speedboat fired a volley of RPGs at the *Dabur*. The grenades inflicted severe damage to the patrol craft and mortally wounded its second mate, Lieutenant Amit Sela. For five minutes the Israelis fought with the terrorists, whom it was later claimed were from Islamic Resistance, before they overcame them and killed the four-man crew. It is thought, although not confirmed, that at least one of the squad was a Palestinian.

Realizing that the high seas were as volatile a battleground as the Golan Heights, the IDF/Navy began to deploy heavily armed *Snapirit* hydrofoils as well as a new craft brought into the fray in 1988: the 'Super *Dvora*' or 'Bee'.§ The 'Super *Dvora* is considered to be the fastest such patrol craft in the world, capable of speeds in excess of 40 knots (almost double that of the *Dabur*). It has a range of hundreds of nautical miles and is armed with two 20mm Oerlikons, two bridge-mounted FN MAG 7.62mm light machine-guns and is built to absorb several other weapons systems such as depth-charges, torpedos and 130mm rockets for bombarding shore targets. Most importantly perhaps is its advanced, Israeli-produced radar system, which is capable of dealing with several small targets simultaneously. According to the then OC IDF/Navy, Major-General Avraham Ben-Shoshan, 'The terrorists are obtaining extremely fast craft and we are obliged to respond in kind in order to defeat the *sea terror*.' Only a few weeks after the new craft were operationally deployed in early 1989, one intercepted and destroyed a rubber dinghy carrying terrorists of the much-feared Abu Nidal Faction towards the Israeli shore.

Perhaps the best indication of the direction Israel's epic war against the Palestinian naval threat might take occurred on 2 August 1988 when an IDF/Navy missile-boat intercepted a 170-ton, 33-metre ferry craft, SS *Doriti* in international waters and captured four officers in the *el-Fatah* seaborne unit. Upon interrogation, the four admitted

§ The original *Dvora* craft was an Israeli-produced hybrid, combining the speed of the *Dabur*, with the *Gabriel* missile-firing capabilities of *Sa'ar*-class missile-boats. An even newer addition to the Israeli fleet was recently unveiled: the *Shaldaq* or Kingfisher, is an eight-man patrol craft with a cruising speed of 45–50 knots. Its weaponry – believed to be light and heavy machine-guns – has not been disclosed, but its existence means that Israel has a triumvirate of vessels in its naval shield with which to combat seaborne infiltration.

that they were *en route* to Libya where, as a result of the IDF/Navy's vigilance, they have been forced to establish their naval training facilities. Only time will tell when, and if, the seemingly impregnable Israeli naval shield will be penetrated and what carnage, retaliation and global repercussions such an incident will entail.

5. 'Select' Operations: Abu Jihad and Ahmed Jibril

'I do believe that commando assault operations are highly successful. They have a strong deterrent impact on terrorists, and therefore, I regard them as a highly important tool. I don't think that Tzahal [IDF] has stopped thinking about them, or that we will stop conducting them'.

Major-General Amnon Shahak, Chief of Military Intelligence
(*Bamachane* – 13 April 1988)

If there was one terrorist incident that sparked a series of unravelling events, it was the hijacking of a bus in southern Israel on 7 March 1988. This affected every one of the 'guards without frontiers' in Israel's all-encompassing war against Palestinian terrorism.

In March 1988, Israel's national security considerations were in a state of transformation. The IDF, the granite foundation of the State's existence, was embroiled in a bitter and controversial conflict against the stone-throwing teenage legions of the Palestinian *Intifadah* in the West Bank and Gaza Strip. Although the *Intifadah* was the Palastinian's spontaneous and undirected declaration of war against Israeli occupation, several Palestinian resistance groups in Lebanon, Syria and Tunis declared responsibility for the international success of the uprising and attempted to assume a dominant role in this opportunistic segment of the struggle. They hoped to do so through the only way known to them – attempted terrorist attacks along Israel's Lebanese frontier.

Such efforts, to cross a border as heavily defended as was the Berlin Wall in its Cold War heyday, were very dangerous to undertake. In 1987 alone, IDF and Border Guard units killed 230 Palestinian terrorists attempting to cross it – for a cost of more than 40 Israeli soldiers and policemen killed in these same incidents. The 'Night of the Hang Glider' was a more conspicuous success; it helped spark the *Intifadah* and it encouraged Palestinian military planners to attempt to end the lackadaisical malaise of the Palestinians, to seize the military initiative on the Lebanese border, and elsewhere if possible. On 20 January 1988, IDF units killed three Palistinian terrorists as they attempted to cut their away across the security fence *en route* to an attack on *Kibbutz* Menara. Two weeks later, on 3 February 1988, a two-man *el-Fatah* team attempted an attack on *Kibbutz* Yiftach, a communal farm approximately one mile from the Lebanese frontier. The terrorists were again detected as they cut their way across the fence, but they maintained an impressive though hopeless twenty-minute defence against a numerically superior IDF paratroop contingent, in which they killed two of the Red Berets.

When the *Intifadah* had broken out in December 1987, Abu Jihad, the PLO's military commander, quickly realized that guerrilla attempts to infiltrate and inflict Israeli casualties would be appreciated by those involved in and bearing the brunt of the festering uprising, as a gesture of support. At that point the Lebanese border was too well-sealed and the local population too hostile to renewed PLO activity to enable attacks to be launched from there; similarly the naval shield was too difficult to penetrate. Therefore, on 26 December 1987, the pro-Arafat Abu Abbas Faction of the Palestine Liberation Front attempted to infiltrate a three-man suicide squad into the Jordan Valley through Jordanian territory. The attack not only failed miserably, but led King Hussein to clamp down on *all* Palestinian military activity in Jordan. With this avenue closed to him Abu Jihad now looked at the most peaceful frontier instead: the border with Egypt, the last possible frontline.

Since the signing of the Camp David Peace Accords between the late Anwar es-Sadat and Menachem Begin in 1978, the Egyptian-Israeli frontier has largely been peaceful and tranquil. With the exception of Bedouin hashish smugglers, lost camel herds and tourists gone astray, the border has been a placid sea of calm in a much turbulent area. A multi-national peace-keeping force patrolled the once heated battlefields of Sinai and feelings of good will and co-operation were prevalent on both sides. Both Egypt and Israel were intent on maintaining the very acceptable *status quo*. Abu Jihad and the Western Command of *el-Fatah*, however, had *other* plans.

In early February 1988, three laden *el-Fatah* terrorists wearing T-shirts and blue jeans left Cairo for a lengthy journey into the Sinai Desert; their destination was the town of El Arish. There they consulted a band of Bedouin smugglers who, after an obligatory payment, helped the three cross into Israel *undetected* at a border position five kilometers north of Mount Harif. The objective of the three-man terror squad was the hijacking of a passenger bus for transportation and the seizure of a desert agricultural settlement. The three were well conditioned and carried two *Uzi* submachine-guns (captured years ago from IDF stocks), one *Carl Gustav* 9mm submachine-gun, thirteen fragmentation grenades, five booby-trapped explosive devices and an assortment of other material including three electronic triggering devices, nine blasting caps, wire-cutters, military issue flashlights, optical gear and combat rations for several days.

Hours later, during a routine security patrol of the frontier, the rare signs of infiltration were noticed by IDF Bedouin trackers and the alert was sounded throughout IDF Southern Command. The isolated desert settlements were notified and IDF units summoned for the chase. Bedouin trackers were instrumental in locating the terrorists in the parched mountain maze of the Negev Desert. Through their dogged foot work and their remarkable skill, they managed to track the *el-Fatah* squad after more than 24 hours of a non-stop manhunt. When contact was made the terrorists resisted for twenty minutes but were overcome by superior IDF firepower and forced to surrender.

This was the third of a spate of incursions in early 1988, but the first on Egypt's side. In 1987, there had been only four *el-Fatah* attempts to infiltrate terrorists into Israel via the peace border with Egypt but in the first three months of 1988 *el-Fatah* were to attempt at least seven such border crossing attempts, a reflection of the boost the *Intifadah* had given the Palestinian organizations outside Israel. Abu Jihad's hastily assembled terrorist squads, a marked departure from the carefully trained covert cells that were his trademark, were virtual 'martyrdom missions'. They were deployed in rapid succession, in the hope that at least one would strike a spectacular blow.

Abu Jihad was outraged by *el-Fatah*'s failure to get a terror squad into Israel and ordered the planning of an even more audacious operation. One month later his vision of destruction would materialize.

In the early morning hours of 7 March 1988, three heavily armed members of *Force 17* crossed the Egyptian-Israeli border. Unlike the squad that had crossed the same frontier a month earlier, these terrorists were Abu Jihad's élite and as such they signified how much such an attack meant to him. The 'professionalism' showed in the way they went about their task.

They cut through the fence and at 0630 hours they stopped a white, IDF-issue Renault 4 on the mountain road three kilometres north of Nafkha Prison in the southern Negev Desert. The car was driven by four *unarmed* officers from the IDF's officer academy, and the terrorists with their AK-47 assault rifles and *Carl Gustav* submachine-guns had little difficulty in seizing it. Foolishly, they allowed the Israelis to escape and they immediately ran towards the nearby prison to inform the authorities.

The efficient Israeli internal security apparatus went into full gear. The isolated desert *Kibbutzim* and *Moshavim* were notified of the terrorist infiltration by telephone short-wave radio and their gates were sealed. Air-raid sirens ordered the women and children into the shelters and the men into defensive positions with weapons to hand. Throughout the Negev Desert, dozens of sleepy-eyed policemen rushed to their vehicles to patrol and set up road-blocks. Heavily armed policemen were stationed at key intersections from the Epyptian frontier to the outskirts of Tel Aviv. As a colossal police pursuit of the white Renault 4 commenced in the beautiful sandy wilderness of southern Israel, a call went through from the National Police operations centre in Jerusalem ordering the Border Guard anti-terrorist commandos to be placed on a full alert.

By 0715 hours the terrorists had reached their first road-block at the Yerucham–Dimona Junction. It failed to stop them; they swerved around the obstacles and sped on their way. A half-hour chase now ensued with the police shooting unsuccessfully at the terrorist's tyres and receiving return fire. IDF forces on manoeuvres nearby joined in the fray, firing unsuccessfully upon the Renault as it passed by. Along the road to Dimona the terrorists ditched their listing, bullet-riddled car and tried but failed to commandeer a semi-trailer. They then set up an ambush, hoping to snare their next means of transportation before the Israelis arrived.

Soon, an inter-city bus carrying workers from their homes in Be'ersheba to the Nuclear Research Centre in Dimona appeared. The driver managed to identify the three figures racing towards his Volvo bus as terrorists and screeched to a hasty stop. He opened his doors and ordered the passengers to leave, but eight women and one male were trapped when the three Palestinians assumed control of the stopped bus. Seconds later the vanguard of the police pursuit force reached the scene, as did OC Southern Command, Major-General Yitzhak Mordechai, and his advanced command team. A stand-off ensued.

In the Renault, IDF officers found a rucksack full of grenades which the terrorists had apparently forgotten, and the semi-trailer's driver was questioned in order to gather some 'impromptu field intelligence'. While the bus was gingerly surrounded by *ad hoc* response teams consisting of dozens of police officers and hastily summoned IDF soldiers, the district police commander, Haim Ben Oyen, commenced the negotiations in fluent Arabic, hoping to gain some time and an invaluable psychological insight.

Within minutes the area had become the busiest location in the country. Scores of men in the Israeli defence community's 'Who's Who?' reached the scene, including Defence Minister Lieutenant-General (Res.) Yitzhak Rabin, Police Minister Lieutenant-General (Res.) Haim Bar-Lev, the National Police Inspector General, Chief of Staff Lieutenant-General Dan Shomron, Deputy C-o-S Major-General Ehud Barak and dozens of lesser known, though highly experienced generals. Helicopters overhead kicked up a sandy cyclone, while the dust kicked up from the dozens of army cars, trucks and ambulances made visual command and control difficult. An élite IDF unit prepared a defensive perimeter surrounding the bus, as well as planning an assault. They were reinforced later by the rescue force from the Border Guard's *Ya'ma'm*. For many of the assembled the incident was a repeat of the No. 300 bus hijacking, although its politically damaging by-products were to be avoided at all costs! This time it would be the *Ya'ma'm* who would be given the job of rescuing the hostages and killing the terrorists.

Unlike the hijackers of the No. 300 bus in 1984, the terrorists holding the Be'ersheba–Dimona bus were well-trained professionals armed with numerous automatic weapons and grenades. Their determination to have a bloody fire-fight was expressed numerous times from 0900 to 1000 hours when they fired bursts of 7.62mm fire at the surrounding crowds and threw fragmentation grenades at encroaching IDF soldiers. Through the hails of gunfire, Ben Oyen attempted a sporadic dialogue with the three Palestinians. They demanded the release of Palestinian prisoners from Israeli gaols and safe passage to a friendly Arab nation. Ben Oyen pleaded with the terrorists to stop the gunfire, but his anguished appeals for calm were ignored with the promise to throw a body out of the bus every 30 minutes.[1]

The decision to act (always difficult to time) was forced on the rescuers when gunfire was heard from inside the bus at 1000 hours. Dissatisfied with the Israeli response to their demands, the terrorists opted to strengthen their position by killing a hostage in cold blood. As Chief of Staff Shomron and OC Southern Command Mordechai (a man already quite intimate with such situations) retreated to a command post in a small sand-hill yards away, the *Ya'ma'm* unit was ordered to prepare its gear and its final assault plan.

For the Border Guard anti-terrorist commandos, wearing bullet-proof vests and carrying the ultra-compact and deadly Mini-*Uzi* 9mm submachine-gun, this was to be their moment of truth as policemen and as a unit. Since their inception, in 1974–5, they had trained incessantly in the art of rescuing hostages, but had never participated in a successful hostage-rescue operation. Since their two tragic incidents in the late 1970s there had been other opportunities but they were passed over. On 7 April 1980, a band of five Palestinian terrorists from the Iraqi-sponsored Arab Liberation Front (ALF) crossed the Lebanese frontier and seized a nursery in *Kibbutz* Misgav Am, killing a worker and an infant. The precise reason why the *Ya'ma'm* wasn't summoned for the operation remains a mystery; instead, a unit from *Sayeret Golani* or Golani Recconnaissance, probably the best 'conventional' reconnaissance/commando force the IDF can field, stormed the nursery and killed the five terrorists.* On 12 April 1984, four terrorists hijacked the No. 300 bus between Tel Aviv and Ashqelon and once again the honed skill of the *Ya'ma'm* wasn't called on, even though they were stationed around the bus and ready for an assault.

The men of the hostage-rescue unit were keen to prove their worth. Composed entirely of veterans from the IDF's élite combat units (such as the paratroops, Golani and other reconnaissance and commando formations), those volunteering into the *Ya'ma'm* are trained in a brutally-paced regime of hand-to-hand combat, cold weapon killing, marksmanship, judo, *Krav Maga* (an Israeli-inspired form of intuitive

---

* Ten months later, on 22/3 February 1981, *Sayeret Golani* avenged the Misgav Am killings in Operation 'New Fitting' (*'Mishlav Hadash'*). A heliborne force attacked the ALF's southern Lebanon HQ in El Kfur in the Nabatiyah Heights, and killed fourteen terrorists.

martial arts) and split-second synchronized assaults on terrorist/enemy-held targets. Each *Ya'ma'm* 'policeman' is trained to proficiency in every type of infantry weapon imaginable: from a K-Bar knife to a hand-gun, from an assault rifle to an RPG-7. Special emphasis is given to urban combat training, by day or night, and to eliminating the terrorists in the first burst of gunfire so that hostages can be rescued unharmed. As a result, each member of a squad is expert in any task he might be called on to perform.

Given their backgrounds, the men were not strangers to participation at the cutting-edge of combat operations. Even as a unit, the *Ya'ma'm* had seen action in Lebanon with the Border Guards (according to an article in the 8 March edition of the Israeli daily *Ha'aretz*); they had also been used inside Israel in support of Shin Bet during delicate security operations, and in August 1985 had helped seize a crazed escaped criminal who was holding hostages in a block of flats.*
But this was to be their first leading role in the task for which they were created. When the decision was issued ordering them into action, it would be a moment of anxious fear each fighter would remember for years to come, especially for the *Ya'ma'm*'s commanding officer, Deputy Superintendent 'A'.

At 1015 hours, after shots were once again heard from inside the bus, the *Ya'ma'm* burst into action in an explosive manner. Seconds later, the three terrorists, wearing T-shirts with the word 'PALESTINE' emblazoned across the chest, were killed. Just seconds prior to the rescue assault, however, the terrorists managed to kill two more hostages, adding a tragic end to a brilliant and decisive operation for the Border Guard commandos.

Because the Be'ersheba–Dimona bus was carrying women labourers to their jobs, the incident has become known as the 'Bus of Mothers'. The entire episode was a stark reminder of the horror and bloodshed a resolute and well-trained terrorist force could still inflict on an unsuspecting civilian population. The operation, conceived and ordered by Abu Jihad, illustrated how such an attack could work as a media bonanza, especially when the *Intifadah* commanded more than its share of Press coverage.

By 1988 Yasir Arafat and his black-and-white *kefiyeh* head-dress was synonymous with the Palestinian revolution. He had become an accepted spokesman for his people and was widely viewed as a voice of moderation in the PLO. These acts of *el-Fatah*, however, exposed the fact that they were still capable of gaining the international spotlight through the murders of innocents. The responsibility for these actions

---

* The *Ya'ma'm*'s anti-terrorist role does *not* restrict them from executing their police duties; in many cases to exciting and spectacular extremes. In February 1990, for example, a *Ya'ma'm* task force left their anti-*Intifadah* and anti-terrorist duties in Israel proper to hinder the lucrative drug-smuggling routes which have sprouted from Lebanon since 1982, when, in many ways, the fates of the two nations became forever intertwined. The *Ya'ma'm* force, heavily armed and disguised as Lebanese fisherman, raided the Christian port of Junieh, north of Beirut, not only to destroy a drug pipeline but gain intelligence as to their connection back in Israel.

lay with Arafat's highly dangerous lieutenants. These were men who cared little for the frivolity of Third World conferences, United Nation tea-parties and positive mentions in the East bloc Press. They also paid little notice to the international diplomatic campaign which had given Arafat new life via the *Intifadah*; instead they saw themselves as soldiers, masterminds of a revolution where the world was their battlefield and all the world's citizens legitimate combatants and casualties in the great 'cause'. Of all the men and *nom de guerres* now equated with terrorism, such as Abu Nidal and Ahmed Jibril, the man who chose to be known as Abu Jihad, or 'Father Holy War', was one of the best.

Abu Jihad was born Khalil Ibrahim Machmud al-Wazir on 10 October 1935 in the town of Ramle, a few kilometres south of Tel Aviv. At the age of 13, during the 1948 War, his family fled to the political hotbed of Gaza, where young Khalil became involved in the students' Movement, forming clandestine cells of Palestinian students to oppose the harsh Egyptian rule. The Palestinian defeat in the 1948 War would leave irreparable emotional pain for the young Khalil who vowed to avenge his nation's humiliation.

Khalil al-Wazir met Yasir Arafat in the 1950s when, together with Salah Khalaf (known by the *nom de guerre* of Abu Iyad), the dreaded PLO internal security chief, he was an 'exiled' Palestinian student enrolled in the University of Alexandria's Philosophy Faculty. The two men were to remain together for more than thirty years. On 10 October 1959, Abu Jihad became Yasir Arafat's second-in-command when *el-Fatah* was founded, a military and political resistance movement which would destroy the State of Israel through armed struggle. Both Arafat and al-Wazir began to recruit Palestinians for their newly founded military resistance organization in Kuwait, where Arafat worked as an engineer and al-Wazir taught in a primary school. In 1963 al-Wazir moved to Algiers where he founded the *Kuwat al-Asifa* or 'Storm Troops', the nucleus of *el-Fatah*'s military wing. He went to the People's Republic of China, North Vietnam and North Korea to receive guerrilla training and invaluable military supplies.[2] After years of preparations and pan-Arab support, Abu Jihad masterminded *el-Fatah*'s first act of armed resistance against the State of Israel. On 1 January 1965, a lone and courageous guerrilla named Mahmud Hijazi infiltrated into Israel and planted an explosive device along the National Water Carrier. To this day, 1 January is regarded as 'Revolution Day' by Palestinian supporters of Yasir Arafat's *el-Fatah*.

During the next 23 years Abu Jihad organized hundreds of operations against Israel, resulting in hundreds of dead and wounded on both sides. He was behind the murderous June 1974 seaborne attack on Nahariya, the March 1975 seizure of the Savoy Hotel, the March 1978 Country Club Massacre and the March 1988 'Bus of Mothers' incident. While many perceive the foiled seaborne attempt to seize the IDF General Staff Headquarters and the Israeli Ministry of Defence on

20 April 1985 as the incident which triggered the Israelis into taking action against him personally, it may well have been the onset of the *Intifadah* that played a more decisive role. According to reports in the foreign Press, Abu Jihad was involved in the planning stage of the establishment of a shadowy Palestinian government for the chaotic Occupied Territories which would make the troubled lands totally ungovernable by the Israelis. His first move was the destruction of Israel's elaborate network of informers in the West Bank and Gaza Strip; a task made possible by the radicalizing effect the *Intifadah* was having on grassroots Palestinians, winning broader support for extreme measures against people deemed collaborators who were now more easily identified.

In addition, there were several reports that hinted that the decision to kill Abu Jihad was reached as a result of a covert 'pact with the devil' he had made with the Libyan leader Muammar Qaddafi.[3] According to these sources, Abu Jihad had negotiated a deal with the Libyans and several eastern European intelligence services, to restore the post-1982 PLO to its former strength through massive supplies of arms, intelligence and logistical support. The process had begun in December 1987, when Abu Jihad made a covert visit to East Berlin. Also instrumental in this arrangement were the Romanians, one of the few East-bloc nations to maintain diplomatic relations with Israel. According to Jon Pachzipa, the former head of Romanian intelligence, the Romanians supplied *el-Fatah* with logistical support to carry out terrorist attacks in Europe, including supplying them with blank western European passports. In addition, the Romanians supplied Abu Jihad with a generous supply of American passports which allowed *el-Fatah* terrorists free access to much of the world.

The East German connection paved the way for a five-day convention in the Libyan desert town of Sabha, where Qaddafi and Abu Jihad attempted to solidify the Iranian–Syrian–Libyan alliance with the onset of an international, Palestinian-led terrorist offensive. In Sabha, Abu Jihad met leaders from the various pro-Syrian and pro-Libyan Palestinian factions to bury their differences and consolidate forces towards the destruction of their common enemy: the loathed Zionist entity. The Libyans were to provide the terrorists with financial, military and logistical support. It was believed that 220 Palestinian and Iranian terrorists had already begun extensive training in newly constructed training camps. Their targets were to include Israeli installations in Europe, and Israeli supporters in Western Europe and the United States. Naturally, the State of Israel was to receive 'special attentions'.

The Israelis therefore viewed Abu Jihad as a dangerous bridge between disparate elements – pro-Arafat Palestinians, pro-Syrian Palistinians, leftist Sunni Muslims, pro-Iranian Shi'ite Muslim fundamentalists and the very capable intelligence services of eastern Europe. It was to shatter the precarious balance of power in the shadowy war of international terrorism.

Abu Jihad's pact for an international terrorist offensive was effectively the rebirth of the *el-Fatah* of the 1970s when the world had watched in horror. Mainly for tactical reasons these actions had been abandoned in the late 1970s by Abu Iyad, probably the most feared in the triumvirate of Abu Jihad, Arafat and Salah Khalaf. The ugly re-emergence of well-trained *el-Fatah* terrorists attacking international targets in tandem with fanatical Muslim fundamentalists supported by the intelligence services of Libya, Syria and Iran, presented Israel with a formidable challenge.

The Israelis also viewed Abu Jihad, a right-wing militant element in the PLO, as representative of the PLO's awkward mixture of wanton violence and pragmatism that makes the organization morally and practically so awkward to deal with. Should pragmatic negotiations ever take place between Israel and the Palestinians, men like Abu Jihad would be definite and deadly stumbling-blocks.

Accordingly, given his record of spectacular operations in the past and the prospects the new arrangements held for the future, together with the growing *Intifadah* which was raising the temperature of the Arab-Israeli conflict once again, a fateful decision was taken to assassinate Abu Jihad.

Before an examination of the assassination of Abu Jihad can be made, it must be stressed that Israel has never officially accepted responsibility for the brilliant 'hit operation'. Although it is widely accepted as fact that Israeli intelligence and military forces were behind the death of Abu Jihad, the Israeli Government has never released any information regarding this operation and has even gone out of its way to prevent new revelations from being unveiled. Several highly esteemed foreign journalists in Israel, for example, had their Press credentials revoked by the IDF Military Censor's Office (an IDF Military Intelligence body which examines all articles, newscasts and book manuscripts concerning the IDF, or Israeli national security matters) for publishing articles and compiling network television newscasts that suggested Israeli complicity in the Jihad assassination. As a result, the following account of the assassination of PLO military commander Khalil al-Wazir is based entirely on information gathered from foreign and Israeli reports. Despite this, the following chronicle of events should still be considered highly accurate and up to date.

For Israel, the most important detail of an assassination operation was deniability, an option which would serve as an escape hatch in the event of an internationally embarrassing public outcry. As a result, another pin-point air raid, like the one on 1 October 1985 which destroyed *Force 17* headquarters in Tunis, was out of the question. The Israelis wanted impact. They wished to strike a devastating blow right in the heart of the enemy's lair and thus serve notice to other terrorist leaders that their lives were in danger too. To succeed it would require the best efforts of Israel's intelligence and military community in a combined and co-ordinated manner. For inspiration, Israel would only have to look back fifteen years to April 1973 and the legendary Operation 'Spring of Youth', the audacious commando raid on Beirut which helped secure Israel's reputation as a special operations master and which had served as a role model for all the effective anti-terrorist operations since.

The killings of Black September's Abu Yusef, Kamal A'dwan and Kamal Nasser in Operation 'Spring of Youth' was a meticulous exercise and a fine example of special operations genius. The commandos wore civilian clothes (including Lieutenant-Colonel Ehud Barak in drag, no less) and carried MAC-10 submachine-guns not traceable to Israel; they entered the apartments of the three targeted figures and killed them in a matter of seconds, and stopping only to gather documents into suitcases brought specifically for that purpose. The covert effort was planned as a deniable incident; it was hoped that the killings could be attributed to inter-PLO rivalry and possibly spark an internal feud as a consequence. But the Israelis had taken casualties and were forced to send in helicopters to evacuate several seriously wounded commandos. This pointed the finger of blame firmly in Israel's direction.

Ironically, Operation 'Spring of Youth' was the act which brought Abu Jihad into the forefront of power, because he was named Abu Yusef's successor as chief of *el-Fatah* military operations. Fifteen years later, both Ehud Barak and Amnon Shahak (in 1988, both were major-generals and the deputy chief of staff and chief of *A'man* respectively) would have a chance to correct their operational errors in Beirut, as well as that operation's odd twist of fate.

It is thought that the scheme grew out of precise and tantalizing information regarding the day-to-day movements of Abu Jihad in Tunis, supplied by an Israeli mole in the PLO. With this reliable data in hand, the wheels were put into motion and planning for the operation commenced.

To conduct such a unique military operation, intelligence is obviously of paramount importance. Israel was in an excellent position as far as Tunisia was concerned. The Israeli intelligence community had been actively and extensively involved in North African collection operations for almost three decades. David Ben-Gurion, Israel's first prime minister and defence minister, masterminded an Israeli policy of 'regional containment' meant to outflank the hostile Arab states by establishing close ties with Turkey (which borders Syria and Lebanon), Iran (which covers Iraq and Jordan) and Ethiopia (which borders Egypt). This 'safe harbour' strategy worked amazingly well.[4]

In the 1950s, the North African states of Libya, Tunisia and Morocco were all colonial bastions and, as a result, generally pro-Western. But when they achieved independence in the early 1960s, Israel moved quickly to cement covert relations with each one, especially Morocco. As a result of King Hassan's tolerance and sometimes open friendship towards Moroccan Jews, relations between Israel and Morocco flourished and the North African kingdom became a safe launching-pad for Israeli intelligence-gathering operations throughout North Africa and the Middle East. The close-knit relationship peaked in the mid-1960s, when the Israelis helped the Moroccans to establish a modern foreign intelligence service, formed along the lines of the Mossad. Israeli advisers also helped create an effective, though sometimes ruthless, Moroccan internal security force which many consider a twin to the Shin Bet. IDF advisers trained the Moroccan Army and Air Force; it is rumoured that the IDF created a tank school for Moroccan armoured units and advanced training facilities for Moroccan Air Force pilots.[5] In a recent exclusive in the Israeli daily *Yediot Aharonot*, it was said that Mossad used their free access to Morocco to recruit countless Arabic- and French-speaking Moroccan Jews, who were later dispersed to various points in the Middle East and North Africa.[6]

According to a report by Professor Neil C. Livingstone and journalist David Halevy, there were 30 Mossad agents and IDF advisers on permanent assignment in Morocco from 1966 to 1975. The annual investment cost of this was between 12 and 20 million dollars, which was reimbursed to Israel by the Central Intelligence Agency.[7] When the pro-Palestinian/anti-Israel movement gained momentum in the Third World just prior to the outbreak of the 1973 Yom Kippur War, Israeli–Moroccan relations cooled and the Israeli intelligence apparatus had to go further underground. Covert intelligence-gathering stations throughout the North African rim were soon established.

When the PLO took refuge in Tunisia in 1982 after being expelled from Beirut by the IDF, the once friendly confines of the North African nation had become a frontline enemy target. The two IDF military intelligence branches, *A'man* and *Ha'man* (acronym for *Heyl Mode'in* or 'Intelligence Corps'), intensified their intelligence-gathering efforts in Tunisia, as did Mossad. Israeli intelligence set up businesses in Tunis which would be able to acquire lists of names, addresses and other data for ostensibly innocent purposes. They recruited Tunisian citizens and, according to the Israeli daily *Ma'ariv*, even Tunisian government ministers.

By 1985, the Israelis had established an elaborate intelligence network in Tunis, including agents and operatives, safe-houses and weapons caches. Their capabilities were so impressive that it has been reported that only *eight* minutes before the IAF F-16s were set to drop their ordnance on the *Force 17* headquarters in Tunis on 1 October 1985, the IDF General Staff was alerted that Yasir Arafat and *Force 17* commander Abu Tayeb had just departed the complex. The IAF operations commander informed Israeli Defence Minister Yitzhak Rabin that Arafat and Abu Tayeb could be *re-targeted*, but the original battle plan was adhered to.

To complement the intelligence *Blitz*, units from the IDF/Navy's élite Naval Commandos or *Kommando Yami*, sometimes referred to as

Shayetet Shlosh-Esrai or 'Flotilla 13', began deep penetration operations in Tunisian waters, mapping Tunisian beaches and possible landing sites. They surveyed the country's naval bases, seaborne detection capabilities and monitored the activities of the small Tunisian Navy. At the same time, reconnaissance commandos from *Sayeret Mat'kal* made frequent deep penetration forays into Tunisia, conducting surveillance of roads, airfields and various other targets, including the PLO headquarters in Hamam-Shat and the homes of top Palestinian leaders in the exclusive suburbs of Tunis. They conducted intelligence-gathering forays against other Palestinian targets and Tunisian troop concentrations, as well as taking a good look at Tunisian military units stationed near the capital. On top of all this, all Tunisian and Palestinian signal communications were conveniently monitored by the IDF in Tel Aviv.

Throughout the turbulent years of Israeli military history, *Sayeret Mat'kal*, the paratroop reconnaissance commando force, answerable *only* to the IDF General Staff, has been synoymous with spectacular operations. Unfortunately, very little of their work has been declassified and remains a deep secret. In July 1969, they joined a Naval Commando raiding party in the assault on the Egyptian Army bastion in the Red Sea called Green Island; on 9 May 1972, their commandos disguised as airline mechanics stormed the Black September-held Sabena airliner on the tarmac at Lod Airport; and in June 1972 they crossed the border into Lebanon and kidnapped several high-ranking Syrian intelligence officers, including a Brigadier-General, who were later exchanged for these IAF pilots shot down years earlier. Perhaps their most technically brilliant operation was the raid on Beirut in April 1973, but their most famous exploit was undoubtedly spearheading the rescue of 103 Israeli and Jewish hostages held in Entebbe in Operation 'Thunderball' on 4 July 1976.

If one of the trademarks of Israeli special unit operations is the 'Follow me!' ethic of command, it comes as little surprise to discover that the *Sayeret Mat'kal* commander flew to Tunis on a commercial flight from Rome, with his authentic Israeli passport, for a look-see of his own. He was met at the airport by the leader of the six-man and one woman Mossad team which had been specifically flown into Tunis to prepare the groundwork for the Abu Jihad killing (to avoid any security leaks, or untimely and unlucky capture by the Tunisian internal security services, all *Israeli* agents were evacuated from Tunis prior to the operation).[8] They drove to Abu Jihad's house in the exclusive Sidi Bouseid surburb of Tunis and then made their way to the landing site that had been chosen: a deserted picturesque beach at Ras Carthage, near the ancient port city of Carthage, approximately 40 kilometres north of Tunis.

In the first week of April 1988, a full rehearsal of the raid was conducted near the port city of Haifa, with the town on Mount Carmel standing-in for the hilly confines of Tunis quite effectively. A rough,

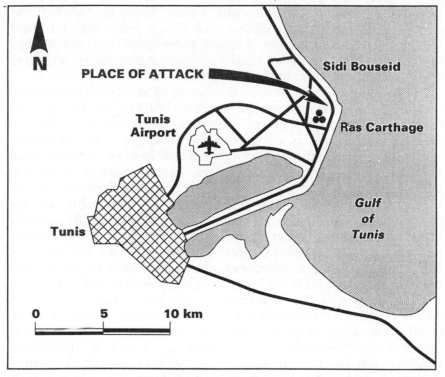

though accurate model of Abu Jihad's home was constructed at a nearby IDF Ordnance base, with 'A Force' – the vanguard team entrusted with the actual killing – supplied with a three-dimensional layout. Training for the hit was conducted at times when superpower satellites would not be flying over Israel and thus would not, it was hoped, discover the pre-raid preparations. After days on intensive, sometimes brutal training the *Sayeret Mat'kal* 'A Force' blasted their way into a model of the Abu Jihad home, found and killed the elusive 'Father Holy War' and exited in an amazing 22 seconds. The 'Chief of Staff's boys', the popular nickname for *Sayeret Mat'kal*, were ready!

Although the operation depended on accurate intelligence obtained by the Mossad and Military Intelligence, the success or failure of the mission hinged on two other equally important components.

The approximately 30–40-man force of *Sayeret Mat'kal* and 'Flotilla 13' commandos were to be ferried to Tunis in four missile-boats; these were four *Sa'ar* IVs, including the INS *Aliyah* and INS *Geula* which carry helicopters. One of the boats would hold two AH-1S Cobra gunships for added fire-support it needed, as well as an advanced field command centre for Major-General Ehud Barak, IDF deputy chief of staff, the Mossad deputy director of operations and the IDF/Navy chief of operations.† The other was outfitted with a full

† There is some conjecture as to the make-up and location of the Israeli commanders. Some reports list all IDF and Mossad chiefs as being present on the two IAF Boeing 707s.

battalion aid station, complete with a surgery and an IAF Bell-206 helicopter able to evacuate serious casualties in haste. Also on board the mini-naval armada were Mossad communications and Tunisia experts, including Mossad's chief communications officer, who had spent years in deep cover in North Africa.[9]

Providing an aerial security blanket of ECM (electronic countermeasures) protection, two specially modified IAF Boeing 707s would be flying over Tunis. One aircraft (international identification number 4X-007) would serve as an airborne reconnaissance and electronic warfare command and control centre; it would have on board the head of Military Intelligence, Major-General Amnon Shahak, a veteran intelligence and special operations officer, as well as Nachum Admoni, the Mossad Controller. The flight would be responsible for the co-ordination of all intelligence matters. The other Boeing 707 (international identification number 4X-497) would serve as a flying headquarters and had OC IAF Major-General Avihu Ben-Nun aboard. Two IAF flying tankers were positioned over the Mediterranean for refuelling operations with a flight of F-15s escorting them as aerial support.

On the ground, the commandos would have to rely on their own well-honed skill. Each commando would wear a black, Nomex coverall, Israeli-made khaki canvas *Patauga* boots and Kevlar bullet-proof vests.‡ Each commando wore a face mask as well as night-vision goggles. Each carried a miniature radio and an emergency homing device – in case of separation from the main force or, worse, capture – which was in constant contact with the flying control and command centres overhead. The force charged with the killing of Abu Jihad carried silenced *Uzi* submachine-guns (odd, since the Israelis generally employ captured Eastern-bloc weaponry such as the AK-47 for such covert operations) and the Israeli favourite the .22 calibre Beretta automatic. The support personnel carried weapons with greater range, such as the *Galil* series of 5.56mm assault rifles and FN MAG 7.62mm light machine-guns. In addition, each commando carried stun grenades and anti-personnel fragmentation grenades.[10]

Under a cloak of secrecy, the missile-boat armada left the safe shores of Israel in early April and proceeded towards their date with destiny. It would be one of the most dramatic military statements ever to be expressed by the State of Israel.

The decision to proceed with the operation was, in fact, a brave one. On 14 April, French intelligence warned the PLO that an impending raid on Abu Jihad was being planned by the IDF. Major-General Barak counted on PLO over-confidence and Abu Jihad's disdain for air-tight security (he was nicknamed the 'Wailing Wall' by his *Force 17* bodyguards who complained of the scores of people who were allowed

‡ According to several reports, the commandos wore Tunisian National Guard uniforms for added camouflage. Although this report appears to be speculative, it calls to mind the Entebbe raid when commandos wore unique, lizard-pattern camouflage fatigues to impersonate President Idi Amin's Palestinian bodyguards.

to visit him every day) when giving the green light for the mission to go ahead. Abu Jihad believed that any attempt on a senior Palestinian leader's life would target Chairman Arafat, and that since Arafat was in Bahrain at this time the French intelligence reports could not be true; it was a costly mistake.

On 15 April, the Israeli cabinet met to give their blessing or prohibition to the operation. Foreign Minister Shimon Peres and Minister Major-General (Res.) Ezer Weizman (the IAF OC during the 1967 War), it was learned later, were vehemently opposed to this assassination of such a top-level Palestinian figure, arguing that it served no positive purpose. They were voted down by ministers from the right-wing *Likud* party. The operation was on!

As darkness fell on the night of 15 April 1988, the armada of IDF-Navy missile-boats rendezvoused just outside Tunisian territorial waters. The two Boeing 707s flew on civilian flight path Blue 21 between southern Sicily and northern Tunisia and blanketed the area with a thick ECM shield which harassed Tunisian radar facilities and frustrated all communications traffic. Simultaneously, Mossad agents on the ground in Tunis managed to tap into the local telephone lines and block any calls that could have alerted authorities to the impending operation.

Two Naval commandos jumped into the choppy Mediterranean and made their way under water towards the deserted beach where they made contact with the waiting Mossad team. The agents made coded contact with the flying headquarters hovering in the skies and the green light was given to dispatch the remainder of the Naval Commando and *Sayeret Mat'kal* force. Five Zodiac craft were thrown into the water and within seconds the vanguard force of frogmen and four teams of commandos landed on the sandy beach.

The Naval commandos remained behind, assuming defensive positions among the palm-trees that lined the beach, while the flotilla of *Sa'ar* IV class missile-boats retreated beyond the range of Tunisian coastal radar.

In an almost carbon-copy of Operation 'Spring of Youth', the *Mat'kal* commandos were loaded on to three rented vehicles (a Peugeot 305 and two Volkswagen mini-buses) and driven towards Sidi Bouseid. The scenic area was a favourite among the PLO leadership and among Abu Jihad's neighbours were Abu el-Chol, *el-Fatah*'s chief of intelligence, and Abu Massen, the man responsible for covert dialogues with Israeli left-wing politicians. As a result, the tree-lined streets were crawling with armed security personnel.

Shortly after 0100 hours on 16 April, the three Mossad vehicles arrived at Abu Jihad's home and linked up with the Mossad agents who had kept the house and neighbourhood under constant surveillance. Unfortunately, and *not* according to plan, Abu Jihad was not at home, but attending a senior PLO meeting in downtown Tunis. 'A Force' remained in their positions around the Abu Jihad home, while the remainder of the men secured escape routes and defensive firing positions. To cover their identities, the commandos and agents spoke to one another in French and Arabic.

At 0130, Abu Jihad's motorcade returned home. Anxiety was replaced by utter fear and tension as the commandos prepared their gear for the last time and awaited the signal to enter the house. As Jihad went in by the front door, his security guards parked the Mercedes and assumed defensive positions with their Beretta 9 mm submachine-guns and AKMS 7.62 mm assault rifles. The plan was to kill Abu Jihad while he was asleep, but the tireless PLO military commander continued to work, examining video reports from the *Intifadah*. For almost an hour, the Israeli task force had to wait.

Finally, at approximately 0230 hours, the lights in Abu Jihad's second-floor bedroom were extinguished and the house was cloaked in silent darkness. H-Hour was at hand.

As 'D Force' deployed on the curb-side approaches to Abu Jihad's house, 'C Force' took up positions at all entrances and 'B Force' moved into assault position, a commando from 'A Force' stealthily approached Abu Jihad's parked car and killed the snoring driver with a shot to the head from a .22 Beretta automatic. The cast iron doors to the home were blasted off their hinges in a virtually soundless and highly classified technique, allowing 'B Force' to enter the house first and secure the basement and ground floor, while 'A Force' headed up the stairs towards the objective, meeting and killing a sleeping *Force 17* guard in the process.

'A Force' assembled outside Abu Jihad's bedroom door, raised their weapons and burst into the room. Abu Jihad, alerted by the noise outside his room, had managed to raise his head a few inches before his body was riddled with 75 bullets. Abu Jihad's wife, Umm Jihad, was beside her husband, but was unharmed.

Slowly and calmly, the commandos evacuated the scene – hoping to escape notice. With the heavily armed 'C and 'D Forces' securing the escape route, the commandos sped in their vehicles towards the Ras Carthage beach which they reached without incident, to be met by the Naval commandos who had prepared an effective defensive perimeter. After ditching their vehicles on the beach in a tell-tale manner, the commandos boarded their Zodiac crafts and sped towards the missile-boats which, alerted to the success of the operation, had re-entered Tunisian waters.

The Mossad agents went directly to the airport, where each boarded a separate flight to various destinations in western Europe, where they switched to connecting flights for Tel Aviv. Although they had participated in one of the more spectacular operations in the history of Israel's war against terrorism, they returned home nameless and unsung.

The entire 'hit' took an astounding 13 seconds from the time the downstairs doors were blown off to the time the first commandos from

'A Force' departed the house. It was remarkable considering that after all the hundreds of man hours that had gone into the planning, pre-operational details and logistical support procedures for the operation, it was over in the blink of an eye. The operation was a rousing testament to the skill of the Israeli intelligence agents who had laid the groundwork for the raid and also to the 'Chief of Staff's boys' who executed it.

Two days later, on 18 April, the Israeli daily *Yediot Aharonot* reported that 'the terminators of Abu Jihad had returned to Israel by sea'. The armada of *Sa'ar* IV missile-boats, covered by an aerial shield of F-15s and F-16s, had indeed reached the Israeli shores without incident and, in fitting fashion perhaps, the commandos they carried returned to Israel on the eve of remembrance services for the thousands of Israeli war dead and the civilian victims of terrorism.

Umm Jihad, herself a senior official in the PLO, responsible for handling the 'martyr's fund' (also known as the 'First Lady of the Palestinian Revolution'), awoke seconds after the assassination only to find her husband's destroyed body lying beside her. She attempted to telephone the authorities, but the lines had been cut. Her daughter, Hanan, raced hysterically to the nextdoor house of Abu Massen, who responded with legions of Palestinian gunmen and Tunisian security men. They were too late, however, and their response capabilities were hampered by the joint IDF-Mossad ECM *Blitz*.

Umm Jihad had managed to get a split-second look at the attackers and, oddly enough, reported to the media that a blonde Israeli woman speaking French with an Israeli accent had worked with the commando team and had video-taped the killing. She also claims to have confronted the Israeli commandos and faced the wall to be killed. She could not understand why the Israelis hadn't killed her and her daughter. During the earlier Beirut raid, commandos had killed Abu Yusef's wife, as she attempted to shield her husband while he reached for his AK-47. Major 'Yoni' Netanyahu was the officer who had killed Abu Yusef and his wife Maha, and it was a bothering footnote to a successful operation and one to be avoided in Tunis at all costs. For propaganda purposes Umm Jihad stated that Abu Jihad had attempted to resist the Israeli force with a revolver he kept in his desk drawer.

What was in fact found in Abu Jihad's drawer was a comprehensive list of hundreds of Palestinian terrorists operating in Western Europe and in Israel proper.[11] The discovery of the list and countless other invaluable documents was an intelligence bonanza and a counterterrorist victory which in itself would rival the killing of Abu Jihad.

Jihad had escaped previous attempts on his life on three occasions, in Lebanon in 1978 and 1982 and in Teheran in 1980. The fourth try had proved successful. His body was taken to Syria for burial in the Martyrs' Cemetery in the Yarmouk Palestinian Refugee Camp § , south

§ Although no official reason was released, Jordan refused PLO requests to have Abu Jihad buried in Amman. After careful 'behind-the-scenes' negotiations, Syria was the only country willing to accept his body.

of Damascus. Approximately 500,000 people attended the political event and observed Abu Jihad's coffin, draped in the Palestinian flag, being lowered into the Syrian earth – a man who had fought for his nation was exiled even in death. Also in attendance were many prominent figures in the Palestinian Movement including the DFLP's Nayif Hawatmeh and the PFLP's Doctor George Habash. Oddly enough, Abu Jihad's closest friend and comrade in *el-Fatah*, PLO Chairman Yasir Arafat, did not participate in the funeral, possibly fearing for his life in Syria. Arafat was in Libya that day, perhaps cementing deals and agreements originally masterminded by the late 'Father Holy War'.

Syrian President Hafez al-Assad was in attendance and Jordan's King Hussein eulogized Abu Jihad with emotional words of praise. It seemed odd that the death of Abu Jihad would serve as a unifying call among the leaders of the fractured Arab world. During 'Black September', Abu Jihad had personally participated in much of the bloody warfare waged between the Palestinians and the Bedouin legions of King Hussein's Royal Jordanian Army. Later, he would play an instrumental role in the Black September Organization's bloody revenge campaign against the Hashemite Kingdom. During the inter-faction political fighting characteristic of the PLO in the mid-1970s, Syrian Intelligence expressed displeasure with the second most powerful man in *el-Fatah* by hurling Abu Jihad's son out of a window from their high-rise Damascus apartment. Jihad never forgave the Syrians for the murder of his son and in the 1975–6 Lebanese Civil War he orchestrated Palestinian military resistance to the brutal Syrian intervention on behalf of the Lebanese Christians, resulting in hundreds of Syrian Army casualties.

Of all the Palestinian terrorist leaders killed since the onset of Israel's undeclared war against Black September in 1972, Abu Jihad was certainly the most important. Among the other leaders assassinated, either by the Israelis or by rival Palestinian factions, the list includes:

■ Kamal A'dwan, Kamal Nasser and Abu Yusef killed in Operation 'Spring of Youth' in April 1973.

■ Sa'id Hamami, the PLO representative in London, shot and killed in his London office on 4 January 1978.

■ A'li Yasin, Director of the PLO office in Kuwait, killed by gunfire on 15 June 1978.

■ Ali Hassan Salameh, Head of *el-Fatah* special operations, former *Force 17* senior officer in Black September and the infamous 'Red Prince' of the Munich Olympics massacre, killed by a car bomb in Beirut on 22 January 1979.

■ Zuheir Muhsin, a senior PLO military commander, shot and killed in Cannes, on 25 July 1979.

■ Samir Tuqan, Second Secretary of the PLO's office in Nicosia, killed by gunfire on 15 December 1979.

■ Na'im Hadjar, PLO representative in Belgium, killed by a burst of automatic gunfire on 1 June 1981.

■   Majir Abu Shrar, PLO Information Minister, killed by an explosion in his hotel room in Rome on 9 October 1981.

■   Kamal Hussein, deputy PLO representative in Rome, killed by a powerful explosive blast in Rome on 17 June 1982.

■   Fald Dani, deputy manager of the PLO office in France, killed by a bomb placed in his car in Paris on 23 July 1982.

■   Sa'ad Sa'il (Abu Waleed), PLO's military chief of staff in Lebanon, killed in a dramatic ambush in Lebanon's Beka'a Valley in September 1982. According to foreign reports, the ambush was the handiwork of *Sayeret Mat'kal*.

■   Issam Sartawi, PLO's political 'Secretary of State', killed in Portugal by Abu Nidal gunmen on 10 April 1983.

■   Ma'amun Mar'wish, one of Abu Jihad's top deputies, killed in Athens on 20 August 1983.

■   Hald N'zal, controller of terrorist activity in the occupied territories and an important member of the Democratic Front for the Liberation of Palestine's central committee, killed in Athens on 10 June 1986.

■   Brigadier Abu Ghazala, naval commander of *el-Fatah* operations, killed in Athens by a bomb placed in his car on 21 October 1986.

Yasir Arafat himself has also been the target in several attempted assassination operations.

In the days following the Israeli victory in the June 1967 Six Day War, *Sayeret Haruv*, an élite paratroop reconnaissance force of the IDF's Central Command, was given the order to seize 'Abu Ammar', *nom de guerre* of Yasir Arafat. Arafat, not then as famous as today, had slipped through Israeli hands in East Jerusalem and the affluent city of Ramallah in 1967 and his capture [or murder] was given serious priority. *Sayeret Haruv* received intelligence reporting Arafat's whereabouts in Jordan, including a description of the vehicle he used – a white jeep with special *el-Fatah* markings. A specially equipped platoon was placed on full, standby alert and they crossed into Jordan on numerous occasions to stop suspect vehicles, but were unsuccessful in locating their man.

An Israeli magazine, *Ha'olam Hazeh* (This World), has recently revealed that Mossad has wanted to assassinate Arafat since the mid-1960s, but claim they have been unable to do so because the 'opportunity never arose'. According to accounts publicized in the Israeli daily, *Yediot Aharonot*, which quoted a book published in Cairo, the Mossad is rumoured to have hatched several assassination attempts on PLO chairman Yasir Arafat in 1978, when Mossad agents were dispatched to the Far East to 'poison' the wily Mr Arafat; and, in 1979, a similar attempt to envenom Abu Ammar in Romania while in a compromising situation. A selective strike was apparently ordered after Israel's invasion of Lebanon in 1982, but it failed due to inadequate groundwork by agents. This seems a curious explanation given that Mossad had managed to organize numerous difficult operations in

Lebanon thanks to its excellent human intelligence sources, not to mention its specially cultivated relationship with the Maronite Christians. It was also said that special aerial units, including pilotless drones, were tasked to eliminate Arafat with a precision strike, but he continued to be an elusive target. It seems that Arafat came closest to death in late August 1982, during the PLO's evacuation from Beirut. As the legions of Palestinian fighters departed, firing volleys of victorious fire into the Beirut sky, an IDF sniper team located the PLO chairman and a marksman placed his head within the cross-hairs of his M-21 7.62mm accurized sniper rifle. Although the young conscript was eager to squeeze the trigger, a senior IDF officer (rumoured to be IDF Chief of Staff Lieutenant-General Rafael Eitan) forbade the killing of Arafat because Israel had promised the United States that it wouldn't violate the cease-fire and take advantage of the Palestinian withdrawal to settle 'old scores'.[12] Once again, Arafat's life was spared.

There has been much speculation as to the 'real reason' why a serious attempt, like the Abu Jihad assassination, has never been attempted on Arafat's life. There are those who believe that killing Arafat would achieve absolutely nothing for Israel; in fact making a martyr out of an ineffective and sometimes laughing-stock leader of the Palestinians – especially with its international repercussions and pan-Arab/pan-Palestinian unifying potential. This theory seems the most logical, especially since to have the Palestinian Movement led by a George Habash and an Ahmed Jibril is certainly *not* in Israel's national interest. Then there are those who believe that Arafat is an Israeli agent; his habit of surviving a turbulent, tumultuous and violent Arab-Israeli conflict serving as the best proof for this. Whatever the true reasons, the fact that he is alive today proves that it is and has been in Israel's national interest to allow Arafat to live.

The death of Abu Jihad was a severe blow to the Palestine Liberation Organization. He was the one of their most intelligent leaders, a man who listened more than he spoke. He was consistent in his beliefs, actions, political affiliations and was known as the 'honest man of the revolution'. While the suicide squads he dispatched to attack targets in Israel were the fodder of the cause, Abu Jihad was its mind and soul. His death hampered the ability of *el-Fatah* to execute terror operations in Europe and Israel, but with hard-liners remaining in the hierarchy of the PLO, such as ex-Black September chieftain Abu Iyad, further acts of terror are inevitable.

Usually, any change in the PLO's delicate balance of power is an invitation to spasms of brutal violence. In the past, more Palestinians have been killed in bitter feuds with other Palestinians and Arabs than by the IDF. The main contenders to assume Abu Jihad's role as PLO military commander are Abu Muatassem and *Force 17*'s commander, Abu Tayeb. There was also outward friction, which had existed for some time, between Arafat supporters and Abu Jihad's private legions of terrorists. The rivalry became public in March 1987 when the *Force 17* commander of southern Lebanon, Hussein al-Haibe, was assassinated by Abu Jihad loyalists in *el-Fatah*. Five months later, the new south Lebanon regional commander of *Force 17* was also killed, this time by an *el-Fatah* death squad from the pro-Abu Jihad 'Ein el-Hilweh battalion'. In Sidon, *Force 17* responded by critically wounding a loyal Abu Jihad supporter, Abu Ali Shaheen, who was the principal liaison officer for Abu Jihad and the fundamentalist Shi'ite and Sunni Muslim groups in Lebanon. In fact, an *el-Fatah* civil war had seemed imminent at the time of the brilliant lightning operation in Tunis. Indeed, many therefore initially speculated that the Abu Jihad assassination could have been an 'inside' job, but such suspicions were quickly dispelled by the emerging details of Israel's involvement. According to one anonymous Western intelligence source, 'If the Palestinians or Syrians were behind the killing, half of Tunis would have been destroyed.'

For the Palestinians in the West Bank and Gaza, the death of Abu Jihad was yet another setback in their search for viable and capable leadership. If in life, Abu Jihad meant to escalate the level of violence in the *Intifadah*, his death achieved that goal with gruesome success. Anti-Israeli demonstrations, stone- and Molotov-throwing incidents to mourn the killing of Abu Jihad resulted in fourteen dead and dozens of wounded. Abu Jihad would soon become yet another martyr in the cause, a man whose name would be adopted by fanatical men of the PLO's *Jaish esh-Sha'ab* (or 'Popular Army') in the occupied territories. Their unit, the *Abu Jihad Commando*, specialized in the brutal murders of suspected Israeli collaborators.

For Israel, denial was and remains the password *vis-à-vis* the Abu Jihad killings, but, obviously, no one expressed any words of sympathy. Jihad was one of the State of Israel's most devoted enemies, a man who was as cunning as he was ruthless and cold-blooded. Jema'a Musa, one of the surviving terrorists from the March 1975 Savoy Hotel incident, told Israeli investigators that Abu Jihad had personally ordered him 'to murder and kill as many Israelis as possible'. Although Abu Jihad's death would not bring about the dismantling of the PLO, it did avenge numerous acts of murder as well as buy valuable time for the overwhelmed IDF. It may have prevented the *Intifadah* from erupting into a bitter all-encompassing life and death struggle.

For the IDF, a proud, conventional army getting bogged down in a frustrating urban conflict against teenage opponents, the assassination of Abu Jihad was a sorely needed morale booster. Just as the 1976 Entebbe rescue operation helped bring Israel out of its shock and malaise from the crushing casualties suffered in the Yom Kippur War, and the June 1981 IAF raid on the Iraqi nuclear reactor helped end an indecisive period of national politics, so too did the Tunis operation bring a sense of pride and a feeling of the nostalgic 'good old days' of brilliantly executed punitive raids back into the ranks of the beleaguered Israel Defence Forces.

The raid did have other repercussions though. According to a 9

July 1988 article in *Al-Ittihad*, an Abu Dhabi newspaper, Tunisian internal security agents arrested approximately 40 members of a Mossad espionage network believed to be responsible in some way for the Abu Jihad assassination. The arrested included Tunisian Jews and several Palestinians and Lebanese living in Tunis, as well as several prominent Tunisians living abroad. At the centre of the arrested Israeli espionage ring was a female night club artist whose house was placed under surveillance by the Tunisian security services because dozens of suspected 'Jews' frequently visited it. After an interrogation, she admitted that she had frequently visited Europe to meet senior Mossad agents and that her contacts with well-placed Palestinians allowed her to collect intimate information on the movements of Abu Jihad. The ring had received in excess of $10 million for their efforts. The fate of those arrested remains unknown.

Perhaps Israeli commando operations may rob the Palestinian revolution of their icon leaders, but it still cannot purchase peace.

And one that failed...

The assassination of Abu Jihad was not the swan-song of the war against terrorism in any way, shape or form. In fact, the spectacular operation could even be viewed as just another salvo in a war characterized by years of incessant and destructive volleys.

In the early hours of 9 December 1988, an IDF task force of Naval Commandos and reconnaissance infantrymen from *Sayeret Golani* landed on the Lebanese coast, three kilometres from the coastal city of Damur. Under cover of darkness they deployed from their Zodiac rubber dinghies and began a fierce forced march towards the suburb of Na'ameh, an exclusive hillside neighbourhood and headquarters of the Popular Front for the Liberation of Palestine General Command, led by Ahmed Jibril. Jibril had proven himself to be a formidable foe; he had masterminded several of the grand tactics used by Palestinian terrorists, including the letter bomb and the airline bombing (*see* page 26). During the 1982 War in Lebanon, Jibril's forces had captured three IDF soldiers whom they held captive until they were exchanged on 20 May 1985 for *1,150* convicted Palestinian and international terrorists in Israeli gaols.*

Ahmed Jibril had also been behind the spectacular 'Night of the Hang-Glider' incident which contributed to the onset of the *Intifadah*.

---

* Among those freed were Ibrahim Tawfik Youssef, Hassan Ali al-Attar and Hasez Dalkemam. The two were originally arrested in Kenya following a bungled attempt to blow an El Al airliner out of the sky with a hand-held SAM-7 surface-to-air missile in 1976. They were secretly smuggled to Israel, tried and sentenced to 18 years imprisonment. Following Jibril's masterfully induced prisoner exchange, they were smuggled to West Germany to establish a terrorist cell in Frankfurt. According to Western intelligence sources, it was the handiwork of these three hard-core PFLP-GC terrorists which brought down Pan Am Flight 103.

Israel chose the first anniversary of the outbreak of the Palestinian uprising for its opportunity to eliminate Ahmed Jibril.

Although Israel has never admitted that the death of Jibril was its objective in the 9 December 1988 raid, numerous non-Israeli reports have listed Jibril's killing as the sole objective of the operation.

Unlike the flamboyant and Press-hungry among the PLO hierarchy, Ahmed Jibril was not an easy target. He rarely ventured outside the immediate safety of Damascus or Syrian-controlled areas of Lebanon and *always* travelled with an entourage of well-paid killers who sported everything from small arms to surface-to-air missiles. As a result, a covert assassination attempt, along the lines of the operations that had eliminated many of Black September's top leadership in the 1970s, was not possible. Air power was also of minimum use, as Jibril's installations were heavily defended and usually within the range of Syrian SAM batteries, especially in eastern Lebanon's Beka'a Valley. In addition, his Na'ameh headquarters was well entrenched in the hills surrounding Damour and his command complex was situated safely underground. A purely military operation was required and this was why a call had gone through to the Naval Commandos and the élite of the Golani Brigade.

Training for the raid on the Jibril camp was carried out in great secrecy. Internal security on such a commando operation was of paramount importance; the prospect of a well-informed PFLP-GC ambushing the vulnerable attacking force would have resulted in a disaster. In the early planning stages of the operation, the two units trained separately. Once the initial skills were mastered they combined their talents under the watchful eyes of their respective commanders, curious generals and the most important judge of all – Chief of Staff Lieutenant-General Dan Shomron. The tireless training continued until perfection and split-second synchronization had been achieved. When all the components of the 'Jibril task force' were ready, the go-ahead was given for Lieutenant-General Shomron to order the date of the assault. It would be one of the largest Israeli operations in Lebanon since the 1982 fighting.†

Just after midnight on 9 December, several dark-grey Zodiac rubber dinghies were lowered into the cold dark waters from the holding pens on an Israeli missile-boat anchored just off the Damur coast. The Naval Commandos wore black rubber wet suits and carried a wide assortment of weapons, including ex-Palestinian RPG-7 anti-tank rockets and *Uzi* submachine-guns fitted with silencers to remove PFLP-GC sentries. Following close behind the Naval Commandos was the Golani force, unaccustomed to the splashing waters and tumultuous waves and eager to reach dry land. After achieving a beachhead and setting up a medevac position, the men set off on the three-kilometre journey to the objective.

† In the spring of 1988, a large-sized paratroop force attacked the *Hizbollah* stronghold of Maidun in southern Lebanon because of their assistance to Palestinian terrorist infiltration teams attempting to attack Israel during its 40th anniversary celebrations.

As the men locked and loaded their weapons and the commanders whispered final instructions to one another, the commando force split into the four sections that would attack four separate positions and awaited H-Hour.

At 0200 hours, they struck. As a PFLP-GC sentry put down his brand-new AKMS assault rifle to light a cigarette, the crackling sound of automatic gunfire filled the air. 'Force A' formed the vanguard of the assault, the group entrusted with killing Jibril. Although encountering heavy enemy fire, they succeeded in approaching the series of two-storey buildings which housed Jibril's headquarters, killing a number of Palestinians in the bitter fire-fight. Intelligence had reported that Jibril employed a labyrinth of Viet Cong-type tunnels (built, it has been rumoured, under the guidance of imported Vietnamese officers) which were used to protect arms caches and PFLP-GC commanders from an anticipated Israeli attack. According to foreign reports, the Israelis responded with a cruel, though effective countermeasure. Instead of engaging the tunnel occupants as American soldiers had done in Vietnam with the 'tunnel rats' (short and agile soldiers armed with .45 calibre automatics), the Golani force used specially trained Dober-manns fitted with knapsacks loaded with high-explosives. Although several dogs made it through the murderous hails of automatic fire to inflict severe damage, including the killing of the PFLP-GC intelligence chief Abu Jamil, they failed to penetrate the heart of the tunnel system where it was thought Jibril lay. After four hours of tortuous combat, the Israelis were surrounded and out of ammunition, so they broke out and headed towards the beach for a heliborne evacuation.

'Force B', commanded by Lieutenant-Colonel Amir Meital, was to attack a series of six adjacent caves in a nearby mountain used as a barracks. The caves were heavily defended and since the only access was through the main base perimeter, this was considered the toughest objective of all to achieve because the terrorists would already have been awakened by the sound of gunfire. Firing incessant volleys from their rifle-launched grenades and 7.62 mm light machine-guns, Meital's men were able to penetrate the darkened caves where they set about destroying them. The defenders had other ideas and fought back with suicidal determination in a fire-fight conducted at point-blank range. Inside the caves, dozens of private, mostly hand-to-hand mini-battles erupted between the Israeli and Palestinian fighters. The automatic fire was so heavy that the engulfing odour of burnt gunpower and cordite choked both attacker and defender alike. As Lieutenant-Colonel Meital co-ordinated his forces for one last push inside the caves, a burst of machine-gun fire ripped through his chest and killed the 29-year-old officer instantly. As had always been the tradition in the IDF, the officer would be the first to fall.

Although 'Force C' (entrusted with destroying the PFLP-GC's training base for international terrorists) and 'Force D' (ordered to destroy a series of anti-tank and anti-aircraft missile emplacements) had executed their objectives perfectly, they had suffered dozens of serious casualties. All the Israeli forces, in fact, had absorbed extremely heavy casualties. As the winter's sun began to rise to betray his men's positions, the commando task force commander ordered a withdrawal toward the waiting Naval Commandos a few kilometres away where a short boat trip would take them out to sea and safety. The severe injuries of many of the wounded prevented this and the frantic order was given for a helicopter rescue to be implemented. Leaving the bodies of more than twenty PFLP-GC fighters killed and dozens more wounded strewn about the Na'ameh base, the Golani force gathered its wounded on stretchers and headed for the rendezous point with the Naval Commandos, taking heavy fire from Palestinian units giving chase.

As the tired fighters began to board their Bell-212 choppers for the quick ride back to Israel, it became apparent that four men had been separated from the main attack force and had been left behind in Na'ameh to face certain capture or death. They were fighting with grim determination, but bullets and time were both running out. With the prospect of four Golani infantrymen in the clutches of a vengeful Ahmed Jibril, Chief of Staff Shomron ordered an immediate rescue operation. One of the most sacred codes of Israeli military ethics is 'never leave men behind' and Shomron was determined to adhere to it religiously. As the transport choppers ferrying the original task force made its way back to Israel, a squadron of Cobra attack helicopters flew towards the besieged men at full speed. Alerted to their position by smoke grenades, several Cobras began blasting away at the encroaching Palestinian units with accurate TOW missiles, while two Cobras proceeded towards a field of wild flowers and the rescue. With no time to secure a rope harness, the helicopter pilots ordered the four soldiers to grab the Cobra's landing boards and hold on for dear life! Absorbing the blasts of air from the chopper's whipping rotor blades, they held on doggedly until safe. Escorting the operation were flights of F-16 and *Kfir*-C-7 fighter-bombers, who used their ordnance to keep the Palestinians at bay.

The raid was a brilliantly planned operation, executed in a courageous fashion and one rivalling the exploits of past IDF special operations. In hours of intense combat, the IDF had dealt a severe blow to the PFLP-GC, but had failed to kill Jibril. Thousands attended the funeral of Lieutenant-Colonel Meital and mourned the death of one of the nation's youngest and most capable officers. The IAF awarded the Cobra pilots medals of valour, for the self-sacrificing courage they had displayed in the rescue of their Golani comrades. Meanwhile, in Damascus, a jubilant Jibril clutched a captured Israeli *Galil* assault rifle and vowed revenge, though not specifying where and when this would materialize. In Washington, the US State Department criticized Israel for the raid and its violation of Lebanese territory.

Two weeks after the attempt on Jibril's life, Pan Am 103 disintegrated over the town of Lockerbie in Scotland. Ahmed Jibril's PFLP-GC left the obscure arena of the Arab-Israeli conflict to take the world stage by striking at a superpower. Had the Israeli operation succeeded, Pan Am 103 might never have been blown out of the sky.

The Israel Defence Forces, and the IAF in particular, have not relinquished the right and the obligation to attack Jibril's PFLP-GC. Following the IDF's December 1988 Na'ameh raid, the IAF had mounted several deep-penetration bombing runs against PFLP-GC headquarters, training camps, and arms depots. Usually the raids targeted PFLP-GC positions along the Lebanese coast but, in March 1989, the IAF bombed a PFLP-GC base deep inside the Syrian-controlled Beka'a Valley in which fifteen people were killed. The fact that the raid was directed against a PFLP-GC base in an area dominated by Syrian SAMs was a concise and direct message to Damascus, warning that its support of terrorist groups responsible for strikes against Israel could *seriously* escalate the level of tension in the volatile Israeli–Lebanese–Syrian triangle.

Most importantly the IAF raid sent an ominous message to Jibril that his time was running out. Because he is the leading suspect as the mastermind behind the bombing of Pan Am 103 he has become 'fair game' as far as the West is concerned – a fact not lost to Israel who will thus suffer fewer public relations losses should Jibril die as a result of their actions. Only time will tell when Ahmed Jibril will indeed be killed for his past actions and martyred for 'the cause'.

Postscript

After years of aircraft seizures, random shootings, bombings and cross-border massacres, on 6 July 1989 Israel witnessed a most unusual terrorist attack.

The No. 405 express bus between Tel Aviv and Jerusalem is perhaps Israel's busiest inter-city connection. A bus leaves the chaotic Tel Aviv Central Bus Station almost every five minutes and is always filled to capacity with off-duty soldiers, pious worshippers heading towards the holy city's synagogues, churches and mosques; and young and eager tourists toting back-packs and visions of history. On the afternoon of 6 July, a crowded bus had as one of its passengers a young Gazan named A'bd el-Ha'di Ghneim. He was a member of the shadowy *Jihad al-Islami* or 'Islamic Holy War' and had taken the 50-minute bus ride frequently during several weeks, judging and calculating every twist and turn of the winding road, memorizing each one like a passage from the Koran. As the bus made its way along the narrow highway lined with eucalyptus trees, white rock hills and skeletal armoured cars from the 1948 War, Ghneim jumped out of his seat and began yelling '*Allahu Akbar*' ['God is Great']. He raced through the narrow aisle screaming and made for the driver's seat. At a carefully selected spot on the road near a steep mountain ravine, Ghneim grabbed the steering wheel from the driver and brought the loaded Mercedes bus crashing down a 200-foot cliff.

The scene was one of death and destruction. As passers-by raced down the steep incline to pull survivors out of the twisted hulk of burning metal, Israel Air Force medevac helicopters ferried the critically injured to hospital. In all, fifteen passengers were killed and 27 seriously injured. Ghneim survived the fall and his home in the Nuseirat refugee camp was duly destroyed by IDF Combat Engineer sappers. Meanwhile, Police Minister Lieutenant-General (Res.) Haim Bar-Lev carefully questioned whether the death penalty should be applied to terrorists. (The last man to be put to death in Israel was Adolph Eichmann, who was killed for his ghastly 'crimes against humanity'.)

As Israel reeled at the horror of religiously inspired acts of terror within its own borders, its military forces were busy preparing the groundwork for a commando operation meant to combat such zealous acts on its northern frontier.

On the night of 28 July 1989, as Muslims throughout the south of Lebanon were preparing to celebrate their Sabbath, three Israel Air Force helicopters landed near the Shi'ite village of Jibchit. While supersonic aircraft staged a mock air raid to muffle the beating of the helicopter rotor blades, about a dozen commandos from, according to foreign reports, *Sayeret Mat'kal* headed towards the home of Sheikh Abdul Karim Obe'id, a senior Muslim cleric and southern Lebanon commander of the fundamentalist Shi'ite guerrilla movement known as *Hizbollah*: The Party of God.

According to foreign reports, the commandos wore combat fatigues darkened by black grease and carried pistols and submachine-guns fitted with silencers. They moved stealthily through the winding alleyways and unpaved roads of Jibchit without attracting the slightest attention of the dozens of heavily armed Shi'ite gunmen who were never very far away. At 0100 hours on 28 July the force of twelve struck, blowing the hinges off Sheikh Obe'id's front door with plastic explosives. After securing the flat, the Arabic-speaking commandos handcuffed Obe'id's wife Mona and five children and taped their mouths shut with electrical tape. A reluctant Obe'id and two of his senior lieutenants were tied up and dragged to a waiting chopper. As he was led away, Obe'id was heard screaming in Arabic, 'Kill me! I won't go with you!'

A neighbour who came to his window upon hearing the commotion was killed by one of the commandos, but no one else was hurt during the operation which lasted less than thirty minutes. Heavily armed gunmen from the rival Shi'ite *Amal* militia attempted to interdict the Israeli operation, but two of the helicopters hovered overhead firing incessant bursts of machine-gun fire, while the third chopper raced back to Israel with its cargo. Many Western intelligence sources would later comment that the Israeli raid exhibited 'healthy doses of genius, resolve and daring'!

Sheikh Abdul Karim Obe'id was an Iranian-educated cleric, who was one of *Hizbollah*'s chief of operations. A fiery orator and devout disciple of the Ayatollah Khomeini's decree for a *jihad* against Israel, the United States and all enemies of Islam, Obe'id's *Hizbollah* was behind dozens of terrorist attacks against the West, including: the April 1983 bombing of the American embassy in Beirut, the October 1983 bombing of the Marine barracks at Beirut International Airport and the November 1983 suicide bombing of the Israeli administration headquarters in Tyre.

They are, however, most notorious for random kidnappings. For various reasons, ranging from the freeing of Shi'ite terrorists in Kuwait to random acts of criminality to express political displeasure, more than a dozen American, French and British hostages have been taken by eight groups whose visiting-cards have ranged from 'Islamic Holy War for the Liberation of Palestine' to the 'Organization of the Oppressed on Earth'. It was the latter shadowy group that kidnapped an American Marine officer, Lieutenant-Colonel William R. Higgins, serving as an observer in the United Nations Interim Force in Lebanon (UNIFIL). All the groups are suspected of being connected to the Party of God.

The day after Sheikh Obe'id had been taken into Israeli custody and was undergoing an intense Israeli interrogation, the 'Organization of the Oppressed on Earth' released a gruesome videotape of a lifeless figure hanging from a noose. The man was identified as Lieutenant-Colonel Higgins. His death, it was claimed, was in retaliation for Israel's abduction of Sheikh Obe'id.

While it is highly improbable that Lieutenant-Colonel Higgins was executed as a result of the Israeli action (*Hizbollah* was known to treat its military and intelligence captives, such as the murdered Beirut CIA Station Chief, William Buckley, in a brutal fashion), many blamed Israel for his death. Calls rang out for Israel to release Sheikh Obe'id immediately in order to spare the lives of other American hostages. In typical fashion, the United Nations censured Israel for its actions, conveniently forgetting that Lieutenant-Colonel Higgins had been working as peace-keeper and had been *murdered* by *Hizbollah*. According to Charles Krauthammer, a syndicated columinist, these calls suggested that, 'The United Nations had progressed beyond impotence to a state of meek and sick complicity with evil.'

Israel, however, stood fast. While such an operation was within the framework of an anti-terrorism strategy meant to punish *Hizbollah* for its bombings, kidnappings and anti-Western/Israeli attacks, *Hizbollah* was holding three Israeli servicemen – two tank soldiers (Yosef Fink and Rami Levi) kidnapped by *Hizbollah* gunmen in southern Lebanon in an abduction operation on 17 February 1986, and Ron Arad, an Israel Air Force F-4E Phantom navigator shot down over Sidon on 16 October 1986 – and they wanted them back (later reports indicated that both Fink and Levi had been killed in captivity).

Israel has an unwritten, though lapidary agreement with its soldiers that should they be captured, the government, the Israel Defence Forces and the shadowy intelligence community will do anything and everything to secure their release. When the *Sayeret Mat'kal* commandos abducted Sheikh Obe'id, it was to gain them an added leverage in the stalled and frustrated efforts to bring their men home. His kidnapping also sent a clear message to *Hizbollah* that its incessant campaign of car bombings and shootings of Israeli soldiers will *not* be tolerated. The operation also dispatched a loud signal to the leadership of *Hizbollah*, especially its spiritual leader, Sheik Fadlallah, that they may feel safe in Beirut, but Israel's commandos have reached there too, more than once.

Yet beyond the scope of spectacular counter-terrorist commando operations, Israel's struggle against terrorism remains a bitter one. In the *Intifadah*, the cavalcade of stone-throwing youths has been re-placed by a shadowy war of terror and fratricide. The emphasis of the uprising has turned from seemingly 'non-lethal' acts of defiance against Israel, such as stones and Molotov cocktails being hurled at Israeli forces, to a PLO-ordered policy of eliminating 'collaborators'. In the two years since the *Intifadah* first erupted, hundreds of Palestinians have been killed by PLO 'enforcer squads', armed with everything from axes to stolen *Uzi* submachine-guns. The deaths of so many collaborators has left the police and Shin Bet with such a shortage of reliable intelligence sources that the Israelis have gone so far as to arm these men and train them to 'stop' the uprising.

As the struggle to keep the *Intifadah* fires burning has turned to small and shadowy cells of highly trained terrorists, extraordinary counter-measures have been taken. One of the newest is a policy called 'Bingo'. IDF infantry and paratroop units are issued with a Shin Bet-supplied list of wanted terrorists and they then conduct midnight heliborne village-hopping forays to capture these men. As the level of violence always increases in the Middle East with such initiatives, rejectionist-front elements of the PLO, such as the DFLP and the Abu Nidal group, have urged the Palestinians in the Occupied Territories to uncover the hidden arms caches and murder thousands of Israelis. In perhaps an ominous move to escalate the violence, the Palestinian groups have begun infiltration attempts from the Jordanian frontier, with more than ten such incidents being reported in 1989 alone.

The Palestinians introduced terrorism as the currency of the modern world almost twenty years ago. Accordingly, Israel's war against that terrorism has been a co-ordinated, all-inclusive effort requiring the might of the nation's military, security, intelligence and police forces. For Israel's guards without frontiers, their epic struggle against hijackings, bombings and cold-blooded killings has on the whole been a victory, and one used by the entire international community as a positive and inspiring example of how terrorism can be fought head-on.

Terrorism has presented Israel with as dire a challenge to her existence as any nation can endure. The very fact that Israel continues to survive as a functioning democracy is a testament to the sacrifice of intelligence agents, counter-intelligence operatives, soldiers, sailors, airmen and policemen. They have operated both on an international stage and in the confines of the streets they call home. They have fought with their minds, their intuitive skills and with heavy fire-power. Yet their hard labour, incessant efforts, technological supremacy and courageous acts under fire cannot protect every Israeli diplomat, aircraft and citizen from harm, nor can it hermetically seal its frontiers and stop terrorists from infiltrating men and material: some acts, like the destruction of the No. 405 bus, are ones of spontaneous hatred for which there is no preventive cure.

For Jews and Palestinians, two peoples whose customs, cultures and language are so similar, the only foreseeable course of history remains one of continuing hatred and violence. With the polarization induced by fanaticism present on both sides, the signs are not encouraging and greater instances of bloodshed seem tragically imminent, be they planned or spontaneous. Perhaps more than ever, Israel's survival as the nation it is now and the nation it strives to be, is dependent on its guards without frontiers.

Chronicle of Terrorist Operations

Year	Incident	Group Responsible
1968		
23 July	Terrorists take over an El Al flight *en route* from Rome to Tel Aviv, forcing it to land in Algeria.	PFLP (Habash)
26 December	Terrorists attack an El Al aircraft in Athens with small arms and grenades. 1 Israeli passenger killed. Terrorists detained by Greeks, but released following the hijacking of an Olympic Airliner.	PFLP
1969		
18 February	Four terrorists attack an aircraft in Zurich with small arms and grenades. Co-pilot killed, and dozens wounded. El Al security kills one terrorist, and others are released in September 1970 following hijacking of Swissair plane to Jordan.	PFLP
8 September	Three terrorists throw grenade into El Al office in Brussels, wounding two.	PFLP
27 November	Two terrorists throw grenade into an El Al office in Athens, wounding 14. Terrorists were released following hijacking of an Olympic flight to Jordan on 22 July 1970.	PSF (Popular Struggle Front) (Dr. Samir Ghosha)
1970		
10 February	Three terrorist fire automatic weapons and throw grenades at passengers about to board an El Al flight in Munich, killing 1 and wounding 8. All the terrorists are released from West German custody after Black September, 1970.	Executive Committee for the Liberation of Palestine (*el-Fatah*)
24 April	Explosion in El Al Office in Istanbul.	PSF
6 September	Abortive attempt to hijack an El Al flight. In mid-air shootout, one terrorist is killed, and Leila Khaled is seized, eventually touching off the Black September hijackings and the Jordanian Civil War.	PFLP
1971		
28 July	Attempt to blow up a Rome–Tel Aviv flight by means of booby-trapped suitcase brought on board by unsuspecting Dutch woman.	PFLP-GC (Jibril)
1 September	Attempt to blow up a London–Tel Aviv flight by means of booby-trapped suitcase brought on board by unsuspecting Peruvian woman.	PFLP-GC
1972		
16 August	Attempt to blow up a Rome–Tel Aviv flight by means of booby-trapped record player (explodes in luggage compartment) brought on board by two British females.	PFLP-GC
13 October	Bomb discovered in Paris El Al office	Unknown

Year	Incident	Group Responsible
1973		
6 March	Attempt to destroy El Al terminal at New York's Kennedy Airport by car bomb.	Black September
4 April	Attempt to blow up an El Al aircraft in Rome.	PFLP
9 April	Attempt to seize *Arkia* (an Israeli charter carrier) aircraft in Cyprus foiled by Israeli security officers.	ANYLP (Arab Nationalist Youth Liberation of Palestine)
11 April	Molotov cocktail hurled at El Al Office in Geneva.	Unknown
19 July	Attempt by terrorists to seize El Al Office in Athens thwarted by El Al's security guards.	PFLP
5 September	Missile attack on an aircraft at Rome Airport thwarted. Five terrorists caught in possession of SAM-7. The terrorists were later released and returned to Libya.	Black September
1975		
13 January	Two terrorists fire RPG rockets at flight taxiing at Paris Airport, but hit Yugoslav airliner parked nearby instead, wounding three.	PFLP
19 January	Attempted attack on El Al aircraft at Paris Airport results in gun fight with police and security agents.	PFLP ('Mohamad Boudia Commando')
1976		
11 August	Three terrorists attack plane at Istanbul Airport, killing four and wounding 21. Terrorists sentenced to life imprisonment.	Wadi Haddad Faction
6 November	Bomb explodes in El Al ticket office in Instanbul.	Unknown
1978		
20 May	Three terrorists attack passengers at El Al terminal at Orly Airport, Paris. Two civilians killed, and all the terrorists killed by El Al security guards and French police.	PFLP
20 August	Five terrorists attack bus carrying 20 El Al crew members in London, killing one stewardess, and wounding 3 others. One terrorist killed by El Al security.	Wadi Haddad Faction
1979		
1 April	Attack on El Al office in Istanbul thwarted by El Al security guards.	*As-Saiqa* (Vanguards of the Popular Liberation War)
16 April	Three terrorists attack passengers at El Al lounge in Brussels Airport with automatic weapons and grenades, wounding twelve.	*el-Fatah*
1980		
18 February	Explosion near Rome El Al office.	ASALA (Armenian Secret Army for the Liberation of Armenia)
21 April	Attempt to blow up Zurich–Tel Aviv flight by booby-trapped suitcase carried by German youth. Bomb, meant to explode in mid air, was discovered by inquisitive El Al security agent.	Wadi Haddad Faction
1981		
15, 16 May	Bombs explode at Rome and Istanbul El Al offices, respectively.	Unknown
9 August	Bomb explodes at Rome El Al office, killing one employee.	Unknown
7 October	Bomb explodes at Rome El Al office, wounding 8.	Unknown
1982		
9 January	Bomb explodes near El Al office in Istanbul.	Abu Ibrahim Group
29 March	Attempt to attack El Al office in Rome thwarted by El Al security.	*el-Fatah*

1983

25 December   Attempt to blow up a flight from West Germany to Israel   Abu Ibrahim Group
thwarted by El Al security guards.

1985

27 August   Bomb explodes at El Al office in Istanbul.   Islamic Jihad
30 September   Bomb explodes at El Al office in Holland.   Abu Nidal Faction

References

Introduction
1. Stewart Steven, *The Spymasters of Israel*, New York: Macmillan & Co., 1980, p. 107.
2. Yosef Argaman, 'How Colonel Hafaz Was Eliminated,' in *Bamachane*, IDF Official Weekly Magazine, 4 November 1987, p. 39.
3. *Ibid*, p. 41.
4. *Ibid*, p. 60.

1. Mossad
1. Jillian Becker, *The PLO: The Rise and Fall of the PLO*, Weidenfeld & Nicolson, London, 1984, p. 41.
2. Edgar O'Ballance, *Language of Violence: The Blood Politics of Terrorism*, Presidio Press, San Rafael, 1979, p. 86.
3. TV Interview, 'Terrorism'.
4. Edgar O'Ballance, op. cit., p. 118.
5. Yosef Argaman, 'Zamir Speaks,' in *Bamachane*, 11 November 1987, p. 33.
6. *Ibid*, p. 34.
7. David Hirst, *The Gun and The Olive Branch*, Faber & Faber, London, 1977, p. 314.
8. Yosef Argaman, '1972: One Year Fifteen Years Ago,' in *Bamachane*, 27 January 1987, p. 7.
9. Edgar O'Ballance, *Language of Violence: The Blood Politics of Terrorism*, p. 188.
10. Stewart Steven, *The Spymasters of Israel*, Macmillan & Co., New York, 1980, p. 321.
11. *Ibid*, p. 43.
12. *Ibid*, p. 311.
13. *Ibid*, p. 337.
14. Michael Bar-Zohar and Eitan Haber, *The Quest For The Red Prince*, William Morrow & Co., New York, 1983, p. 152.
15. *Ibid*, p. 152.
16. Edgar O'Ballance, *Language of Violence: The Blood Politics of Terrorism*, p. 177.
17. *Ibid*, p. 177.
18. See Michael Bar-Zohar and Eitan Haber, *The Quest For The Red Prince*, p. 196.
19. Edgar O'Ballance, op. cit., p. 230.
20. Michael Bar-Zohar and Eitan Haber, op. cit., p. 213.
21. *Ibid*, p. 216.
22. *Ibid*, p. 220.
23. Stewart Steven, *The Spymasters Of Israel*, p. 354.
24. Rolf Tophoven, *GSG-9: German Response To Terrorism*, Bernard Graefe Verlag, Germany, 1984, p. 67.
25. Yosef Yaffe and Michael Na'emen, 'The Darkened Triangle,' in Weekly Supplement to *Ha'aretz*, 16 November 1987, p. 7.
26. *Ibid*, p. 9.
27. *Ibid*, p. 42.
28. Anat Tal Shir, 'Memory of Ya'akov,' in Weekly Supplement to *Yediot Aharonot*, 6 July 1987, pp. 38–9.
29. Shafi Gabay, 'From The PLO's Files: How The *Mossad* Killed Abu Shrar,' in *Ma'ariv*, 18 September 1987, p. 5.
30. Simon Shiffer, *Snowball: The Story Behind The Lebanon War*, Yediot Aharonot Books, Edanim Publishers, Israel, 1984, p. 21.
31. Various editors, *The War Against Terror: National Policy and Security of Israel 1979–1988*, Revivim Publishing House Ltd., Tel Aviv, 1988, p. 120.
32. Neil Livingstone and David Halevy, 'Striking Back: Oliver North's Secret War On Terror,' in *Soldier of Fortune Magazine*, December 1989, p. 60.
33. *Ibid*, p. 61.
34. *Ibid*, p. 69.
35. Uzi Machniami, 'The Palestinian Agent Was Also An Agent For The *Mossad*,' in Supplement A to *Yediot Aharonot*, 17 June 1988, p. 9.
36. *Time Magazine*, 23 March 1987, p. 32.

2. The Shin Bet
1. Haim Raviv and Colonel Gadi, 'The Terror,' in *Bamachane*, 22 July 1987, p. 20.
2. Interview with senior Western Intelligence officer, commenting on article in

212   REFERENCES

the *Jerusalem Post*.

3. Haim Raviv and Colonel Gadi, op. cit., p. 20.
4. Yossi Melman, ed., *CIA Report: Israeli Foreign Intelligence and Security Survey*, Tel Aviv: Zmora, Bitan Publishers, 1982, p. 60.
5. Interview with a senior Israeli military official.
6. Uzi Benziman, *Sharon: An Israeli Caesar*, Adama Books, New York, 1985, p. 115.
7. Ron Ben-Yishai, 'Gaza 1988: Sharon's Methods Wouldn't Be Efficient Now,' in Weekend Supplement to *Yediot Aharonot*, 22 January 1988, p. 8.
8. Michele Mayron, 'Israel's Watergate,' in *Penthouse Magazine*, January 1987, p. 50.
9. *Ibid*, p. 54.
10. Various editors, *The War Against Terror: National Policy and Security of Israel 1979–1988*, Revivim Publishing House Ltd., Tel Aviv, 1988, pp. 134–5.
11. Michele Mayron, op. cit., p. 154.
12. Government of Israel, Report of the Commission of Inquiry (Jerusalem, 1987), p. 33.
13. Yoram Binur, *My Enemy, Myself*, Doubleday, New York, 1989, p. 152.
14. Article, 'The Houses of Two Terrorists in the Gaza Strip Were Destroyed For Their Role in the Murder of Two Palestinian Collaborators,' in *Yisrael Shelanu*, 24 March 1989, p. 29.

3. The Border Guards and the Police Sappers

1. Amos Navo, 'Kfar Kassem: 1956–86,' in Weekend supplement to the weekend edition of *Yediot Aharonot*, October 1986, p. 20.
2. *Ibid*, p. 22.
3. Eilan Bachar, 'Protection Without Boundaries,' in *Ma'ariv*, 19 November 1982, p. 11.
4. Interview with Gabi Last, Ramle, 17 December 1985.
5. Interview with senior Border Guard officer, 11 December 1985.
6. Eilan Bachar, 'Protection Without Boundaries,' in *Ma'ariv*, 19 November 1982, p. 13.
7. Yair Ben-David, 'The *Ya'ma'm* Terminated the Terrorist Chief In His Bed,' in *Bamachane*, 24 September 1982, p. 25.
8. Interview with Gabi Last, Zichron Ya'akov Police Station, 11 January 1985. All the facts were read off official National Police/Border Guard files; read, incidentally, while in the company of an officer from the IDF Military

Censor's Office.

9. Richard A. Gabriel, *Operation Peace For Galilee*, Hill & Wang, USA, 1984, p. 111.
10. Emanuel Rozen, 'I Found All Of My Friends And They Were Dead One Next To Another,' in *Ma'ariv*, 11 November 1983, p. 13.
11. Interview with Israeli officer serving in the Gaza Strip, Tel Aviv, 12 May 1988.
12. '*Shin Bet*'s Secret Drive,' in *Time Magazine*, 29 August 1988, p. 37.
13. Gil Ronen, 'The Head Underneath The Green Beret,' in *Kotrot Roshit*, 27 August 1986, p. 18.
14. Paul Wilkinson, *Terrorism and the Liberal State*, John Wiley & Sons, New York, 1977, p. 105.
15. Yosef Argaman, '1972: One Year Fifteen Years Later,' in *Bamachane*, 27 January 1987, p. 42.
16. Interview with Shlomoh Aharonishky, Sheikh Jarakh, Jerusalem, 19 April 1988.
17. Michael Dewar, *The Weapons and Equipment of Counter-Terrorism*, Arms & Armour Press, London, 1987, p. 84.
18. Interview with a veteran National Police *Hablan*, South Holon Police Station, 11 May 1988.
19. Robert Rosenberg, 'Holy City Sappers: Jerusalem Bomb Squad Defuses Arab Terror,' in *Soldier of Fortune Magazine*, January 1989, p. 83.

4. Israel's Naval and Air Campaign Against Terrorism

1. Christopher Dickey, Milan J. Kubic and Theodore Stanger, 'Cutting Arafat's Sea Link: A Widening Secret War,' in *Newsweek Magazine*, 1 December 1987, p. 46.
2. Various editors, *Tzahal Be'heilo: Encyclopedia for Military and Security, Volume No. 4*, Revivim Publishing House Ltd., Tel Aviv, 1981, p. 166.
3. 'Sailors of Terror,' in *Bamachane*, 12 December 1984, p. 22.
4. Haim Raviah and Eilan Kfir, 'The Objective: A Massacre At General Staff Headquarters,' in *Hadashot*, 23 April 1985, p. 3.
5. Israeli Ministry of Foreign Affairs, 'The Threat of PLO Terrorism,' Jerusalem, 1985, p. 17.
6. Neil C. Livingstone and David Halevy, 'Israeli Commandos Terminate PLO Terror Chief,' in *Soldier of Fortune Magazine*, December 1988, p. 75.
7. William E. Smith, John Borrell, and Dean Fischer, 'The Voyage of the *Achille Lauro*,' in *Time Magazine*, 21 October 1985, p. 33.

5. 'Select' Operations: Abu Jihad and Ahmed Jibril

1. 'I Pleaded For The Hostages Not Be Harmed; He Threatened To Throw Out A Body Every 30 Minutes,' in *Davar* 8 March 1988.
2. Jerusalem Post Staff and Agencies, 'Father of the Holy War,' in *Jerusalem Post*, 17 April 1988, p. 15.
3. Special Reprint from US News and World Report, 'Abu Jihad Was Terminated Because Of A Pact With Qaddafi,' in *Yediot Aharonot*, 4 May 1988, p. 8.
4. Neil C. Livingstone and David Halevy, 'Israeli Commandos Terminate PLO Terror Chief,' in *Soldier of Fortune Magazine*, December 1988, p. 76.
5. *Ibid*, p. 76.
6. Ron Dagoni, 'Ministers In Tunisia Served The *Mossad*,' in *Yediot Aharonot*, 18 November 1988, pp. 1–2.
7. Livingstone and Halevy, op. cit., p. 76.
8. *Ibid*, p. 77.
9. *Ibid*, p. 78.
10. *Ibid*, p. 78.
11. *Yediot Aharonot* Staff Writers, 'Israel Captured a List Of PLO Agents in Israel and Abroad,' in *Yediot Aharonot*, 8 May 1988, p. 1.
12. Various editors, *The War Against Terror: National Policy and Security in Israel 1979–88*, Revivim Publishing House Ltd., Tel Aviv, 1988, p. 70.

Bibliography

Amir, Aharon. *Lebanon, Country, People, War.* Hadar Editors, Israel, 1979.

Awad, Tawfik Yusef. *Death in Beirut.* Mifras Publishing House, Jerusalem, 1983.

Bar-Zohar, Michael, and Haber, Eitan. *The Quest for the Red Prince.* William Morrow & Co. Inc., New York, 1983.

Batelheim, Avi. *GOLANI: A Family of Fighters.* Ministry of Defence Publishing, Tel Aviv, 1980.

Bavly, Dan, and Salpeter, Eliahu. *Fire In Beirut: Israel's War in Lebanon With the PLO.* Stein & Day, New York, 1984.

Becker, Jillian. *The PLO: The Rise and Fall of the Palestine Liberation Organization.*

Ben Amnon, Shlomoh. *Following the Arab Terrorist.* Madim Books, Tel Aviv, 1978.

Ben David, Ofer. *Hama'aracha Belevanon.* Israel, 1985.

Benziman, Uzi. *Sharon: An Israeli Caesar.* Adama Books, New York, 1985.

Bermudez, Joseph Jr. *North Korean Special Forces.* Janes Publishing Co. Ltd., England, 1988.

Binur, Yoram. *My Enemy, Myself.* Doubleday, New York, 1989.

Blitzer, Wolf. *Territory of Lies.* Harper & Row, New York, 1989.

CIA: Translator and Editor – Mellman, Yossi. *Israeli Foreign Intelligence and Security Services Survey.* Zmora, Bitan, Tel Aviv, 1982.

Clifton, Tony, and Leroy, Catherine. *God Cried.* Quartet Books, London, 1983.

Cobban, Helena. *The Palestine Liberation Organization, People, Power and Politics.* Cambridge University Press, London, 1984.

Dan, Uri. *Fingers of God: Terror Incorporated.* Massada Ltd., Israel, 1976.

Dan, Uri, and Ben-Porat, Y. *The Secret War: The Spy Game in the Middle East.* Sabra Books, New York, 1970.

Deacon, Richard. *The Israeli Secret Service.* Sphere Books Ltd., London, 1979.

Dewar, Michael. *The Weapons and Equipment of Counter-Terrorism.* Arms & Armour Press, London, 1987.

Dietl, Wilhelm. *Holy War,* Macmillan Publishing Co., New York, 1984.

Dimbleby, Jonathan. *The Palestinians.* Quartet Books Inc., New York, 1980.

Dobson, Christopher, and Payne, Ronald. *The Carlos Complex: A Study in Terror.* Hodder & Stoughton Ltd., London, 1977.

—*Counterattack.* Facts on File Inc., New York, 1982.

—*The Terrorists: Their Weapons, Leaders and Tactics.* Facts on File Inc., New York, 1982.

Dupuy, Trevor, N. *Elusive Victory: The Arab Israeli Wars 1947–1974.* Harper & Row Publishers, New York, 1978.

Eisenberg, Dennis, Dan, Uri, and Landau, Eli. *The Mossad: Israel's Secret Intelligence Services Inside Stories.* Signet, New York, 1979.

Eitan, Rafael. *Raful: A Soldier's Story.* Ma'ariv, Tel Aviv, 1985.

El-Rayyes, Riyad, and Nahas, Dunia. *Guerrillas for Palestine.* St. Martin's Press, New York, 1976.

Emerson, Steven. *Secret Warriors: Inside the Covert Operations of the Reagan Era.,* G. P. Putnam and Sons, New York, 1978.

Frangi, Abdallah. *The PLO and Palestine.* Zed Books Ltd., London, 1983.

Gabriel, Richard A. *Operation Peace for Galilee.* Hill & Wang, USA, 1984.

Goren, Roberta. *The Soviet Union and Terrorism.* George Allen & Unwin, London, 1984.

Groussard, Serge. *The Blood of Israel: The Massacre of Israeli Athletes in the 1972 Olympics.* William Morrow & Co. Inc., New York, 1975.

Haber, Eitan. *Today War Will Break Out: The Reminiscences of Brigadier-General Israel Lior, Aide-de-Camp to Prime Ministers Levi Eshkol and Golda Meir.* Edanim, Tel Aviv, 1987.

214

Harel, Isser. *Soviet Espionage and Communism in Israel*. Edanim Publishers, Tel Aviv, 1987.

—*Security and Democracy*. Edanim Publishers, Tel Aviv, 1989.

Herzog, Chaim. *The Arab-Israeli Wars*. Arms & Armour Press, Lionel Leventhal Ltd., London, 1982.

Hirst, David. *The Gun and the Olive Branch*. Faber & Faber Ltd., London, 1977.

Israeli National Police. *Bravery Award Recipients in the Israeli National Police 1985*. National Police Publications, Jerusalem, 1986.

Israeli, Rafael. *The PLO in Lebanon: Selected Documents*. Weidenfeld & Nicolson, London, 1983.

Iyad, Abu, and Rouleau, Eric. *My Home, My Land: A Narrative of the Palestinian Struggle*. Times Books, New York, 1978.

Katz, Samuel M. *Follow Me! A History of Israel's Military Elite*. Arms & Armour Press, London, 1988.

Kimche, David, and Bawly, Dan. *The Sand-Storm. The Arab-Israeli War of 1967: Prelude and Aftermath*. Stein & Day Publishers, New York, 1968.

Kramer, Martin (ed.). *Protest and Revolution in Shi'ite Islam*, United Kibbutz Publishing, Tel Aviv, 1985.

—*The Moral Logic of Hizballah*. Occasional Papers, The Shiloah Institute, Tel Aviv University Press, Tel Aviv, 1987.

Laffin, John. *The War of Desperation 1982–1985*. Osprey, London, 1985.

Lanir, Zvi. *Fundamental Surprise: The National Intelligence Crisis*. United Kibbutz Publications, Tel Aviv, 1983.

Laquer, Walter. *Terrorism*. Abacus, London, 1977.

—*A World of Secrets: The Uses and Limits of Intelligence*. Basic Books Inc., New York, 1985.

Livingstone, Neil C., and Halevy, David. *Inside The PLO: Covert Units, Secret Funds, and the War Against Israel and the United States*. William Morrow & Co. Inc., New York, 1990.

Martin, David C., and Walcott, John. *Best Laid Plans: The Inside Story of America's War Against Terrorism*. Harper & Row, New York, 1988.

Melman, Yossi. *The Master Terrorist: The True Story Behind Abu Nidal*. Adama Books, New York, 1986.

Melman, Yossi, and Raviv, Daniel. *A Hostile Partnership: The Secret Relationship Between Israel and Jordan*. Yediot Aharonot Publications, Israel, 1987.

Merari, Ariel, and Elad, Shlomi. *The International Dimension of Palestinian Terrorism: JCSS Study No. 6*. The Jerusalem Post and Westview Press, Jerusalem, 1986.

Milstein, Uri. *A History of the Paratroopers, Vols. 1–4*. Shalgi Publishing House Ltd., Tel Aviv, 1985.

Netanyahu, Benjamin. *Terrorism: How the West Can Win*. Farrar, Strauss & Giroux, New York, 1986.

O'Ballance, Edgar. *Arab Guerrilla Power 1967–72*. Faber & Faber, London, 1974.

—*Language of Violence*. Presidio Press, California, 1979.

—*Terrorism in the 1980s*. Arms & Armour Press, London, 1989.

O'Brien, Conor-Cruise. *The Siege: The Saga of Israel and Zionism*. Simon & Schuster, New York, 1986.

Ohana, Arnon-Yuval, and Yodfat, Arieh. *The PLO: Portrait of an Organization*. Ma'ariv Library, Israel, 1985.

Parry, Albert. *Terrorism: From Robespierre to Arafat*. Vanguard Press, New York, 1976.

Perry, David. *Diary of A Prison Warden*. Sifriat Poalim Publishing House Ltd., Tel Aviv, 1986.

Posner, Steve. *Israel Undercover: Secret Warfare and Hidden Diplomacy in the Middle East*. Syracuse University Press, New York, 1987.

Ronen, David. *The Year of the Shabak*. Ministry of Defence Publishing, Israel, 1989.

Rosie, George. *The Directory of International Terrorism*. Mainstream Publishing Co. Ltd., Edinburgh, 1986.

Rozental, Rubik. *Lebanon: The Other War*. Sifriat Poalim Publishing House Ltd., Tel Aviv, 1983.

Schiff, Zeev, and Rothstein, Raphael. *Fedayeen: Guerrillas Against Israel*. David Mckay Co. Inc., New York, 1972.

Schiff, Zeev, and Ya'ari, Ehud. *Israel's Lebanon War*. Simon & Schuster, New York, 1984.

—*Intifada: The Palestinian Uprising – Israel's Third Front*. Simon & Schuster, New York, 1990.

Schoenberg, Harris O. *A Mandate For Terror: The United Nations and the PLO*. Shapolsky Publishers Inc., New York, 1989.

Sharon, Ariel, with Chanoff, David. *Warrior: An Autobiography of Ariel Sharon*. Simon & Schuster, New York, 1989.

Shiffer, Simon. *Snowball*. Yediot Aharonot Books, Edanim Publishers, Israel, 1984.

Sinai, Anne, and Pollack, Allen. *The Syrian Arab Republic*. American Academic Association for Peace in the Middle East, New York, 1976.

Sterling, Claire. *The Terror Network: The Secret War of International Terrorism*. Berkley Books, New York, 1982.

Steven, Stewart. *The Spymasters of Israel*. Ballantine Books, New York, 1982.

Stevenson, William, and Dan, Uri. *90 Minutes and Entebbe*. Bantam Books, New York, 1976.

Susser, Asher. *The PLO After the War in Lebanon: The Quest for Survival*. United Kibbutz Publications, Israel, 1985.

Thompson, Leroy. *The Rescuers: The World's Top Anti-Terrorist Units*. Dell Publishing, New York, 1988.

Tinnin, David B., and Christensen, Dag. *The Hit Team*. Dell Publishing Co. Inc., New York, 1976.

Tophoven, Rolf, *GSG-9: German Response to Terrorism*. Bernard Graefe Verlag, Germany, 1984.

USGPO. *Terrorist Group Profiles*. US Government Printing Office, Washington D.C., 1986.

Various editors. *Tzahal Be'heilo: Encyclopedia for Military and Security – Volumes 1–18*. Revivim Publishing House Ltd., Tel Aviv, 1981.

Various editors. *The War Against Terror: National Policy and Security of Israel 1979–1988*. Revivim Publishing House Ltd., Tel Aviv, 1988.

Journals

Bamachane – IDF Weekly Magazine

Biton Heyl Havir – Israeli Air Force Magazine

IDF Journal – Bi-monthly English-language military magazine

Skirat Hodshit – Monthly magazine for IDF Officers

Ma'arachot – IDF-published military history magazine

Documents

Government of Israel, 'Report of the Commission of Inquiry into the Methods of Interrogation of the General Security Service regarding Hostile Terrorist Activity – Part Three'. (Jerusalem, 1987)

Index